Preposterous Virgil

NEW DIRECTIONS IN CLASSICS

New Directions in Classics is a series of short monographs on Classical antiquity and its reception, covering subjects from across the entire spectrum of ancient Mediterranean culture, including its literature, history, material survivals, and their afterlife in diverse media. These volumes move the discipline of Classics forward by breaking new ground, whether in their combination of sources or their method, and by presenting pluralist studies that blend and transcend modes of analysis that have enriched Classics, broadly defined, in recent decades. As fresh and stimulating takes on their topics they are characterized by their dynamism, intellectual energy, and interdisciplinary scope, and are accessible without compromising on academic rigour.

Preposterous Virgil

Reading through Stoppard, Auden, Wordsworth, Heaney

Juan Christian Pellicer

BLOOMSBURY ACADEMIC

LONDON • NEW YORK • OXFORD • NEW DELHI • SYDNEY

BLOOMSBURY ACADEMIC
Bloomsbury Publishing Plc
50 Bedford Square, London, WC1B 3DP, UK
1385 Broadway, New York, NY 10018, USA
29 Earlsfort Terrace, Dublin 2, Ireland

BLOOMSBURY, BLOOMSBURY ACADEMIC and the Diana logo are trademarks of
Bloomsbury Publishing Plc

First published in Great Britain 2022

Cover design: Terry Woodley
Cover image: 'El Campo', 1984, gouache on paper, by Carlos Pellicer López

A catalogue record for this book is available from the British Library.

A catalog record for this book is available from the Library of Congress.

ISBN: HB: 978-1-8488-5651-6
       PB: 978-1-8488-5652-3
       ePDF: 978-1-3501-9822-7
       eBook: 978-1-3501-9823-4

Series: New Directions in Classics

Typeset by RefineCatch Ltd, Bungay, Suffolk NR35 1EF, UK

To find out more about our authors and books, visit www.bloomsbury.com
and sign up for our newsletters.

For Helene and Elias

Contents

Acknowledgements

This book has taken so long that I must not only express gratitude but offer apologies to those who have aided me in the course of writing it. Heartfelt thanks to the original series editors, Charles Martindale and Duncan Kennedy, and to Alex Wright, then editor at I B Tauris, for their kindness. Charles's encouragement and criticism have sustained me from first to last. My other guiding light is Tim Saunders, treasured friend and reader. I am profoundly grateful to Fiachra Mac Góráin for his erudite guidance and unsparing help, which have been critical to the enterprise, and to Nora Goldschmidt for her invaluable comments on the manuscript when it was nearing completion. Lily Mac Mahon at Bloomsbury has been extremely helpful, as has been Alice Wright. Warm thanks to Lisa Carden for her skilful copy-editing, and to the anonymous reader, whose generosity is keenly felt. John Goodridge and David Fairer, heroes of long standing, have also cheered me on and commented on parts of the manuscript at various stages. Alison Martin helped greatly with Sackville-West. Peter Davidson introduced me to Ian Hamilton Finlay. All these readers and supporters have improved my work. The remaining blights are someone else's fault entirely.

I should also like to thank the following for various kinds of help, generosity and encouragement: Monika Asztalos, Silvio Bär, Kathleen Coleman, Tom Jones, Jakob Lothe, Anastasia Maravela, Cathinka Neverdal, Kirsti Sellevold, Mathilde Skoie, Richard Thomas and Abigail Williams, as well as colleagues at the Department of Literature, Area Studies and European Languages at the University of Oslo, my Naples of the North.

Warm thanks to the staffs of the Humanities Library at the University of Oslo and the Bodleian Library, Oxford. I especially cherish the memory of the late Vera Ryhajlo of the Upper Reading Room.

The members of my family have been characteristically supportive. I would especially like to thank my parents, Juan and Holly Pellicer, for lighting my way. My uncle, Carlos Pellicer López, whose art gives me great joy, gave permission to reproduce the painting on the cover of this book. I am sustained by friendships of many years: Knut Andreas Strøm-Gundersen, Richard Burrows, Øivind Bratberg. The book is dedicated to my children, who make my life delightful.

Introduction: Reception and the Figure of Allusion

The gigantic gilded head of a handsome youth with flowing locks stands in a garden wood, giving the illusion that the rest of the golden colossus lies buried in the ground beneath. The inscription across its brow reads, 'APOLLON | TERRORISTE'. Since the legend is in French, and since the garden features many commemorations of the Jacobin leader Louis Antoine de Saint-Just (1767– 94), we are invited to identify this golden figure under the sign of a historical moment, the Reign of Terror of 1793–4. A prolific legislator and close ally of Robespierre, Saint-Just is famous for his aphoristic defences of revolutionary justice, as well as for his zealous prosecution of the opponents of the revolutionary government, typically to the steps of the guillotine. But what is Saint-Just doing in the guise of Apollo? We find him elsewhere in the garden, too. By its central Temple of Apollo, there is a Roman *lararium* or household shrine with a small statue of the youthful god, modelled on Bernini's famous statue of Apollo and Daphne in the Galleria Borghese in Rome. This fleet deity gracefully extends a machine gun. The plinth inscription reads 'A SJ', or Apollo as Saint-Just. Apollo is, among other things, a god of purification, which is the aim of revolutionary justice according to Saint-Just.[1] As the garden historian Jessie Sheeler observes, the statue's 'bringing together of the ideals of integrity and truth with violence requires a judgement about the role of violent action in our or any world view'.[2] The Apollo with a machine gun suggests that terror is more than The Terror. Terror is also a timeless, universal phenomenon, transcending historical contingency. The statue reminds us too that Apollo is a god of many parts. He is not only the god of the lyre, which is how he is most comfortably remembered, but also 'the distant marksman' (*hekaébolos*, his Homeric epithet) whom Virgil places at the centre of Aeneas' shield, where from on high, Apollo of Actium scatters the Oriental opponents of Octavius Caesar (Augustus) as they panic before his bow (*Aeneid* 8.704–6). Virgil's Shield of Aeneas also represents Caesar/ Augustus celebrating this victory over Antony and Cleopatra at Actium (31 BC) in his triple triumph in Rome in 29 BC. On the shield, Augustus is seated before the white marble temple to Apollo that he built close to his own house on the Palatine Hill in Rome, surveying the line of captives who represent the conquered peoples (8.720–3).³ In Little Sparta, the Temple of Apollo bears this dedication: 'TO APOLLO | HIS MUSIC | HIS MISSILES | HIS MUSES.'

The garden is Little Sparta, created by the artist and poet Ian Hamilton Finlay in the Pentland Hills, southwest of Edinburgh. On the entrance path, the visitor passes a section of low brick wall with a brass plaque inscribed with a refrain from Virgil's eighth Eclogue, in English translation. The plaque reads 'FLUTE, BEGIN WITH ME ARCADIAN NOTES' (*incipe Maenalios mecum, mea tibia, versus* [lines 21, 25, 31, 36, 42, 46, 51, 57], 'Begin with me, my flute, a song of Maenalus!').⁴ This refrain in turn echoes the refrain of the first Idyll of Theocritus, '*Begin, my Muses, begin the herdsman's song*' (trans. Verity). These incantations sound a keynote of pastoral verse. In Virgil, the literary herdsman's invocation of his 'flute' or pipe (the *tibia*, Greek *aulós*, a reed instrument with stops) further identifies the genre of his song as pastoral.⁵ On Finlay's plaque in the wall outside Little Sparta, the Virgilian inscription is illustrated by a bas-relief depicting a machine gun with prominent vent holes in its barrel. The holes are designed to look like the stops of a pipe. This fusion of martial and pastoral imagery is startling. It introduces the motif we have already observed in the garden temple's alliterative dedication to Apollo's music, missiles and muses. A smaller plaque inset below reads 'FEBRUARY 4 1983'. The date commemorates the first victory in a long-running dispute between the artist and the local council over tax rates on the garden temple. (The council wanted to tax the temple as an art gallery. Finlay insisted it should be taxed as a religious building.) When the council authorized a sheriff's officer to confiscate art works from the Temple of Apollo, Finlay's supporters rallied in defence. Finlay celebrated the skirmish as 'The First Battle of Little Sparta' and dubbed his defenders 'the Saint-Just Vigilantes'.⁶ The serio-comic tone of Finlay's extravagant titles and inscription of the date captures the inherent instability of mock heroic. Even the name 'Little Sparta', which humorously signals opposition to Edinburgh, 'the Athens of the North', also recalls Sparta's more fearsome qualities as the most radically militarized of the Greek city-states. (It is ironic, in this connection, that the Spartans subjugated the Arcadians.) The tone of the garden's signature juxtapositions is similarly unstable. With its visual conflation of music, missiles and muses, the bas-relief of the machine gun pipe with its pastoral inscription is genuinely disconcerting. As Alessandro Barchiesi has said of an allusion that involves Apollo in a different context, we learn 'how to read Apollo the killer in Apollo the musician'.⁷

Disconcerting too are the garden's many references to Saint-Just and the Apollonian figures with whom he is associated. The already complex issue of what these figures may be taken to mean is always complicated by the question of how seriously they should be taken. The reader of the garden (who may be a reader first and foremost, if the garden is visited through the medium of an illustrated book) is prevented from making a conclusive judgement of the garden's tone.

If Saint-Just is figured as Apollo in Finlay's garden, or vice versa, does this necessarily have anything to do with Virgil? Not necessarily; it depends on the context. Which is to say, it depends on contextualization. Like texts themselves, contexts are what a reader puts together. In the context I made from my reading of Finlay's Virgilian inscription 'FLUTE, BEGIN WITH ME ARCADIAN NOTES' and its engraved figure of the machine-gun flute, which I joined with Finlay's Temple dedication 'TO APOLLO | HIS MUSIC | HIS MISSILES | HIS MUSES', the Saint-Just Apollo takes on a Virgilian significance. Once this idea is established, further questions suggest themselves. Since the figure of Apollo not only pervades Virgil's works but appears in many forms and guises, which 'Virgilian' versions of Apollo should we discern in the figures of Finlay's Saint-Just? These questions touch on a condition of literary interpretation to which this book will continually return, namely the instability at the heart of reading itself. For even as readers and critics need to make interpretative decisions that take them one way or another, these decisions do not (or should not) remain frozen but must be remade with each reading. The tonal indeterminacy that characterizes mock-heroic (how seriously do we take Finlay's composite Apollo?) sensitizes readers to a fundamental aspect of literary interpretation, namely its ongoingness, its provisional state.[8]

Apollo plays a programmatic role in Virgil's *Eclogues*, not only as presider over the golden age announced in the 'Messianic' Eclogue 4 (10, *tuus iam regnat Apollo*, 'Your own Apollo now is king!'), but also as the poet's own mentor in Eclogue 6, where the speaker recalls Apollo's admonishment against entertaining epic ambitions. Virgil has Apollo instruct the poem's speaker that a shepherd (i.e., a pastoral poet) should instead sing 'a fine-spun song' (*deductum carmen*), a description that becomes a figure of pastoral poetry (3–5).[9] This Apollo is an arbiter of literary style.

Apollo also plays a key role in the development of another of Virgil's central themes throughout his works, namely the relation between the muses and the missiles, between poetry and power. At the centre of the *Georgics*, Apollo is invoked as a pastoral deity (the 'famous shepherd of Amphrysus') at the head of

Virgil's description of the temple to Caesar he announces he will build – an imaginary temple that represents Virgil's projected future poem to the emperor (3.2, 16, 36). Timothy Saunders has drawn attention to Virgil's use of the same verb, *deducere* (to 'draw down' or 'draw out'), in the phrases he uses for the exemplary shepherd's song (*deductum* carmen, *Ecl.* 6.5, a song 'drawn out' like wool being spun into yarn) and for his own ambition to *draw down* the Muses from Hesiod's Helicon (*Aonio rediens deducam vertice Musas, Geo.* 3.11; see also *Eclogues* 6.70–1), as though drawing down the Muses from the headwaters of Greek poetry into Roman literary channels were like directing troops in a military operation. The figure of Apollo features significantly in the links Saunders traces in the *Eclogues* between Virgil's representation of contests over bucolic song and contests over bucolic land, including the confiscation of land from shepherds to reward demobilized soldiers in Eclogues 1 and 9.[10]

Apollo was cultivated as a literary patron by the Hellenistic poet Callimachus, and later by Callimachus' admirers in Augustan Rome, Virgil foremost among them. The god was also reverenced as a political patron by Octavian/Augustus.[11] Finlay's connection between Apollo's muses and his missiles therefore touches a nerve. What is the relationship between the lyre and the bow, between the sculptor and Ozymandias? Does art collude with violence when they are mutually supportive? What is the relationship between the artists and the men of might, especially when they cultivate the same god?[12]

Virgil concludes the *Georgics* with a 'seal' of his authorship (the Greek term is *sphragis*), identifying himself by name as the poet who composed in Naples, flourishing in the arts of peace while Caesar thundered in war by the Euphrates (4.559–66). While Callimachus had written pointedly that it was for Zeus to thunder, not for him (*Aetia* fr.1.20), Virgil acknowledges that the peace he enjoys to write Callimachean verse is largely thanks to the avatar of Jupiter currently pacifying the hosts of Asia.[13]

Octavian/Caesar was not only thundering on the Euphrates while Virgil wrote the *Georgics*. He was also building the Temple of Apollo on the Palatine in Rome.[14] When Virgil's Aeneas at Cumae vows to Apollo that he will build a temple to him in Latium (*Aeneid* 6.69–70), the reader may construe this as a prefiguration of Octavian's dedication of the Palatine temple to Apollo in 28 BC.[15] Scholars have traditionally located Evander's settlement of Pallanteum on or around the Palatine Hill, and have taken Virgil's description of Evander's modest dwelling, which Aeneas visits in *Aeneid* 8, as a prefiguration of Augustus' house in the same area. Virgil's mythic figure of Evander is a son of the Arcadian god Hermes/Mercury and a king of the Arcadians (8.138–9), whose passage out of the east and settlement in Italy prefigures the story of Aeneas and his Roman descendants. Virgil thus emphasizes Rome's Arcadian, as well as Trojan, origins. Clearly, then, Finlay's Scottish Temple of Apollo (who was Troy's patron, Virgil reminds us at *Georgics* 3.36, *Troiae Cynthius auctor*)[16] in a garden that everywhere recalls the (mainly post-Virgilian) notion of Arcadia, is pregnant with traces of Virgil's reception.

The fact that Finlay's temple is a repurposed cow byre might be taken as occasion to discern deep continuities among the Virgilian genres. Virgil's *Eclogues* were entitled *Bucolica*, the Greek for songs of the *boukolos* or cowherd. Pastoral singers are herdsmen of oxen, sheep or goats. As I have mentioned, Virgil invokes Apollo as shepherd (*pastor*, 3.2) at the turning-point of the *Georgics*, in the central proem that promises to build a temple to Augustus, understood as an allegory of his future epic (3.1–39). Across his three works Virgil is concerned to project the composite, even paradoxical character of Rome, at once rustic and imperial, Greek and Latin, from the vantage-point of the humblest as well as the divine sources of life. (Visiting Evander's modest dwelling, where we are told that Hercules had once spent the night driving his bulls homeward, Aeneas looks out on the bucolic scene of cattle grazing on the site of the future Roman Forum, 8.359–63.)[17] How is it, we are prompted to wonder, that the Romans, who can trace their descent from the rural Arcadians (so Aeneas tells Evander as they celebrate their common ancestry, *Aeneid* 8.127–42) as well as from the urban Trojans who arrived in Italy as Eastern refugees, can be destined to rule as *rerum dominos*, lords of all, whose *imperium* ('dominion') will be *sine fine*, without end? (*Aeneid* 1.282, 279; compare Apollo's similar prophecy at 3.97–8.)[18] The aspect of Augustan culture that Finlay's Temple specifically highlights is the Virgilian juxtaposition of arts and arms, each typically figured with regard to the idea of conquest, either by culture or contest, by music or missiles.

The argument of this book, or rather the thesis it puts to the test of literary criticism, is that such encounters between modern and ancient art can occasion two-way channels of interpretation that serve a valuable critical purpose. '*Preposterous Virgil*' alludes to T. S. Eliot's argument that, in reading, the past is altered by the present. No one should find this idea preposterous, says Eliot, though literally speaking, that is precisely the word that describes his reversal of the expected order.[19] Eliot does not say his idea is new, only that it needs to be taken seriously. David Lodge pays it the compliment of making a serious joke of it in his novel *Small World* (1984), where his protagonist Persse McGarrigle mischievously misrepresents his own MA thesis as being 'about the influence of

T. S. Eliot on Shakespeare', explaining that '"we can't avoid reading Shakespeare through the lens of T. S. Eliot's poetry. I mean, who can hear *Hamlet* today without thinking of 'Prufrock'?"'. (Lodge's heroine concedes that the fictional thesis sounds 'more interesting' than the conventional real one.)[20] Lodge's joke worked in the 1980s (and I think remains funny) because the assumption dies hard that reception obeys time's arrow. In classics, the proposition that reading Greek and Latin poems though their subsequent receptions 'opens up fresh hermeneutical possibilities' was the radical challenge issued by Charles Martindale's influential *Redeeming the Text* (1993), and has won acceptance as a premise of reception studies.[21] My own approach is doggedly empirical. There is no better way to determine whether the hermeneutic possibilities advertised by reception studies are in fact worth realizing than to sound them out. This book is therefore an experiment in reading, or rather a series of tests. Whether Tom Stoppard's *Arcadia* – to take one of my own experiments – can prompt us into new ways of reading Virgil's *Eclogues* 'which might otherwise have remained invisible to us' (as Martindale proposes a similar ambition) strikes me as an extravagant and possibly quixotic hope, but not a dishonourable one.[22] Let us continue to turn over this idea, and return to the Scottish garden.

Finlay's Little Sparta 'prompts us' to read a number of Virgilian texts, quite literally since it physically presents textual fragments to the visitor-reader, as we've seen in the inscription 'FLUTE, BEGIN WITH ME ARCADIAN NOTES', a translation from Virgil's Eclogue 8. Placed at the garden's entrance, the quotation reminds us that the verb *begin* is a bucolic trope. A reader may reflect further that the trope of beginning is also a characteristic of georgic (*hinc canere incipiam, Georgics* 1.5) as well as epic. (Recall the opening invocations of Homer, Hesiod and Apollonius; and Virgil's asking the Muse to say the cause, *Aeneid* 1.8, likewise implies starting from the very beginning). Finally, a reader may wonder how this knowledge will bear on his or her experience of the garden. Each inscription asks to be situated in a range of possible contexts, only some of which will be realized at any time by any reader. Each encounter entails a recontextualization, a new challenge to interpretation. In another part of Finlay's garden, for instance, two round plaques, each the bullseye of a circular stone sett girdled with trees of various kinds, are inscribed with three lines each from Virgil's description of the trees grown by the old Corycian gardener in *Georgics* 4.141–6.[23] Here readers must 'situate' Virgil's text in an uncommonly literal sense.

But Finlay's garden also requires us to 'read Virgil' in a more extended sense, since the act of contextualizing fragments and allusions engages a range of experience that encompasses so many other texts, and since these interpretative acts cannot be predicted or contained. Yet another inscription in Finlay's garden, this time carved on the inside of a gate so it describes a broad view of the agricultural moorland *outside* the garden, reads '*das gepflügte Land* • *the fluted land*'. This challenges us to consider not only the implications of the German language in this location, and of the wider European contexts that the German fragment introduces, but also the implications of the act of translation itself, and further, of the act of passing physically between two kinds of space (as here, between garden and pasture), and the implications of the way in which the garden's pastoral codes have been deployed to control the way the viewer perceives the agricultural land beyond.[24]

The garden is full of allusive fragments. A garden urn inscribed 'CO GITATIO | SUB UMBRA | LATINAE | CELATA' ('A thought hidden under the shade of Latin') provocatively restages and translates ('back'?) into Latin a complex dialogue between Virgil's *umbra*, a key word in the *Eclogues*, and two of this Latin word's richest receptions in English, Andrew Marvell's poem 'The Garden' ('Annihilating all that's made | To a green thought in a green shade') and John Keats's 'Ode on a Grecian Urn' (which represents, on the eternally silent urn, the youth beneath the trees piping melodies *unheard*).[25] What happens if we accept the challenge of Finlay's urn to read these English and Latin texts together and anew? The trial of whether or not the conjunction of Finlay's garden and Virgil's work is critically 'valuable' consists in elaborating readings from the encounter, and judging these new permutations by their results.

Or shall we say, judge the grafts by their fruits? As John Henkel has observed in an article on the metapoetic dimension of Virgil's treatment of arboriculture in the *Georgics*, grafting often serves modern critics too 'as a metaphor for allusion and intertextuality'.[26] Celebrations of hybridity quickly run to cliché, especially on the routine assumption that any new graft must be wonderful. But wonderment has its place in this metaphor's company, together with a sense of humour. Virgil describes a grafted tree that 'marvels at its strange leafage and fruits not its own' (*miratastque novas frondes et non sua poma, Georgics* 2.82). Henkel finds Virgil's grafted tree 'an apt metaphor for allusions that are especially conspicuous or extensive', the 'most famous' of which in Virgil's own work 'is surely Aeneas' excuse to Dido in the underworld (*invitus, regina, tuo de litore cessi, Aen.* 6.460), which Vergil takes nearly unchanged from the speech by Berenice's lock in Catullus (*invita, o regina, tuo de vertice cessi,* Cat. 66.39)'.[27] This allusion is famous precisely for presenting readers with a perennially astonishing puzzle. What on earth was Virgil doing, lifting a mock-heroic line from a poem famous above all for its allusive brio, and inserting it into his own epic at precisely the spot where the line needs to sound absolutely pure, a single unbent note of gravest pathos? How could Virgil hope to so inoculate his old stock but we should relish of it? As Richard Thomas observes, 'no amount of hermeneutical activity has been able to remove' the subversive charge of recognizing Virgil's theft from Catullus.[28] Nor will any amount of hermeneutical activity finally establish what Virgil was up to, or decide how a reader should interpret Virgil's stolen line, much less how readers will continue to interpret Virgil's open theft. Wit and wonder strive in its reception. In this regard the grafting metaphor seems apt, for Virgil's grafted tree that 'marvels at its strange leafage and fruits not its own' is a figure of wit as well as wonder. How seriously should we take Virgil's description of the grafted tree, all agog at its own strange leaves and fruit? Humour is a key element in the reception of georgic.[29] John Philips (1676–1709), the first English poet to imitate Virgil by writing a full-scale formal georgic, is also the wittiest. His two-book poem *Cyder* (1708) in Miltonic blank verse treats grafting not only extensively, as required by his subject of apple cultivation, but with a genial irony no less befitting his topic. 'What loss', he asks tongue in cheek, to 'search how far | Two different Natures may concur to mix | In close embraces, and strange Off-spring bear?' (*Cyder* 1.300–3). 'At diff'rent times | Adopted *Plums* will aliene Branches grace', and Herefordshire apple stocks may yet bear quinces, pears, and even peaches (1.297–309). Philips's ironic amusement is also a form of seriousness. It allows him to keep an open mind. The thing about grafting – what makes this metaphor relevant to allusion – is that it is entirely a matter of experience. 'Let sage Experience teach thee all the Arts | Of Grafting, and In-Eyeing', Philips advises (1.326–7). 'In-Eyeing' is budding, or Hamlet's 'inoculation', a traditional grafting technique. Virgil explains the main difference between grafting, *inserere*, and budding, *oculos imponere*, in *Georgics* 2.73–82. 'Experience' is Philips's word for *experiment* (*OED* s.v. 'experience', 1.b), so his phrase 'sage Experience' combines the 'sageness' accumulated through past experience with the anticipatory drive of probing or testing that distinguishes 'experience' in the sense of experimental inquiry.[30] Allusion is much like this, 'experience' in both senses of that Janus-like word.

When readers come upon an 'engraftment' such as Virgil's *invitus, regina* – a rare occasion, of course – they face a host of interpretative choices. In *Cyder* such a moment occurs when Philips apostrophizes the Redstreak apple:

Hail *Herefordian* Plant, that dost disdain
All other Fields! Heav'n's sweetest Blessing, hail!
Be thou the copious Matter of my Song.

                                                         1.524–6

Apostrophes beginning with the word 'hail' are formulaic in Milton's *Paradise Lost*, but 'copious Matter' takes us straight to 'Hail, Son of God, savior of men, thy name | Shall be the copious matter of my song' (*PL* 3.412–13). Philips's borrowing is shockingly, delightfully perverse, teetering on the brink of blasphemy. Philips's late-eighteenth-century editor, the learned clergyman Charles Dunster, was embarrassed enough to construct an elaborate apology, arguing that Philips could not possibly have been conscious of the borrowing, but had so thoroughly assimilated his model that he took Milton's words to be his own.[31] We are more likely to think that Philips was indulging his own lighthearted brinkmanship in a game not unlike the Italian humanist Marco Girolamo Vida's avowed predilection 'to play with and to allude to phrases from the ancients, and, while using precisely the same words, to express another meaning.'[32] Philips's appropriation is an impishly conspicuous theft for the erudite to detect, a graft that flaunts its own engraftedness.

This book will not be much concerned with that kind of allusion. But the example from Philips's *Cyder* is instructive inasmuch as it identifies allusion as a kind of experiment that puts literary experience to the test. Confronted with a text that looks or sounds allusive, we respond with our past experience, experimentally trying out configurations of elements old and new. Parts of this experiment will confirm or merely add to what we already knew, and parts may change the way we know them. This is true of reception generally. While we may hope that reading through reception will prompt us into new ways of reading ancient poems 'which might otherwise have remained invisible to us', we should not expect the experience to bring only new discoveries. Modern works of art such as Little Sparta, for instance, will often recall things already known, and so draw our attention to facts that may well be familiar, but which also need to be experienced and contextualized afresh. Experience, after all, is mainly a process of repetition, recognition, and variation, not a chain of radically new discoveries. Most readers of this book will long since have realized that Virgil's work is not sealed off from other poets and genres, if indeed they ever doubted this truism. But our knowledge is only as good as the experience that sustains it, and experience is necessarily a work in progress.

Re-experiencing Virgil though new encounters in art can lead one to make discoveries that give specificity to general ideas, modifying them in the process. One does not need to visit Little Sparta and see Virgilian texts and figures set among a host of other literary presences to realize 'that Virgil's work is not sealed off from other poets and genres'. But the garden's many reminders may well draw our attention toward a related characteristic of Virgil himself, namely his poetic inclusiveness and centripetal force – not only his ability to synthesize his own literary culture, but also the capacity of his work to absorb later creative responses that Virgil himself could not have anticipated. We see that Finlay's main temple is dedicated to Apollo. But just opposite, there is a smaller temple dedicated to Baucis and Philemon, whose story is best known from Ovid's *Metamorphoses* (8.618–724).[33] That Ovidian story of the gods welcomed into a humble dwelling (in Ovid's narrative, Jupiter and Mercury are travelling incognito) is of the same kind as the story of Evander's hospitality to Hercules in the inset narrative in *Aeneid* 8.[34] Finlay's garden reminds us not only that Virgil's text is allusive or intertextual (as Virgil himself constantly reminds us) but that we read Virgil with our whole experience of the literature that comes after him. In Finlay's Little Sparta, 'Apollon Terroriste' is near another statue of Apollo, this one chasing the figure of Daphne. Like Finlay's small statue of the machine-gun-bearing Apollo, this large red-and-green statue (in modern 'cut-out' style) is modelled on Bernini's famous statue of Apollo and Daphne, and like its seventeenth-century model it represents the Ovidian episode of the erotic pursuit of Daphne. While my own reading of 'Apollon Terroriste' has been shaped by the Virgilian perspective of my project in the present book, others have read differently, and naturally will again. Jessie Sheeler, for instance, reads the legend 'Apollon Terroriste' of the gilded head as Apollo/Saint-Just with reference to the Ovidian narrative of Apollo's torture of the satyr Marsyas, which opens new perspectives that are not incompatible with my reading. Indeed, Suetonius records that sometime in the famine years 40–36 BC, Octavian attended an ill-advised private banquet dressed up as Apollo as part of a divine masquerade, and his enemies sarcastically dubbed him 'Apollo Tortor', probably with reference to the god's flaying of the satyr Marsyas.[35]

The juxtaposition of Finlay's two temples may also cause us to reflect how each represents two kinds of encounter with the gods, the one ceremonial and the other homely, and how both are represented in various ways in the episode of Aeneas' encounter with Evander. As should now be clear, Finlay's garden is full of memorializing structures that either invoke Virgil or evoke him, constantly prompting new contextualizations and interpretations. A stone grotto represents the cave in which Virgil's Aeneas and Dido shelter from the storm and consummate their passion in *Aeneid* 4.160–72. The lightning bolt engraved on the keystone above the door makes the storm appear a sign of Jupiter's power, rather than of Juno's as in Virgil (4.166–7). Finlay's bolt may be a witty concretization of the term *coup de foudre*, but it also invites us to consider how Jupiter is implicated in the Virgilian episode (he is prompted to separate the lovers by the complaint of the Numidian king Iarbas, 4.198–221, who goads Jupiter with a taunt about his thunderbolts at 208–9), not least because the Jovian lightning bolt above the grotto's door separates a letter A for Aeneas from a letter D for Dido.[36] The lightning stroke looks menacing, too, the design of its single bolt reminiscent of the double-bolt *Siegrune* of the Nazi SS. This stylized lightning does not betoken any merely benevolent god. In Finlay's garden, classical emblems are everywhere combined with figures of modern trauma. And the tone is always unstable. Paradox operates by wrong-footing, by *trompe l'oeil*. A broken column that at first sight appears to commemorate Queen Dido turns out to commemorate the 'TRAGEDIES | of the | DIDO | class cruisers' sunk during the Second World War, with a famously pathetic inscription from the Virgilian underworld, TENDEBANTQVE MANVS | RIPAE VLTERIORIS AMORE' (*Aeneid* 6.314).[37]

Finlay's broken column presents the illusion of a ruin. The garden is full of artificial ruins. Lying lopsided on the grass near a toppled column, a stone block is engraved, 'THE WORLD | HAS BEEN | EMPTY SINCE | THE ROMANS | *SAINT-JUST*'. Elsewhere, a monumental-scale arrangement of eleven separate rough-hewn blocks with a single word carved in each reads, 'THE | PRESENT | ORDER | IS | THE | DISORDER | OF | THE | FUTURE | SAINT- | JUST'. (As Sheeler observes, by switching the position of two of the huge blocks, the opposite meaning would be given.)[38] A stone plaque inscribed *hic gelidi fontes, hic mollia prata*, 'here are soft springs, here soft meadows' (*Eclogues* 10.42) is artfully made to look as though it has been worn quite through by the garden spring that now pours through it. These artificial ruins, especially those with Virgilian inscriptions or associations, provide occasion to reflect on the combination of the framed and the fragmentary in our own readings of Virgil, and how each reader must actively compose and recompose the various temporal elements of that inherently unstable combination.[39]

At the heart of this book's experiments in reading is the figure of allusion. I prefer this term to 'reference', which signals authorial intention more strongly still, but also to 'intertextuality', which describes an inherent property of texts rather than a cognitive event.[40] Stephen Hinds proposes that instead of thinking of memory as 'really a way of talking about allusion', one can think of allusion as 'really a way of talking about memory'.[41] 'Allusion' may serve as a way to speak about an interpretative event in the mind of a given reader at a given time. Allusion is thus a figure of instability, indeed cannot be otherwise, since (as a mentor once wrote to me) 'it depends on a dialectic of difference and sameness whose relationship can always be reconfigured by a new interpreter'. Perhaps the term is best used as an adverb. Instead of speaking of allusion as though it were a thing, one may speak of 'reading allusively'.

To read allusively is to read a text through one's reading of other texts. These interposing texts are spectral presences. There is a sense in which allusions are illusions; they are not really 'there'. I would associate the figure of allusion not with Apollo's gilded head, but rather with the figure underneath. Allusion, the underground colossus, is not really buried there, it is a projection of one's own imagination. Necessarily, its construction depends on the interpretative processes and creative procedures of the individual reader.[42] This is why allusion always raises questions about its own normative force. As one classicist says to another, 'Your artistic allusion is someone else's chance resemblance'.[43] Questions about the limits of allusion are central to the enterprise of reading itself.[44] They are not incidental, they do not go away, and cannot be finally resolved but must always be encountered provisionally, not to mention practically. So let me try another example, this time guided by the gilt of the giant head under which I imagine the allusive/illusive body.

Robert Frost's poem for the presidential inauguration of John F. Kennedy in 1961, presaging 'The glory of a next Augustan age . . . A golden age of poetry and power | Of which this noonday's the beginning hour', has proved an embarrassment to many lovers of Frost, if not to lovers of Virgil. (As R. J. Tarrant has remarked, Frost's poem is precisely 'a specimen of the kind of commemorative poetry that Virgil successfully avoided writing'.)[45] Frost's inauguration poem alludes to Anchises' prophecy to Aeneas in Elysium that one day Augustus would 'again establish a golden age in Latium amid fields once ruled by Saturn' (*aurea condet | saecula qui rursus Latio regnata per arva | Saturno quondam, Aeneid* 6.792–4). Frost also has his eye on Virgil's excited announcement in Eclogue 4.4–10 of an imminent renewal of the Saturnian age with the rise of a new golden people (*gens aurea*) under the reign of Apollo. Paul Muldoon's poem 'Gold' (in *Meeting the British*, 1987) critically examines Frost's inauguration poem of 1961 and the historical moment it represents by reading it through an earlier poem by Frost that undermines it, 'Nothing Gold Can Stay' (1923).[46] Muldoon's poem is dedicated and addressed to his friend Gerard Quinn, Muldoon's English teacher in 1962, when 'just a year earlier | old Frost | had swung the lead || while hailing Kennedy – | *A golden age* | *of poetry and power*'. The expression 'to swing the lead' means to shirk by pretending to be occupied; here Muldoon implies that Frost shirked his duty as a poet. But the expression is chosen specifically to introduce the idea of lead, which is gold's opposite in the pseudo-science of alchemy. In *The Dunciad*, Pope memorably represents Dulness 'with mighty wings out-spread |

To hatch a new Saturnian age of Lead' (1.27–8), and explains in his own note, 'The ancient Golden Age is by Poets styled *Saturnian*; but in the Chemical [i.e., alchemical] language Saturn is Lead'.[47] 'Twenty years on' from 1962, Muldoon represents his onetime teacher and abiding friend Quinn reaching 'into the breast | of a wind-cheater || for [his] blue pencil: | 'All cancelled; | *Nothing gold can stay*.''. The lead of Quinn's editorial blue pencil cancels 'gold', playing on the tension suggested between Frost's 'stay' and the shorthand *stet* ('let it stand'). Muldoon further develops the notion of lead as gunshot, figuratively evoking the shot that would soon kill Kennedy ('Not the dead weight | of a grouse | flaunted from an open car'), before reconnecting with the motif of gold with a reference to Chaïm Soutine's painting *Hare on a Green Shutter* (1925–6, a gold-and-green composition), a reference that not only plays on Frost's first lines – 'Nature's first green is gold | Her hardest hue to hold' – but also recalls Kennedy's 'green' or Irish origins. (The Irish flag is sometimes described as 'green, white and gold'.) Frost's green/gold motif also engenders an earlier poem by Muldoon about the same school year, 'The Geography Lesson' in *Why Brownlee Left* (1980), in which bananas transported from Africa 'would hanker after where they'd grown', and how from either 'the depths of a ship' or from under the counter in an Ulster shop, their greenness 'turned to gold | Through unremembering darkness, an unsteady hold'.[48] Here the ambiguity of gold and green is shared with 'hold', noun as well as verb. Paradoxically, 'the hardest hue to hold' is a figure of unsteadiness, yet also of something capable of sustaining an unseen, unbreakable hold. (Muldoon's 'unremembering' opens up further paradoxes, especially with regard to allusion.)

Now all this is traditional allusive practice. How far should it be pursued? And can it be read 'backward' into readings of Virgil? In an interview, Muldoon proposes a reading of Frost's inauguration poem in which the surface meaning of Frost's reference to a golden age is taken as intentionally sabotaged by the ironic force of the word 'gold' elsewhere in Frost's poems. In 'A Peck of Gold' (1928), for instance, Frost reflects on the ironies of what he was told as a child in San Francisco, namely that the dust blown about by the wind was gold ('"We all must eat our peck of gold."'). Besides, Muldoon argues, the word 'noontide' in Frost's inauguration poem implies that, as in 'Nothing Gold Can Stay', organic decline must immediately follow on from that ephemeral first instant associated with noontime and gold. 'So old Frost was up to his tricks at Kennedy's inauguration'.[49]

The only part of this reading that seems at all problematic to me is Muldoon's implication that 'old Frost' was being subversive by design, and even this is problematic only if absolute certainty about the author's intention is taken as a necessary part of the reading, as a validating 'proof'. Otherwise, a reading that takes Frost's inauguration poem to be complicated or subverted by the implications of his earlier poems seems unexceptional. If we wished, we might allow ourselves to find subversive meanings even in aspects of the reception of Frost's inauguration poem that are patently accidental, such as the fact that during the noontime inauguration ceremony, Frost was so blinded by the glare of sun and snow that he was forced to skip his planned reading of the new poem and instead recite from memory 'The Gift Outright'. Frost himself joked that he detected the jealous hand of Apollo, god of poets and the sun.[50] If one relinquishes to know authorial intention, or indeed the mind of every reader, one often finds that little was lost by the concession.

But can Muldoon's subversive reading of Frost's inauguration poem inform readings of Virgil – perhaps comparably subversive ones? Richard Thomas's reading of Anchises' prophecy *aurea condet | saecula qui rursus*, '[Augustus,] who will again establish a golden age' (6.792–3) focuses on the verb *condere*, which Virgil's predecessor Lucretius uses in a sense that 'is precisely the opposite of that "required" in the sixth *Aeneid: proinde licet quot vis vivendo condere saecla*, 'therefore by living on you may lay to rest as many generations as you wish"' (*DRN* 3.1090).[51] In this context *condere* means to close out, even as in others it means to establish. As is well known, Virgil uses the same verb, *condere*, at the beginning of the *Aeneid* to describe the founding of the Roman line (1.33) and at the poem's close when Aeneas sinks (*condit*) his sword into the breast of the suppliant Turnus (12.950). Pope's *Dunciad* begins and ends with this very ambiguity. The 'new Saturnian age of lead' heralded at the beginning of the poem finally ushers in the 'universal darkness' that 'buries all'. Now Thomas does not say that Virgil's *aurea saecula condere* actually means 'bring a golden age to a close', but argues that Virgil's phrasing is ambiguous, as attested by the critical reception of this passage, and that the scholars who propound an 'Augustan hermeneutics' have tried in vain to suppress this historical ambiguity.[52] My own approach is less polemical and historicizing, more speculative and tentative. Let us try a few more examples of reading Virgil through his modern reception, and see what happens.

We can begin with the reading of Frost in Muldoon's 'Gold', which as we have seen understands gold (with the Frost of 'Nothing Gold Can Stay') as a fundamentally ambiguous sign, at once denoting the stasis of perfection and the onset of decline. The noblest of materials, gold is always shadowed by its antithesis, sometimes lead, sometimes dust (compare the gold and lead caskets in *The Merchant of Venice*, or the famous lines from *Cymbeline*, 'Golden lads and girls all must, | As chimney sweepers, come to dust', 4.2.262–3).[53] Of course Muldoon does not take Frost to imply that gold is not truly 'golden', but only that as a metaphor, 'gold' is always qualified by its figurative and intertextual implications. The final word of Muldoon's poem (rhyming with the first line's comparison of Quinn to 'Merlin') is 'Marilyn', whose life, like Soutine's, was brief; whose blondness was fake; who describes a figure of illusion/disillusion, of transience, artifice, pathos, and loss. (The triangulation of Kennedy–Marilyn–Frost is suggestive too, as is the ambiguous evocation of Camelot in Muldoon's reference to Merlin.) One needn't take this as encouragement to systematically review the full gamut of evidence that gold in Roman poetry is correspondingly compromised by implications of deceptiveness in Latin literature.[54] It may suffice to consider, even briefly, how gold is figured in Virgil.[55] Take the goldenness of the Capitol at *Aeneid* 8.348, where Aeneas at Pallanteum is shown the Capitol, *aurea nunc, olim silvestribus horrida dumis*, 'golden now, then bristling with woodland thickets'. Now gold, but green before? Or gold now, to be green once more? As Martindale explains, Virgil's superimposition of the Roman Capitol on a prehistoric scene invites alternative readings, one producing a narrative of progress from wilderness to gilded temple, and another of culture's eventual degeneration to its primal origins:

> the *nunc/olim* figure [...] is itself ambiguous since *olim* can refer to past or future: either 'golden now, once densely wooded' or 'golden now, one day to be densely wooded'. So it is not only a matter of whether we prefer woods or gold; the trajectory of history is itself unclear, either from gold to woods or vice versa, and the lines might allow us to see beyond Augustan grandeur to a return to the wild.

Moreover,

> *Nunc* may introduce a further wavering, since it could mean 'now in Virgil's day' or 'now in Aeneas' day', and 'golden' could be literal or metaphorical, 'belonging to a golden time' or 'made of gold/gilded'.[56]

In brief, the significance of 'gold' depends of the way it is contextualized. So too with the Saturnian golden age of *Aeneid* 6.792–3. Common sense requires the passage to mean that a golden age will yet once more be inaugurated in Latium by Augustus. To read *condere* in the opposite sense, as 'bring to a close' (an option Thomas does not recommend, but would preserve unsuppressed) causes problems that many find unnecessary.[57] But to read Virgil's *condere* through

Muldoon's reading of Frost in 'Gold' is only to perceive transience itself ('nothing gold can stay') as a qualification of *condere* in the sense of 'inaugurate', allowing us to see the end in the beginning. There is no need to invoke intentionality, no need to imagine any poet 'up to his tricks'. We might describe such an ambiguity of reception as qualitative rather than logical. That is to say, what distinguishes this kind of ambiguity is not its ideas but its allusive character, unlike the subject of Empson's more strictly logical kind of analysis in *Seven Types of Ambiguity* (1930), a study much appreciated in R. A. Brooks's 1953 article on Virgil's most famous and complex representation of gold (*Aeneid* 6.201–9), '*Discolor Aura*. Reflections on the Golden Bough'.[58]

The goldenness of Virgil's golden bough, which Aeneas must secure to gain passage to the underworld, is ambiguous not so much for any quality of gold itself, but for the way in which the strange bough is represented as a link between the world of organic life and the world of the dead. The bough is dead gold growing like a miraculous graft on living green (6.206). This gold, *aurum*, is described as an *aura*, a breath of air (6.204). 'The ancient critics did not know what to make of the expression, and no wonder', remarks Virgil's twentieth-century commentator R. G. Austin.[59] One way to approach this marvel is through its reception. What have poets made of Virgil's golden bough? We might read Virgil's bough through Muldoon's two responses to Frost's 'Nothing Gold Can Stay', each of which can be said to be responding only obliquely to Virgil. Or for a direct response to Virgil, one that is characteristically local and localized, we may turn to Seamus Heaney. His version of the golden bough is the bunch of glittering oat stalks, each grain wrapped in foil from chocolate bars, customarily carried to births as well as funerals in 'Route 110', the twelve-part poem that recasts *Aeneid* 6 as an autobiographical lyric sequence in Heaney's final collection, *Human Chain* (2010).[60] But as Rachel Falconer has observed, Heaney's evocation of the golden bough recapitulates distinctive aspects of his own work every bit as much as Virgil's: 'Some readers might remember how gleams of light in dark, muddy places are a feature of Heaney's verse even before they are pulled into the aura of Virgil's bough.'[61] So Heaney's late version of the golden bough celebrates Virgil, but corroborates the earlier Heaney as well. Reception's retrospection searches through many provinces.

'Corroborate' is a term Heaney taught his critics, and it seems a useful verb by which to acknowledge that the act of reading through reception does not always discover things that were entirely unknown before. And yet it does not find things, or indeed leave them, exactly as they were. The golden head in Finlay's garden – does it mean more, does it mean 'better' after the series of readings I have sounded out, in which gold is simultaneously a figure of permanence and impermanence? A mere thickening of interpretative texture is not necessarily an improvement in reading. With luck, however, an ancient text may be recontextualized through its reception in ways that may 'enrich' subsequent readings, not in the sense of loading them with critical gold, but rather in the sense of proposing new ways for them to mean again, in readings that will depart and differ from the previous ones.[62]

'Enrichment' is Stephen Harrison's term for the way in which Augustan poems amplify their own scope for meaning by incorporating elements from different genres within the text's 'host' genre, allowing the reader to generate meaning from these orchestrated confrontations between the genres.[63] In a more prosaic vein of intertextual close reading, my book aims to investigate key areas of Virgil's texts by focusing on points of poetic reception. While reception is bidirectional, the form of reading I test in these chapters faces mainly towards the classics. That is to say, I am mainly concerned to inquire whether, for instance, Muldoon reading Frost can help me read Virgil in a way that might seem useful or interesting to others. I am not asking how Virgil might enable us to understand Stoppard's *Arcadia*, but instead how *Arcadia* can help us find ways that lead to Virgil through his reception. I read Auden's 'The Shield of Achilles' to search out traces of Homer in Virgil's Shield of Aeneas, and Wordsworth's 'Tintern Abbey' to interpret the paradoxical or equivocal 'double *makarismos*' passage in *Georgics* 2, where Virgil twice juxtaposes the blessings of intellectual glory against the blessings of obscure piety (475–94). In the final chapter I interrogate Seamus Heaney's lifelong engagement with Virgil, testing apparently Virgilian springs without presuming that they can be traced back to a knowable source in Heaney's imagination, but asking instead how Heaney can lead the reader to Virgil.

In each of these comparative exercises I have tried to find value in elements of difference – the ways in which Auden or Heaney differ from Virgil – quite as much as in the elements of similarity I propose. I have done so partly to temper an occupational bias of literary studies in favour of demonstrating points of likeness. One is too easily inclined to say 'this is like Virgil' instead of the opposite. Yet the freedom of negative judgement is vital to the enterprise. I have found that reservations are greatly sped by the confidence that, like any other critical judgement, they will never be the final word.

The chapter sequence needs a word of explanation. Though each chapter can be read on its own, the book is also intended to work cumulatively. Since the book focuses mainly on Virgil, and since it is a work of literary criticism rather than history, the chapter sequence does not observe chronology in the order in which modern authors are discussed. The book's pattern might instead reflect the paradigm of the hierarchy of Virgilian genres, beginning in pastoral and culminating in epic, and the corresponding notion of generic ascent throughout (and in each of) Virgil's works. As Harrison explains in *Generic Enrichment*, this ascent is not a mere matter of graduating from lower to higher genres as though each phase were simply a stepping-stone to the next, or a rung on a ladder. Instead, each phase involves the others and requires an awareness of the full cycle. The principle of generic ascent operates within individual works, regardless of their place in the conventional hierarchy, as each work develops poetic complexity through its own progression through a series of intertextual encounters. My book would ideally describe an analogous widening of scope through its progression of intertextual encounters, in that the first three chapters discuss single works in relation to Virgil, before the final chapter surveys an entire *oeuvre*, namely Heaney's. But I do not strictly follow the order of Virgilian genres, if only because the order itself matters less than the principle of progression or ascent. After the first chapter on Stoppard's *Arcadia* and pastoral, I pass on to Auden's 'Shield of Achilles' and epic, before focusing on a key aspect of georgic in the third chapter on Wordsworth's 'Tintern Abbey'. My chapter sequence reflects the principle of ascent inasmuch as it aims to trace a widening of scope.

The sequence should not be taken to imply any notion of qualitative hierarchy among the texts discussed, either modern or Virgilian. (Put crudely, epic is not 'better' than pastoral.) The first chapter on *Arcadia* is the book's next longest because it concerns a whole Virgilian or post-Virgilian tradition, the pastoral, and because I think the complexities of Stoppard's magnificent play lend themselves to introducing the basic issues of reading through reception. The final chapter on Heaney is the book's longest, because it traces his engagement with Virgil throughout his whole career. The middle pair of chapters are relatively concentrated, and aim to show how reading through reception can serve to concentrate on specific points in Virgil's work. The book's structure describes a chiastic pattern. The long chapters on Stoppard and Heaney bracket a central pair that are each relatively short and concentrated. The Introduction and Conclusion are relatively broad-ranging bookends. The Conclusion, a coda on the ways in which modern literature can help us become better or at any rate happier readers of Virgil, focuses on the genre of didactic epic as developed in V. Sackville-West's two georgics, *The Land* (1926) and *The Garden* (1946).

Virgil in Stoppard's *Arcadia*

*I shall no longer resist the passion growing in me for things of a natural kind,
where neither art nor the conceit or caprice of man has spoiled their genuine
order by breaking in upon that primitive state. Even the rude rocks, the mossy
caverns, the irregular unwrought grottos and broken falls of waters, with all
the horrid graces of the wilderness itself, as representing nature more, will be
the more engaging and appear with a magnificence beyond the formal
mockery of princely gardens.*

Shaftesbury, *Characteristicks* (1711), 'The Moralists, a
Philosophical Rhapsody', part 3, section 2

*'Allow me,' said Mr Gall. 'I distinguish the picturesque and the beautiful, and I
add to them, in the laying out of grounds, a third and distinct character, which
I call* unexpectedness.'

*'Pray, Sir,' said Mr Milestone, 'by what name do you distinguish this
character, when a person walks round the grounds for the second time?'*

Thomas Love Peacock, *Headlong Hall* (1815), ch. 4

What can Tom Stoppard's *Arcadia* (1993) help us see in the *Eclogues*? The attempt
to find a positive answer may seem bold to the point of folly, or simply naïve. The
removes between Virgil and Stoppard are innumerable. They are not even fully
recoverable; what is more, they do not hold still. What interposes between Virgil
and Stoppard is scarcely less than the whole pastoral tradition in the arts – an
extraordinarily varied set of generic permutations. But if there is a route to be
traced from Stoppard to Virgil – and I wish to investigate whether there is – we
cannot seek to bypass the intervening pastoral tradition, if only because
Stoppard's play comprehends and reconfigures so many elements of that
tradition. To approach Virgil through a modern playwright and a complex post-
classical tradition is not only preposterous but perverse, insofar as it courts
insurmountable difficulties. Some classicists have felt that the reception of the

Eclogues is precisely what has 'made interpretation difficult', as a scholar has remarked specifically of Eclogue 4, since Virgil's poems are long since 'encrusted by tradition'.[1] Richard Jenkyns, for instance, urges that we rather scrape away 'the barnacles of later tradition' the better to see the *Eclogues* 'in their true shape'.[2] Proponents of reception studies take the opposite view. They insist that, on the contrary, the 'barnacles' are actually vital to the organism, vital even to our capacity to perceive it in the first place. The very ideal of a pristine original, they contend, is inconceivable without the mediation of tradition itself. Reception scholars have argued that since anachronism and diachrony cannot be avoided, the resources associated with these should be used creatively. In the past three decades, reception-oriented studies in Classics have influentially proposed an understanding of the pastoral genre as a dynamic complex of historical processes that mediates each realization of the *Eclogues*.[3] Genres themselves, it is proposed, 'are best thought of as processes'.[4]

I shall be discussing the many ways in which Stoppard's *Arcadia* draws attention to distinctive aspects of the *Eclogues* as well as Virgil's reception. Above all, *Arcadia* helps us appreciate the historical 'jointedness' of pastoral, its growth through branching out, through creative accretions and points of contact with other traditions: the processes by which both pastoral and 'Virgil' prove their integrity by the trial of articulation.[5]

The play's title evokes the motto *et in Arcadia ego* made famous by Nicolas Poussin's two versions of *The Arcadian Shepherds* (Chatsworth, *c.* 1628–9; Louvre, 1638–40). The motto itself is not Virgilian, yet its meanings are integral to our sense of what 'Virgilian' means. Just so, the fundamental problems of mortality, loss, and the passage of time that lie at the heart of Stoppard's play describe a province of pastoral that is 'Virgilian' greatly by virtue of the Renaissance reception that informs the *Eclogues*. *Arcadia* introduces its audience to several intellectual traditions that have been understood as 'versions of pastoral', most importantly eighteenth-century theories of landscape gardening, where pastoral and georgic converge. Through its own structure, the play also reworks many of pastoral's distinctive structural tropes, such as recurrence, antithesis, and ironic suspension. But it should be stressed that Stoppard incorporates aspects of the pastoral tradition in order to consider something extra-literary, something even more fundamental or universal than pastoral itself. *Arcadia* traces the ways in which historical processes unfold. As one of Stoppard's characters puts it, 'The unpredictable and the predetermined unfold together to make everything the way it is' (62/64).[6] The speaker, a young mathematician studying population dynamics, is explaining the area of modern mathematics known as nonlinear dynamics or deterministic chaos or chaos theory. Mathematics and pastoral might seem unlikely bedfellows, at any rate until one remembers a basic feature they share common, the principle of economy that governs their typically stylized and abstracting modes of representation.[7] Mathematics, like Keats's 'cold pastoral', operates at a remove from reality, or rather a series of removes. Chaos theory is 'not about the behaviour of fish. It's about the behaviour of numbers' (60/62); and as Stoppard's mathematician Valentine also observes, modelling fractals is 'not a way of drawing an elephant' (62/64). Given this common tendency towards abstraction, mathematical elegance may not seem so far removed from the pastoral aesthetic of *gracilitas* and *tenuitas*. One might almost describe mathematics as another art of 'putting the complex into the simple', William Empson's famous formulation of the pastoral process.

Mathematics and pastoral

Of course, there is no literal relation between mathematics and pastoral. It is the figurative link that *Arcadia* suggestively explores. Chaos mathematics is described in the play in order to imply analogies with processes of historical change and loss, dramatically illustrated by the unfolding of a strange kind of double plot on two time levels that reworks many features and motifs associated with the pastoral tradition. Stoppard's treatment of chaos theory in *Arcadia* suggests new ways to reconfigure Empson's fix on the essential relationship in pastoral between simplicity and complexity.[8] Certainly Empson's model is not crudely reductive: his formulation need not imply that pastoral *collapses* the complex into the simple, or that reduction entails a loss of meaning. If anything, compression tends to *increase* a text's potential for meaning and ambiguity. But Empson's 'putting the complex into the simple' does describe a figure of substitution whereby the complex appears to be *replaced by* the simple. Empson's figure offers no idea of how the simple and the complex might work together. To suggest an outline sketch of such processes, such unfoldings, is the representative function of nonlinear dynamics in *Arcadia*.

Thematically, Stoppard uses the concepts of chaos theory to explore a fundamental philosophical question that has preoccupied him throughout his career, namely the relationship between determinism and free will. As Stoppard's Guildenstern defines determinism (parodying Wilde's Miss Prism), 'Each move is dictated by the previous one – that is the meaning of order'.[9] Chaos theory aims to describe the behaviour of deterministic systems in states when 'you can't say what [the system is] going to do next'.[10] But Stoppard's version of chaos mathematics also provides a suggestive analogy for the processes of generic change in seeking to describe how patterns can be glimpsed in the turbulence of mixture, or to explain 'what happens in a cup of coffee when the cream goes in' (62/64).[11]

Et in Arcadia ego

To suggest how Stoppard's play draws us toward many conduits of the pastoral tradition and their points of confluence with other aesthetic traditions, we need only linger over the play's title. The notion of Arcadia is remarkably complex, and its centrality in the pastoral tradition, which is inseparable from Virgil's modern reception, is mainly a post-medieval development.[12] Above all Arcadia is a composite idea, inspired by many poets and artists besides Virgil – all of whom were in some way inspired by Virgil, but by no means purely or exclusively. In Virgil, Arcadia is the distant Greek upland of pastures, peaks and pine forests, a chilly climate – the primitive domain of Pan, virile god of herdsmen and bucolic song. Virgil's Arcadia is thus a mythic region as well as a geographical terrain, and its mythical dimension itself betrays its literary constructedness. Even in the exceptional case of Eclogue 10, the only Virgilian eclogue arguably 'set' in Arcadia, the Arcadian setting is actually *in*set. It is presented at a remove, framed by the primary scene of the pastoral singer's performance (1–8, 70–7).[13] Placed within the poem's programmatic framework, the Arcadian motif provides a scenic context for the elegiac poet Gallus' love-sufferings.

In fact Virgil may be said to evoke Arcadia most characteristically in Sicilian and Po Valley settings, accentuating his typical juxtaposition of mythic Greece and contemporary Italy, as when a pair of shepherds capping verses by the northern Italian river Mincius (Mincio) are said to be *Arcades ambo*, 'Arcadians both' (7.4). Similarly in *Aeneid* 8, Evander's people on the banks of the Tiber came to Italy from Arcadia. Virgil's Arcadia is a figure of originary purity, yet typically he uses it to highlight the compositeness of his own contemporary world. Stoppard too reminds his audience, through the mouthpiece of Hannah Jarvis, the play's landscape historian, that the notion of an 'Arcadian' English landscape – 'the real England' – is an 'invention', the result of derivative composition:

Bernard   Lovely. The real England.

Hannah   You can stop being silly now, Bernard. English landscape was invented by gardeners imitating foreign painters who were evoking classical authors. The whole thing was brought home in the luggage from the grand tour. Here, look – Capability Brown doing Claude, who was doing Virgil. Arcadia!

34/36

Hannah's remarks dismiss the notion of 'the real' English landscape, but they also unsettle the whole notion of Arcadia as a figure of points of origin – whether the origins of a landscape, or of poetry, or of civilization. Stoppard's play is concerned precisely with the reality of loss, the difficulties of recovery, and the impossibility of return. The common notion of 'Arcadia' stands for a stasis that always proves illusory, ever receding before examination, like the past itself. Stoppard's Lady Croom invokes Arcadia to veto the proposals of the landscape architect Richard Noakes, employed by her husband to redesign the grounds in the new picturesque style, and Lady Croom's notion of a providential 'Arcadian' English landscape reflected in the layout of her estate is precisely the cliché dismissed by Hannah. When the landscape architect attempts to defend the picturesque, Lady Croom interrupts:

> But Sidley Park is already a picture, and a most amiable picture too. The slopes are green and gentle. The trees are companionably grouped at intervals that show them to advantage. The rill is a serpentine ribbon unwound from the lake peaceably contained by meadows on which the right amount of sheep are tastefully arranged – in short, it is nature as God intended, and I can say with the painter, '*Et in Arcadia ego!*' 'Here I am in Arcadia,' Thomasina.

16/19

Lady Croom here unwittingly betrays a paradox that also concerns the classical Arcadia, which, too, is 'already a picture'. The Arcadian point of origin once more recedes as the dichotomy of nature and art breaks down. For Lady Croom, Arcadia simply represents stasis, a timeless idyll, a refuge from change. Yet Arcadia is also associated with the loss that accompanies all change, and indeed the passage of time itself. In the play, Lady Croom's complacent mistranslation of *Et in Arcadia ego*, the motto Poussin derived from the Italian painter Guercino, serves to dramatically suggest the entropic process by which art loses its definition as it seeps into life, for her invocation of the motto has already been anticipated by a comically debased version spoken (unwittingly) by the poetaster Ezra Chater, a figure as innocent of his own bathos in praising the fortunate results of his wife's infidelity as he is of evoking Arcadia/Eden and the happy fall (*felix culpa*):

Chater   It was all a nonsense, sir – a canard! But a fortunate mistake, sir. It
brought me the patronage of a captain of His Majesty's Navy and the brother of
a countess. I do not think Mr Walter Scott can say as much, and here I am, a
respected guest at Sidley Park.

12/14

Lady Croom's mistranslation of Guercino's motto as 'Here I am in Arcadia' is
immediately called into question by Thomasina, who knows as well as Septimus
that the 'correct' translation implies that the speaker is a personification, Death
himself: '"Even in Arcadia, there am I!"' (18/21). Either of the historically
established translations of *Et in Arcadia ego* (discussed in Erwin Panofsky's
famous article on Poussin) acknowledges a kind of irrevocable loss.[14] The
melancholy 'I too lived in Arcadia', understood as spoken by the shepherd from
the grave, mourns an irrecoverable past. The *memento mori* sentiment as spoken
by Death insists on the absoluteness of mortality. (Each of Poussin's two paintings
may be said to illustrate one of the alternatives: 'Louvre' the melancholic,
'Chatsworth' the dramatic.) Yet the notion of Arcadia, unchanging though
vulnerable to intrusive loss through the passage of time, suggests not only
absoluteness but also recurrence. This is what the conceit of Stoppard's stage
setting is meant to suggest: *Arcadia* is set entirely in a single room, alternating
between two periods. As Stoppard's stage direction to Scene Two explains, '*The
action of the play shuttles back and forth between the early nineteenth century and
the present day, always in the same room. Both periods must share the state of the
room, without the additions and subtractions which would normally be expected*'
(19/22). When ideas, motifs, phrases and situations from the action of the
Regency era scenes are echoed (with intriguing variation) by characters in the
present-day scenes, this oscillation between the two periods suggests patterns of
(near-)recurrence. The invisible traffic between the time periods is tangibly
represented onstage by the room's large table, which accumulates objects from
both eras and thus effectively shares them across time, enabling discoveries and
rediscoveries by supplying lost information. The 'state' of the room (the revised
text of 2009 reads 'stage'), its fixed parameters hosting the action of two periods
in a version of 'the double plot', suggests the palimpsestic character of the stylized
setting associated with Arcadia in Renaissance poetry, where the standard
backdrop of painted meadows and purling streams serves to frame a potentially
infinite set of fine variations played on the conventions of pastoral. As Thomas
Rosenmeyer observes of Theocritus' 'bucolic landscape' in his famous study of
the pastoral lyric (*The Green Cabinet*, 1969), 'the clarity with which the landscape
is articulated suggests the limited confines of an interior'.[15] The 'limited confines'

and timeless arrest of the Renaissance Arcadian setting typically foreground a process of recalibration. By common consent the most conventional of modes, pastoral works by repetition and echo, iterating its simple codes to produce variation and (at its best) complexity.[16] 'Already a picture', Arcadia must nevertheless always be reconfigured anew. The stylized boundaries described by pastoral convention serve, moreover, to offset processes of change, whether the regular passage of days and seasons or the more abrupt incursions of mortality and historical events. The repetitions of convention are never identical, but serve to suggest patterns of recurrence. Recurrence casts light before as well as after; but time's arrow is irreversible, as the finality of death typically serves to recall. In Stoppard's play, time's irreversibility raises quite specific philosophical and scientific questions about apparently universal patterns or possibilities of recurrence.

'Time conquers All, and we must Time obey'

Time's paradoxes are Stoppard's main concern. If time is the medium of plot, it is also the medium of loss, *Arcadia*'s fundamental theme. As Stoppard's Rosencrantz observes, 'for all the compasses in the world, there's only one direction, and time is its only measure'.[17] In the English eclogue tradition, it is Spenser who introduces the structural principle of the Calendar and so establishes the seasonal paradigm.[18] Marlowe's lyric 'The Passionate Shepherd to his Love' (printed 1600) elicited the retort of Raleigh's nymph that pastoral's illusion of suspended pleasure is contradicted by the very fact of mutability: 'Time drives the flocks from field to fold' ('The Nymph's Reply to the Shepherd', 5). But it is Alexander Pope who, enshrining Spenser's calendrical order in his own *Pastorals* (1709), identifies transience as pastoral's distinctive philosophical concern. 'Time conquers All, and we must Time obey' ('Winter', 88). This climactic statement of Pope's work echoes the sense of *omia fert aetas*, 'age robs us of everything' (Moeris' remark in Eclogue 9.51, Heaney's translation), but inhabits the form of the resonant line spoken by Gallus in Virgil's Eclogue 10, *omnia vincit Amor: et nos cedamus Amori* , 'Love conquers all; and we must yield to Love' (69, trans. Dryden).[19] In *The Winter's Tale*, Shakespeare's pastoral tragicomedy of reconciliation and restoration, personified Time plays the pivotal role, introducing himself as he 'that makes and unfolds error' (4.1.2). Shakespeare thus highlights Time's double nature as the agent of restoration as well as loss, juxtaposing the disconcerting vagaries of fortune (where 'chance rules all', as the embittered Moeris complains in Eclogue 9.5) with the play's providential implications, powerfully buttressed by its symmetrical design. The reconciliation of accident and design ('the fortuitous and the ordained', as Stoppard's Guildenstern puts it) is precisely what Stoppard's use of chaos theory aims to suggest.[20] This convergence is given emblematic expression in *Arcadia*'s final scene, in which the play's two time periods overlap. The play ends with two couples dancing in the play's single room, one couple from each of the periods, each unaware of the other, each dancing to music from their respective period.[21] While the Regency couple waltzes 'fluently', the modern couple dances 'rather awkwardly'. The scene has reminded critics of Poussin's famous allegorical painting known as *The Dance to the Music of Time*.[22] For a mediating text we may look to Anthony Powell's *A Dance to the Music of Time*, the sequence of novels that widely familiarized Poussin's painting in twentieth-century Britain, specifically the narrator's seminal observations on the painting in Powell's opening pages:

> These classical projections, and something in the physical attitudes of the men themselves as they turned from the fire, suddenly suggested Poussin's scene in which the Seasons, hand in hand and facing outward, tread in rhythm to the notes of the lyre that the winged and naked greybeard plays. The image of Time brought thoughts of mortality: of human beings, facing outward like the Seasons, moving hand in hand in intricate measure, stepping slowly, methodically, sometimes a trifle awkwardly, in evolutions that take recognisable shape: or breaking into seemingly meaningless gyrations, while partners disappear only to reappear again, once more giving pattern to the spectacle: unable to control the melody, unable, perhaps, to control the steps of the dance.
>
> *A Question of Upbringing*, 1951, ch.1, second paragraph[23]

The oscillations observed by Powell's narrator between apparent randomness and apparent order, between the disappearance and reappearance (or rediscovery) of patterns, make this passage seem strikingly relevant to what one might call *Arcadia*'s 'chaos paradigm' and Stoppard's fascination with the loss and partial reappearance of information. Poussin's painting has also been discussed in other pastoral contexts, for instance as a possible influence on the design of Pope's *Pastorals*. The links between time, mutability, chance and design are recurrent themes in the reception-history of Poussin's work, signs of its deep affinities with pastoral.[24] And Poussin looms large in Stoppard's dramatic meditation on pastoral, reminding us of the painter's centrality in the literary tradition. Stoppard's most powerful evocation of Poussin's *Arcadian Shepherds* occurs when the audience is made aware that there exists a memorial to

Thomasina in the Park. The motif inevitably recalls the tomb in Arcadia (101/104). With a decorum and perhaps a sensibility we might call 'Virgilian', the play's key allusion to an Arcadian motif refers to a location *offstage*.

Loss. And recurrence?

Stoppard's main ideas about loss and recurrence centre on the brilliant adolescent Thomasina herself. The first lesson her tutor sets her may itself be taken as a kind of parable about loss and rediscovery. With witty disregard for pedagogical fair play, Septimus challenges Thomasina to work out a proof for Fermat's theorem ('when x, y, and z are whole numbers each raised to power of n, the sum of the first two can never equal the third when n is greater than 2'; 4/6):

> **Septimus**   [...] Fermat's last theorem has kept people busy for a hundred and fifty years, and I hoped it would keep *you* busy long enough for me to read Mr Chater's praise of love with only the distraction of its own absurdities.
>
> 2/4

Fermat's problem was never strictly a theorem but rather a conjecture, since he never produced the proof he famously claimed he did not have the space to write down in the margin of his *Arithmetica* (7/10). This alerts us to a crucial point about Fermat's theorem, which remained unproved until two months after the première of *Arcadia*, when on 23 June 1993 the Cambridge mathematician Andrew Wiles finally presented his proof. (A flaw was soon discovered, but Wiles perfected his proof the following year.) Stoppard could not have foreseen that this Holy Grail of mathematicians would ever be found. Fortuitously, though, Wiles's discovery highlights a simple truth adumbrated by Stoppard's representation of chaos theory in *Arcadia*, namely that Wiles's proof cannot be identical with the proof Fermat claimed to have discovered, if only because the articulation of any proof is necessarily unique. *That* particular proof cannot recur (except perhaps statistically on an impossible timescale); *it* is truly lost. In an important early speech, Septimus optimistically denies the ultimate reality of historical loss, countering Thomasina's anguish over 'all the lost plays of the Athenians' and the burning of the Great Library of Alexandria:

> We shed as we pick up, like travellers who must carry everything in their arms, and what we let fall will be picked up by those behind. The procession is very long and life is very short. We die on the march. But there is nothing outside the march so nothing can be lost to it. The missing plays of Sophocles will turn up

piece by piece, or be written again in another language. Ancient cures for diseases
will reveal themselves once more. Mathematical discoveries glimpsed and lost to
view will have their time again.

51/53

What Septimus is describing is a fantasy of history as a closed system, as it might
appear to someone unaware of the second law of thermodynamics. In some
respects Septimus's fantasy also adumbrates Henri Poincaré's recurrence
theorem, which proposes that some closed systems (including the universe) may
– given sufficient time – return to states very close to their initial state.[25] But
history is not a closed system. Rather it is an open system, like the weather. Its
motions are caused by the flow of energy from the sun, and they are sensitive to
initial conditions, or feedback. *Arcadia* ironically – teasingly – bears out
Septimus's prophecy that 'Mathematical discoveries glimpsed and lost to view
will have their time again'. But Septimus also comes to experience that loss is
more humanly real as well as more absolute and final than he first allowed. From
its privileged perspective, the audience observes how key aspects of Thomasina's
discoveries and even traces of her character appear to recur in the present-day
scenes. But what gives this partial recurrence its poignancy is the stubborn,
obvious fact that Thomasina herself cannot recur. We might take this as a parable
of the scholarly quest for historical recovery – of an 'original' text, for instance, or
a historically 'authentic' reading. These too leave traces that may be realized
variously, perhaps in some ways fulfilled, in the passage of time. But the
arrow of time guarantees that the point of origin always recedes. It is always
irretrievably lost.

Entropy

Stoppard's concern with the problem of loss is broached early in the play's
first scene, where Thomasina shows her prescient grasp of the significance of
entropy. In thermodynamics ('the theory of the relations between heat and
mechanical energy', *OED*), entropy is a measure of the loss of available energy,
notwithstanding the absolute physical law of the conservation of energy. To
adopt Stoppard's imagery, heat dissipates throughout the universe like a spoonful
of jam stirred into a rice pudding. As Thomasina observes, the mix is irreversible:
'you cannot stir things apart' (6/8). No more can a Latin translation of Shakespeare
be translated back into its original, for as Septimus's second witty lesson in
futility demonstrates, poetry is what is lost in translation (46–52/48–54). You

cannot put the 'lost poetry' back in (47/49), any more than you can collect up the heat from the smash of a broken window (125/128). Thomasina's provocatively naïve question 'How is a ruined child different from a ruined castle?' elicits a ludicrous response – 'A ruined castle is picturesque, certainly' (14 – 15/17) – only to offset the unspoken tragic answer. Yet however fundamentally these processes of 'ruin' differ from each other, they are equally irreversible.

Energy dissipates. As Peter Atkins explains, while the total quantity of energy is conserved, its quality, measured as the energy available for work, degrades with each exchange.[26] Lost heat 'goes into the mix', observes Valentine, gesturing '*to indicate the air in the room, in the universe*' (126/128). He is explaining the diagram of heat exchange that shows Thomasina's anticipation of the second law of thermodynamics. The total state of the universe moves inexorably in one direction, towards maximum entropy or thermodynamic equilibrium:

> **Valentine**   Heat goes to cold. It's a one – way street. Your tea will end up at room temperature. What's happening to your tea is happening to everything everywhere. The sun and the stars. It'll take a while but we're all going to end up at room temperature.
>
> 104/106

When the implications of this principle were realized in the nineteenth century, contemporaries generally drew Septimus's gloomy conclusion that 'we are all doomed!' (125/127, echoing/echoed by Valentine, 87/89).[27] Yet as Thomasina appears to anticipate (she assents to Septimus '*cheerfully*', 125/127), the principle of irreversibility has come to be recognized as fundamental to the organizing principles of life itself. Even as energy dissipates, as systems are disorganized and information is lost, 'nature forms patterns'.[28] Anticipating Sadi Carnot's pioneering work in thermodynamics, Thomasina intimates too that entropy is itself a precondition for change, indeed for life itself. (Atkins describes entropy as the 'spring' of change).[29] She attributes the unpredictability of deterministic systems to the entropic dissipation observed in Joseph Fourier's early analysis of heat flow in the prize-winning essay Septimus has been reading, *Mémoire sur la propagation de la chaleur dans les corps solides* (1807, on 'the action of bodies in heat', 111/114). Loss itself can thus be seen as the source of creative feedback.[30] Valentine's remark that 'the heat goes into the mix' occurs in the final scene in which the play's two periods converge, so that Thomasina's immediately following line, inflecting the *carpe diem* sentiment, sounds like a rejoinder to her twentieth-century family descendant: 'Yes, we must hurry if we are going to dance' (126/128).

'Like seeing a picture'

Entropy and energy are often thought of as mutually opposed, but the processes
they denote are always concurrent, indeed mutually implicated. ('As the universe
ebbs toward its final equilibrium in the featureless heat bath of maximum
entropy', writes James Gleick, 'it manages to create interesting structures'.)[31] The
study of nonlinear dynamics or mathematical chaos aims to understand the
principles of design that inform the pattern-generating processes in nature, as
well as the recursive patterns observable in 'any phenomenon which eats its own
numbers – measles epidemics, rainfall averages, cotton prices' (60/2),[32] reflecting
processes that deterministically yet also quite unpredictably combine elements
of repetition and irregularity (62–3/64–5). Septimus's tragic fate – or tragic
choice – is to devote the remainder of his life after Thomasina's death to the futile
task of finishing the final exercise he set her: 'For your essay this week, explicate
your diagram [of heat exchange]'. 'I cannot', Thomasina replies, 'I do not know
the mathematics' (117/119) – a shortcoming her future relative Valentine
echoingly observes: 'She didn't have the maths, not remotely' (125/127). Septimus
asks Thomasina to explain 'Without mathematics, then' (117/119). But without
'the maths', Thomasina's insight into 'what things meant, way ahead' must remain
expressed as a diagram (125/127). The maths is what Septimus attempts to work
out, and although the results are lost – at the end of his life he destroys his
thousands of sheets of paper in a bonfire (36–7/38–9) – his anticipation of
twentieth-century chaos mathematics is tantalizingly suggested by the
uncomprehending and contradictory (and fictional) Victorian accounts of his
work, cited in the play. On the fictional evidence of Thomas Love Peacock,
Hannah reports that the hermit of Sidley Park had 'covered every sheet with
cabalistic proofs that the world was coming to an end' (36/39). A Peacock letter
quoted later in the play represents the hermit's labours as an effort to bring
together the gloomy predictions of 'Frenchified mathematick' (a reference to the
mathematical implications of the second law of thermodynamics) with 'the
restitution of hope through good English algebra' (87/89) – a description in
which the audience has been taught to recognize the self-organizing processes
and principles associated with mathematical chaos and fractals.[33]

What Victorian science cannot grasp (but Stoppard's audience is primed to
discern) is the connection between entropy and self-organization. Thomasina
discerns time's arrow in both, and she realizes that irreversibility must have
fundamental implications. This is what Valentine means when he says 'she saw
[...] way ahead, like seeing a picture' (125/127). What Thomasina grasps is that

whereas the classical heat equation is linear, *real* heat flow is not, and that the irreversibility anyone can observe in processes of cooling or mixing has important scientific implications.[34] She anticipates chaos theory in surmising that many natural processes are nonlinear (i.e., systems in which the outcome is not proportional to the input), and that all living things, like all real heat engines, are open systems. Against Septimus's fantasy of human history as a closed system in which recurrence is bound to happen ('there is nothing outside the march so nothing can be lost to it', 50/53), Thomasina's nonlinear algebraic geometry describes systems that are familiar to common experience in that *patterns* of recurrence are not to be confused with literal or identical recurrence. *Arcadia* fully acknowledges the reality of loss – its effects appear by turns farcical, poignant, and devastating in the play's tragicomic mode – even as Stoppard also intimates the operation of universal patterns of recurrence on discontinuous scales.

The kaleidoscope of genre

How can *Arcadia*'s treatment of loss and recurrence aid us in reading Virgil afresh, besides offering a series of meta-perspectives? I have already suggested some ways in which *Arcadia* draws attention to essential aspects of Virgil's *Eclogues*, such as the dramatic cast of the eclogue form that foregrounds herdsmen's conversation in a *tableau vivant*-like scene, referring to offstage larger-scale events. The play's single stage setting is a version of 'the pastoral space' that 'has no unique landmarks', reflecting a form whose 'history [...] is one of revisitings, repeatings, and superimpositions'.[35] The aesthetic self-reflexiveness of Stoppard's play too suggests a kinship with Virgil as well as the broader pastoral tradition. Further, the structural doublings of *Arcadia* (echoes, recurrences, bifurcations) seem germane not only to the symmetries of Renaissance pastoral drama (again, consider *The Winter's Tale*) but also to Virgil's palimpsestic reworking of Theocritus. I shall now try to offer still more detailed readings of Virgil through Stoppard's play.

'The world's great age begins anew'

Reception studies must appreciate distance and difference as well as proximity and similarity. When Valentine celebrates the advent of a new age of scientific inquiry heralded by chaos theory (62–3/64–5), he does so in terms that seem considerably removed from Virgil's 'Messianic' Eclogue 4, the poem that hails a new golden age to be ushered in by the birth of a miraculous boy. 'It's the best possible time to be alive', enthuses Stoppard's young mathematician, 'when almost everything you thought you knew is wrong' (63/65).[36] Here we catch an echo of Wordsworth's famous reminiscence in *The Prelude* of his ardour in the early 1790s at the birth of the revolutionary era, 'Bliss was it in that dawn to be alive, | But to be young was very heaven!' (1805, 10.692–3). Stoppard is an allusive writer; we may well be intended to hear the Wordsworthian undersong.[37] Comparison to this tangible intertext makes Virgil's Eclogue 4 seem relatively distant, the intervening centuries dense with intermediary tradition. Yet other immediate contexts telescope that distance. Wordsworth's passage associates 'the beauty … of promise' with 'Paradise itself' (10.702–4), and Valentine's celebration of chaos theory evokes a similarly Edenic state of expectancy that derives from golden age metaphors in Stoppard's own sources in the popular science writing of the 1980s, notably Gleick's *Chaos*.[38] The metaphor of a golden age, ultimately derived from Virgil's millenarian expectations in Eclogue 4 as well as other classical sources, is a common trope in the narrative of scientific disovery. Gleick's chapter on the beginnings of chaos research in the 1960s and 70s (evocatively titled 'Revolution') observes that physicists came to realize that the pioneering mathematicians had ushered in 'a golden age', a 'paradigm shift of paradigm shifts'.[39] The Kuhnian concept of the 'paradigm shift' posits a cyclical dialectic that brings out the etymological sense of 'revolution'. As Gleick puts it, 'A new science arises out of one that has reached a dead end'.[40] Valentine's sense of liberation in the discovery that 'almost everything you thought you knew is wrong' echoes the mathematical physicist Mitchell Feigenbaum's remark, reported by Gleick, that as a mathematician observing turbulent phenomena in nature, 'you know that you really don't know anything'.[41] Or as Valentine puts it earlier in his speech, 'It makes me so happy. To be at the beginning again, knowing almost nothing' (62/64). The paradoxical idea of scientific renovation through the avowal of ignorance, of progress as a radical return to epistemological origins, has a pronounced New Age flavour. Perhaps it also owes something of its style to the mode of Christian paradox, specifically the disourse of sublime humility Erich Auerbach finds distinctive of 'the world of Christianity'.[42] (The affinity between the biblical *sermo humilis* and the sublime *humilitas* of Virgil's Messianic Eclogue goes a fair way to explain that most important historical convergence of Christian and Virgilian pastoral traditions.) Pastoral has often served as a vehicle for imagining a fresh start, a return to basic principles, for instance during the age of Romanticism and revolution. Shelley's reworking of Eclogue 4 in the final Chorus of *Hellas* provides a memorable example: 'The world's great age begins anew, | The golden years return'. As Stephen Hinds has observed, pastoral is among the most capacious of genres precisely because it is Janus-faced, harking back to points of origin even as its own condition of continual renewal suggests futurity.[43]

Renewal and return

What such examples make immediately apparent is the sheer familiarity of the tropes associated with golden age tradition – a kind of familiarity that also impinges on readings of Virgil. In Ian Du Quesnay's 1976 reading of Eclogue 4, this sense of recognition or familiarity serves as a foil for discerning an elusive but no less distinctive aspect of the poem, namely its heightened sensitivity to the unpredictable, a feeling of genuine suspense that is naturally much more difficult to recover or even describe than the more familiar sense of recognizing commonplaces. The poem's appeal, he argues, is

> its emotion and pure excitement. The emotion it conveys, that of relief, of the overwhelming incredulous joy, which accompanies the passing of a crisis and the glimpse of a better tomorrow, is an extremely difficult one to handle in words. The choice of details used to characterise the new age makes a large contribution to establishing the emotional tone. On the one hand, they are familiar [. . .] Yet they are so fantastic that there is never a question of believing that they will really happen. It is the mood that is important, the feeling that anything might happen.[44]

This intimation of the unexpected ('the feeling that anything might happen') is very close to the sense of excited wonder conveyed by Valentine's speech, in which the build-up of declarative statements pushes towards the epigrammatic and paradoxical. 'The future', he explains, or rather announces, 'is disorder'. Valentine's speech (62–3/64–5, quoted below) not only catches something of Virgil's oracular tone, and perhaps too of the eclogue's 'stichic' manner,[45] but the analogy of modern science allows Stoppard to invest this annunciatory style with a fresh expectancy of the imminent yet unpredictable. We may here have an instance of reception's capacity to rediscover, if not recover, distinctive aspects of the seminal text.

Shelley's chorus 'The world's great age begins anew' demonstrates the pastoral tradition's capacity to project expectations of renewal as recurrence or return.

What Stoppard's Valentine celebrates is a renewal of science by the process of rediscovering the mystery of everyday things:

> **Valentine**   People were talking about the end of physics. Relativity and
> quantum looked as if they were going to clean out the whole problem between
> them. A theory of everything. But they only explained the very big and the very
> small. The universe, the elementary particles. The ordinary-sized stuff which is
> our lives, the things people write poetry about – clouds – daffodils – waterfalls
> – and what happens in a cup of coffee when the cream goes in – these things are
> full of mystery, as mysterious to us as the heavens were to the Greeks.
>
> 62–3/64–5

Valentine's simile suggests a comparison between chaos theory and ancient Greek science, implying that they are equally distinguished by their commitment to an 'ordinary' human scale and their refusal to draw a boundary between The Two Cultures, between science and 'the things people write poetry about'. The play's idea that an empirical return to the scale of human sensory perception enables the recognition of deep affinities between science and the arts, especially as represented by Romantic art, may owe something to Gleick's biographical account of the young Feigenbaum, who found inspiration in Goethe's heterodox colour theory, which failed to displace Newton's but has nevertheless had a rich afterlife.[46] Throughout *Arcadia*, Stoppard teases his audience with the possibility that, to repeat Septimus's words, 'discoveries glimpsed and lost to view will have their time again' (51/53): Thomasina's fictional insights, lost to history, all anticipate later scientific discoveries.

Occasionally Stoppard's fascination with recurrence is given a millennarian inflection, as when Valentine speculates that, although this world remains 'doomed' by the second law of thermodynamics, the principles of fractal structures offer hope for a (very) distant future: 'If this is how [the world] started, perhaps it's how the next one will come' (103/106). Valentine's remark appears to reflect Stoppard's awareness of the recurrence theorem of Poincaré, who suggested further that the state of maximum entropy 'will not be the final state of the Universe, but a sort of slumber, from which it will awake after millions of centuries'.[47] Again, this may seem a great distance from Virgil's expectations of a returning Saturnian dispensation in Eclogue 4. Yet it may also help us rethink Virgil's panegyrical yet ambivalent prophecy of another Argo, a new Achilles, a second Troy (31–6). Virgil is using these tropes rhetorically, as figures of transition to an age of new beginnings,[48] and his immediate aim seems to have been to celebrate the auspicious beginnings of his patron Pollio's consulship in the reconciliation of Antony and Octavian. But still we are invited to wonder, what *would* a second Troy be like, another expedition of the Argonauts? The number of ways in which these things may be imagined are limitless. What is certain is that a new Achilles would differ from as well as resemble his prototype. In mathematical chaos, some kinds of systems display recurrent behaviour. But in human experience, recurrence is never identical repetition. What Valentine's remark about a new world after this one might help us to see in Virgil's Fourth Eclogue is that renewal – *nascentia,* line 5 – is not the same as identical recurrence.

Binaries

Pastoral's hospitality to figures of recurrence and doubling generously indulges Stoppard's long-standing predilection for figures of doubleness and binary constructions. Does pastoral also discipline this propensity as an analytic tool? Stoppard has explained that the inspiration for *Arcadia* occurred when his reading of Gleick's *Chaos* met with a concurrent urge to exploit, for analytic as well as dramatic purposes, the binary opposition of the Classical and the Romantic:

> [**Interviewer**]   To return to *Arcadia,* where did it begin? With the book, *Chaos*?
>
> [**Stoppard**]   I think so. On the other hand, I must have been reading *Chaos* because of something else I read, maybe in a magazine or a newspaper. It's like a river with more than one source. There's no 'where' about it. You just mentioned the Chaos mathematics book. At the same time, I was thinking about Romanticism and Classicism as opposites in style, taste, temperament, art. I remember talking to a friend of mine, looking at his bookshelves, saying there's a play, isn't there, about the way that retrospectively one looks at poetry, painting, gardening, and speaks of classical periods and the romantic revolution, and so on. Particularly when one starts dividing people up into classical temperaments and romantic temperaments [. . .]. The romantic temperament has a classical person wildly signalling, and vice versa.[49]

With its penchant for contrastive pairings and symmetrical constructions, the pastoral tradition proves remarkably congenial to Stoppard's affinity for figures of antithetical complementarity. *Arcadia* describes the dichotomy of the classical and the romantic as a set of formal contrasts between regularity and irregularity, order and disorder, restraint and extravagance, logic and intuition, and so on.[50] Stoppard's Hannah explains the contrast with regard to landscape design, delivering a narrative of 'predetermined yet unpredictable' decline:

> **Hannah**   The history of the garden says it all, beautifully. There's an engraving
> of Sidley Park in 1730 that makes you want to weep. Paradise in the age of
> reason. By 1760 everything had gone – the topiary, pools and terraces,
> fountains, an avenue of limes – the whole sublime geometry was ploughed
> under by Capability Brown. The grass went from the doorstep to the horizon
> and the best box hedge in Derbyshire was dug up for the ha-ha so that the fools
> could pretend they were living in God's countryside. And then Richard Noakes
> came in to bring God up to date. By the time he'd finished it looked like this
> (*the sketch book*). The decline from thinking to feeling, you see.
>
> 36 – 7/39

However, Hannah's early opposition of classical and Romantic is not the play's
final word on the subject – or indeed her own final opinion in the play. Developing
the contrast between the classical and romantic as a critical tool in his Postscript
to *Appreciations*, Walter Pater introduces a refinement that anticipates Stoppard's
understanding of these terms as complementary and concurrent rather than
mutually exclusive opposites:

> But, however falsely those two tendencies may be opposed by critics, or exaggerated
> by artists themselves, they are tendencies really at work at all times in art, moulding
> it, with the balance sometimes a little on one side, sometimes a little on the other,
> generating, respectively, as the balance inclines on this side or that, two principles,
> two traditions, in art, and in literature so far as it partakes of the spirit of art.[51]

Pater seems to be thinking of the interplay between the 'two principles' as
patterns described by processes that are 'really at work at all times in art'. (These
patterns might equally seem abstracted not from art itself but from its
appreciation.) Stoppard represents chaos theory, which explains how the
unpredictable emerges from the deterministic, as a paradigmatic abstraction of
the interplay between the classical and the romantic, or the regular and the
irregular. The play's main *human* figure of this dichotomy is its most important
offstage character, Byron, described by Bernard as 'an eighteenth-century
Rationalist touched by genius' (79/81). The play's main conceptual illustration of
chaos theory is achieved through the figure of fractals.

Fractals in the green cabinet

Fractals operate by iterating an equation. This mathematical procedure, an
algorithm known as a mapping, is a kind of feedback associated with recursive

processes and self-similar behaviour. The solution to each equation in the series is fed into the next equation (see Valentine's explanation to Hannah, 56–8/59–60). As we have seen, Thomasina calls her algorithm the 'rabbit equation' because it 'eats its own progeny' (103/105). Fractals are suggestive in *Arcadia* because they illustrate how a very simple kind of mathematical procedure (the algebra 'you did at school', 57/59) underlies very complex structures, the mathematical shapes that come closest to resembling the shapes observable in nature. Fractals are not themselves chaotic, but their infinitely complex structure appears in the irregular processes associated with chaos, all predicated on the principle of 'sensitive dependence on initial conditions' that determines the shape and behaviour of 'clouds – daffodils – waterfalls', as well as such similarly unpredictable processes as coffee mixing with cream. Thomasina grows dissatisfied with the Euclidean geometry of her lessons because it projects a 'world of forms' composed exclusively of regular figures: 'nothing but arcs and angles' (49/51; compare her similar remarks on 112/114). 'Do we believe nature is written in numbers?', she demands. 'Then why do your equations only describe the shapes of manufacture? [. . .] Armed thus, God could only make a cabinet' (49/51). Stoppard appears to be playfully alluding to *The Green Cabinet*, Thomas Rosenmeyer's famous study of pastoral. The book's title, Rosenmeyer writes in his preface, 'is a misnomer':

> Theocritus does not, as a rule, calls his pleasance green, nor does he think of it as an enclosure. But 'green cabinet' caught my eye when I read it in Spenser's 'December' [line 17], as '*vert cabinet*' had caught Spenser's eye when he found it in Marot's 'Eglogue au Roy' [Clément Marot, *Eglogue du Marot au Roy* (1539), line 13]. It is the sort of phrase which is at home on a title page. And, with a bit of squeezing, it can be made to fit the *locus amoenus* of Greek pastoral poetry.[52]

Rosenmeyer's explanation of his own title as a suggestive misnomer might be taken to illustrate Richard Jenkyns's description of 'the whole notion of Arcadia' as 'a kind of mistake', its story 'another chapter of accidents' in pastoral's 'odd and accidental history'. As Jenkyns observes – though we needn't share his disapprobation – the more we know about this fortuitous history, 'the better we shall understand why it has been so various and elusive'.[53] Stoppard gives a further twist of the accidental to the phrase *green cabinet* by making Thomasina use 'cabinet' in the modern sense of a piece of elegant carpentry – a display case – instead of evoking the rustic house or 'cabinet' in which Spenser and Marot placed their pastoral singers (the sixteenth-century poets' cabinet is the obsolete diminutive of 'cabin'; cf. the lowly hut, *casa humilis*, of Virgil's Eclogue 2.29).

Stoppard's wit unexpectedly gives new life – or a new meaning – to the notion of a 'green cabinet' by associating the phrase with Thomasina's fractal 'New Geometry of Irregular Forms' (56/59). What made Marot's phrase attractive in the first place, and eventually emblematic of pastoral itself, was its joining of opposites, setting nature (represented by the colour green) against culture (the cabin or cabinet). The notion of unbounded nature – which includes figures of irregularity, like the 'little lines | Of sportive wood run wild' of Wordsworth's 'Tintern Abbey' – is thus combined with the idea of carefully defined space, as in Wordsworth's 'pastoral farms | Green to the very door' (lines 16 – 18), or indeed Hannah's description of grass helped by the ha-ha to appear to stretch 'from the doorstep to the horizon' (36/39). We have seen that Rosenmeyer chose his book title to suggest the convergence of the natural world with 'the limited confines of an interior': if only for this reason, *The Green Cabinet* might make a suggestive alternative title for *Arcadia*, a play set in a single room that concerns the revelation of nature 'through number alone' (56/59). With regard to fractals, which run to literally infinite detail within a bounded space, 'the green cabinet' is evocative because the phrase joins the idea of natural irregularity (to infinity) observable, for instance, in a leaf, with the notion of craftsmanlike regularity and finitude suggested by 'cabinet': a conjunction, and also a conflation, of nature and the arts; of growth and manufacture; the infinite and the finite; chance and design; the accidental and the predetermined. When Thomasina pregnantly describes her mathematical procedure for deriving fractal shapes from algorithms as the method of 'trial and error' (112–14), that interplay between the regularity implied by *trial* and the irregularity implied by *error*, in the Latinate sense of a wandering course, is entirely accurate. (Septimus's dry response – 'Trial and error perfectly describes your enthusiasm, my lady' – is the wit of a classical temperament. Yet the romantic 'wildly signalling' in this character will eventually sacrifice his life and sanity in the futile quest to prove Thomasina's conjectures by hand, in an age before the computer made it possible to carry out iteration on the necessary scale.) With regard to the pastoral tradition, 'the green cabinet' serves as a reminder, not only that pastoral develops by allusion and echo throughout its 'odd and accidental history', but also that allusion and echo are figures of instability as well as continuity.

With a bit of squeezing, in Rosenmeyer's phrase, Stoppard aligns the principles of fractals with Coleridge's notion of 'organic form' and the infinitude of forms in nature. 'What a faint-heart!', Thomasina chides Septimus when he tries to temper her disdain for the notion of a cabinet-making God (elsewhere she remarks that 'God must love gunnery and architecture if Euclid is his only geometry', 112/114).

Septimus primly parries that God 'has mastery of equations which lead into infinities where we cannot follow' (49/52; echoing Pope's *Essay on Man*, but also adumbrating Laplace's description of a supreme intelligence, often referred to as 'Laplace's demon'). But Thomasina will have none of this. 'We must work outward from the middle of the maze', she insists. 'We will start with something simple. (*She picks up the apple leaf.*) I will plot this leaf and deduce its equation' (49/52). While theoretically it may be be possible to derive the algorithm that will give a very close approximation to the mathematical shape of a given individual leaf, it is not possible to deduce the equation that will give the shape in perfect detail, partly because detail goes to infinity, and partly because sensitivity to initial conditions means that a final output cannot be traced backward to an original input. The leaf itself is the result of an unpredictable interplay between deterministic processes (which *can* be described by an algorithm) and environmental conditions that together *cannot* be 'played backwards' or recovered with accuracy. As Thomasina comes to realize, the very principle of irreversibility that makes the universe 'a one-way street' also sees to it that determinism – without of course ceasing to be deterministic – 'leaves the road at every corner' (111/114). Despite Thomasina's self-confessed mathematical limitations (117/119), Valentine acknowledges her uncanny prescience ('She saw what things meant, way ahead, like seeing a picture', 125/127). To the audience, however, Thomasina's ideas may also echo literary theories familiar from her own period. The 'picture' of 'work[ing] outward from the middle of the maze' seems suggested by Coleridge's remarks on the 'organic form' that 'develops itself from within', in his eighth lecture on Shakespeare:

> The true ground of the mistake [about putative irregularities and incongruousnesses in Shakespeare] lies in the confounding mechanical regularity with organic form. The form is mechanic when on any given material, we impress a predetermined form, not necessarily arising out of the properties of the material, as when to a mass of wet clay we give whatever shape we wish it to retain when hardened. The organic form, on the other hand, is innate; it shapes as it develops itself from within, and the fullness of its development is one and the same with the perfection of its outward form. Such is the life, such the form. Nature, the prime genial artist, inexhaustible in diverse powers, is equally inexhaustible in forms.[54]

Coleridge's notion of the inexhaustibility of forms in nature is obviously adaptable to the subject of fractals: what Stoppard is here (as everywhere) at pains to underscore is the cardinal thesis of chaos theory, that nature's infinite variety, like Cleopatra's, results from the combination of the predetermined and the unpredictable.[55] Stoppard's playful conceit that sex is the Cleopatra-like 'strange attractor' in the human universe – the fractal multi-scale trajectory toward which human error unpredictably gravitates – should hardly be taken solemnly. In fact partly for this very reason, Stoppard's handling of the theme of *eros* may cast light on Virgil and the role of love in the pastoral tradition.

Cleopatra's nose

'I hate Cleopatra!', declares Thomasina. 'Everything is turned to love with her. New love, absent love, lost love – I never knew a heroine that makes such noodles of our sex' (50/52). In the pastoral tradition, the conventions of love poetry have at times played a similarly stultifying role, and have similarly been held to account for periods and modes of decadence and exhaustion. 'Oh, damn your soul, Chater!', Septimus tells the hapless author of *The Couch of Eros*. 'Ovid would have stayed a lawyer and Virgil a farmer if they had known the bathos to which love would descend in your sportive satyrs and noodle nymphs!' (55/57). Love has indeed made poets of many who never wrote before, as Theocritus' friend Nikias of Miletus commented good-humouredly of the Cyclops Polyphemus' surprisingly poignant love complaint in *Idyll* 11.[56] But since 'generic possibilities' soon became 'generic expectations',[57] pastoral has also made its share of poetasters. As an exceptionally conventional genre, pastoral's very conventions have been accused of lowering the bar, as in Samuel Johnson's famous dismissal of the code as 'easy' and 'vulgar'.[58] Pastoral has been accused of trivializing its perennial themes of love and loss. The risk is palpable: Virgil's blend of playfulness and pathos is delicate and volatile, and therefore vulnerable to the hardening of convention. Moreover, love poetry risks bathos even without the liability of sportive satyrs and noodle nymphs. What Stoppard's treatment of love and loss in *Arcadia* may help us rethink is Virgil's complex engagement with the conventions of love in the *Eclogues*. For although it is not until the Renaissance that we find 'the Arcadian community – which in Virgil and Sannazaro could scarcely contain the passionate lover – [transformed into] a community *of* such lovers',[59] it can also be said that Virgil's lovesick shepherd Corydon, the speaker of Eclogue 2 modelled on Theocritus' Cyclops, represents 'the true prototype of the Passionate Shepherd of the later pastoral tradition'.[60] There is a sense, after all, in which the *Eclogues* 'are also a species of love poetry'.[61] Moreover, if Virgil's blend of playfulness and pathos is indeed delicate and volatile, it would be wrong to try and pin it down: better to approach it through a tender and witty play.

Eros and elegy

'Tender and witty' is one way of translating Horace's description of Virgil's early poetry, *molle atque facetum* (*Satires* 1.10.44); 'delicate and witty' has often been proposed – or one may prefer Guy Lee's "'sensitive and witty', or even 'sensitive and ironic"'.[62] Like the *Eclogues* themselves, Horace's phrase has proved remarkably hard to fasten to any single interpretation of sense, tone and inflection – not least regarding the theme of love, which *molle* has been taken to suggest.[63] From the opening line of Stoppard's play – 'Septimus, what is carnal embrace?' – sex serves mainly to drive the plot's farcical elements and the dialogue's play of ideas. In the exceptional case of Thomasina, however, the play's comic sexual theme is sublimated by the tragic preservation of her chastity, which gives elegiac poignancy to her moral innocence – an innocence distinct from the merely factual knowledge of sex she rapidly acquires. Septimus is similarly sublimated by Thomasina's fate. Indeed he is transfigured. During most of the play, Septimus exhibits all the worldliness, sangfroid, wit and intellectual poise associated with Enlightenment sophistication, above all in the theatre, where the Restoration casts a long shadow. From this paragon of polish, Septimus will be transformed, just beyond the play's staged action, into the hermit of Sidley Park. This fixture of the pre-Romantic rage for the picturesque ('No landscape garden of the eighteenth century was complete without its hermitage or even its hermit') is rendered tragic and real by the kind of rage associated with love-elegy, namely the passion of dying for love.[64] In other words, the tragic *eros* of love-elegy appears unexpectedly amidst the stage business of witty farce; true pathos forms alongside the enjoyable trivialities of sexual comedy, yet in distinct juxtaposition to them. A comparison with the *Eclogues* will not seem far-fetched, given that the blend of humour and pathos in Corydon's complaint in the second Eclogue's begins Virgil's development of a pastoral repertoire of love poetry that culminates in the tenth Eclogue's very different blend of humorousness and pathos in describing the elegiac poet Gallus, 'in a concretisation of a common erotic trope', as dying of love.[65]

'Love conquers all; and we must yield to Love': Gallus' final words bring to a climax the only Eclogue allowed by Rosenmeyer to 'dramatize a love that asks to be taken seriously'.[66] With his last words Gallus abandons the prospect he briefly entertained of seeking a cure for love in the distractions of an Arcadian life of hunting and poetry (10.50–69). The cruelty of Love is not in question: on the contrary, this is the common theme of elegy (recall Pan's admonishment that love is insatiable, 10.28–30). But ultimately Gallus does not seem to want a cure. The elegist needs love's wound to be kept green. Theocritus' *Idyll* 11, addressed to the doctor-poet Nikias, observes that the Cyclops Polyphemus sought and found the only cure for love – neither drink nor drug, but the cure offered by the Muses (1–18) – though the 'cure' of song is also described as a symptom of his ailment (13, 39). In conclusion, Polyphemus is said to have 'shepherded' his love, i.e., brought it under control through song (80).[67] But even this cure is doubtful, and the speaker's comment need not be taken to express the view of his author, whose final *Idyll* closes with an elaborate denial that love will ever submit to discipline (30.25–32).[68] With even greater insistence, Virgil guards against the delusion that love may be controlled. His Corydon is a hopeless case, as the hapless shepherd himself admits in self-reproach (2.58). While his plight is partly of his own making (and his final solace entirely so), Virgil seems mainly concerned with illustrating the wretchedness caused by the passion he suffers. Corydon's complaint is doomed, not as one might suppose because it is misdirected towards the empty woods when Alexis is not there to listen, unlike Theocritus' Cyclops who pours forth his song above the sea where the nymph Galatea might possibly hear. The crucial point is that in Virgil, the animate woods – whose echo he establishes as a marker of pastoral community – remain unresponsive to Corydon's speech (contrast 1.5, 5.62–4, and the emphatic 10.8, *non canimus surdis, respondent omnia silvae*, 'We sing to no deaf ears; the woods echo every note'). Now Corydon's shortcomings are comically evident, like the Cyclops' on which they are mainly based. Yet what these comic shortcomings serve to underscore is not, as in Theocritus, the power of love to turn an unlikely figure into a poet, but rather love's power to abase its victim (curiously, this power may appear all the more impressive, as well as pathetic, when the afflicted was humble to begin with). And when Corydon asks rhetorically, *quis enim modus adsit amori?* (2.68, 'what bounds can be set to love?'), the question no more admits an answer than when Pan makes the nearly identical demand of the lovesick Gallus in Eclogue 10: *'ecquis erit modus?'*, 'Will there be no end?' (10.28). By definition, love respects no *modus* or bound; its inordinateness is axiomatic. In Eclogue 8, the *amor* that drove Medea to murder her own children is described as positively feral (*saevus*, 47). In this connection the boy-god Amor is described as *wickedly* transgressive (*improbus*, 49–50, with emphatic epanalepsis). For Virgil, there seems to be no cure for love (lovers' dreams are delusive, 8.108). *Amor* destroys at will.

Gallus submits to love's power in a spirit of philosophical concession. Virgil presents his graceful submission in contrast to the rawer defeat suffered by his model Daphnis, Theocritus' defiant master-singer, who keeps up a spirited vituperation of Venus even as he lies dying of unrequited love (*Idyll* 1.100 – 13).

Virgil keeps love out of his other version of The Death of Daphnis in Eclogue 5 (except insofar as the repetition of the adjective *crudelis* at lines 20 and 23 suggests the trope of love's cruelty), concentrating instead on nature's mourning for Daphnis and his apotheosis. Eclogue 10 casts Gallus in the role of Daphnis in a remarkably self-conscious way (the correspondence is announced in lines 9–10, which commence Virgil's adaptation of *Idyll* 1.66ff.). The figure of Gallus wasting away for an unrequited or unworthy love (*indigno amor peribat*, 10) may be taken as partly tongue-in-cheek, especially since the poem is explicitly directed to Gallus' mistress Lycoris as well as the elegiac poet himself. Casting Gallus as the dying Daphnis is in part a playfully fantastic conceit. It pays Lycoris a compliment that is at once elegant and extravagant. As already observed, Virgil is revitalizing a figurative expression by literalizing it. In Eclogue 8, Virgil invests the trope with a remarkable intensity by placing it in the context of the famously delicate recollection of falling in love with a little girl picking dew-chilled apples with her mother in a garden in one of the fragmentary stanzas that make up Damon's song. *ut vidi, ut perii, ut me malus abstulit error!*, comments the speaker (41): 'I looked and I was lost. How fantasy misled me!' (trans. Lee).[69] Here the hyperbolic trope of dying of love may be felt to derive a special poignancy from the shift in tone as a conspicuously adult perspective breaks in on the speaker's sensitive memory of himself as an adolescent. But in Eclogue 10, the dying Gallus is presented at an ironic remove, however sympathetically – precisely because the real Gallus is *not* dying of love. There is general agreement that Virgil's real subject is the genre of love-elegy that Gallus appears to have invented: Gallus' poetry is represented by his life (in a kind of reverse metonymy, the whole stands for the part). And yet this fiction is remarkably intense, precisely because elegy operates by erasing the boundaries between the life and the work. And so Virgil's lament for the dying Gallus achieves a pathos perceived as heartfelt even by – or perhaps especially by – readers who are also sensitive to Virgil's ironies.

Elegy and pastoral

By common consent, the metapoetic argument of Eclogue 10 concerns the relationship between Roman love–elegy and pastoral. Gallus decides to rewrite his elegies in the pastoral hexameter and adopt a strenuous Arcadian life designed keep at bay the pangs of disprized love, but finally changes his mind and resolves to abide by the sacrifice required of the elegiac poet-lover. Even a pastoral dream that acknowledges mortality –

hic gelidi fontes, hic mollia prata, Lycori,
hic nemus; hic ipso tecum consumerer aevo.

                                                                    10.42–3

Here, Lycoris, are cool fountains, here soft fields,
Here woodland, here with you I'd be Time's casualty.

                                                                    Lee

– is found incompatible with elegy: perhaps, as Gian Biagio Conte puts it, the harsher 'reality of the elegiac life lacerates the [bucolic] dream'.[70]

Yet Virgil's poem is precisely an attempt to confront the 'the reality of the elegiac life' within the confines of bucolic poetry in a final test of pastoral's limits, thus bringing his *Eclogues* to a kind of consummation (if not a resolution) of the generic rivalry between elegy and pastoral as distinct poetries of love. The Eclogue begins with a programmatic representation of elegy and pastoral in the aetiological myth of Arethusa, originally a nymph in Arcadia. Pursued by the Arcadian river god Alpheus, she was turned into a stream by her rescuer Artemis/ Diana, and mingling with Alpheus, travelled untainted through the Ionian Sea to surface as a freshwater spring in Sicily (Ovid, *Metamorphoses* 5.572–641). The underwater passage between Greece and Sicily can be taken to allegorically represent Greek literature as a living source of Latin. The stream's miraculous purity and the trope of connection without commingling make this image emblematic of pastoral. Virgil describes the sea (*Doris*) as bitter (*amara*, 5), inviting an allegorical identification with elegy, inviting the inference that pastoral may engage with elegy without contamination.[71] In Eclogue 10, pastoral serves Virgil as a means to fully acknowledge 'the reality of the elegiac life' even as he holds himself off from it.[72] He can sing the song of Gallus as he himself weaves 'a frail of slim hibiscus' (*gracili fiscellam hibisco*, 71, trans. Lee). In fact Virgil, or pastoral, achieves what Gallus, or elegy, could not. Gallus found he could not rewrite his elegies in epic metre (or hexameter) without betraying his commitment to elegiac love. The ironic removes of pastoral, by contrast, allow Virgil to compose a hexameter poem that incorporates untold fragments of Gallus' (lost) elegies, most famously the climactic phrase *omnia vincit Amor*, thought to be the second half of an elegiac pentameter by Gallus. Eclogue 10 finds several ways to redeem or sublimate the failures of earlier Eclogues. In Eclogue 2, Corydon ended his complaint by proposing to give up his inchoate passion (*dementia*, 'madness', 69) and instead weave something useful out of osiers and rushes (71–2). His callow, sad attempt to reassure himself in the final line, echoing the words of Theocritus' Cyclops but placing the beloved's name in emphatic end position, sounds painfully inauthentic: *invenies alium, si te hic fastidit, Alexin,* 'If this Alexis sneers at you, you'll find another' (73). In Eclogue 10, Virgil manages to rework these elements. Gallus, echoing no one's words but his own, remains true to his unrequited love (*indignus amor,* 10) – there is no question of 'another Lycoris' – and Virgil honours the attendant cost or waste in human spirit by crafting a graceful, modest (and all the more complimentary) work of art instead of the concrete object by which he represents it, in pointed contrast to Corydon's utilitarian basket. The dangerous realities of erotic passion, then, are fully acknowledged at a series of aesthetic removes, with a humorous, ironic sympathy that combines wry affection with solicitous regard.

What drives Septimus mad?

In *Arcadia* too there is no question of 'another Thomasina'. Her loss is what drives Septimus to madness. Now let us briefly pause, for this needs proof. Is it really bereavement, guilt and a belated realization of love that turn Septimus into the embodiment of a Romantic/elegiac cliché? After all, Septimus's obsession is also mathematical. Yet his quest to prove Thomasina's conjectural procedure for developing a fractal geometry from 'good English algebra' is also (unreliably) reported to have a metaphysical objective – nothing less, in fact, than 'the restitution of hope' in the face of the implications of the second law of thermodynamics (87/89). It is perhaps Septimus, not Thomasina herself, who truly grasps the implications of her fractal geometry and her understanding of entropy, and what is more, surmises the connections between them, anticipating chaos theory. In the play's final scene, Thomasina assures Septimus that the conjecture she wrote in her primer three years earlier, in 1809, had been 'a joke' (123/126). Lightheartedly imitating Fermat, she had written: 'This margin being too mean for my purpose, the reader must look elsewhere for the New Geometry of Irregular Forms discovered by Thomasina Coverley' (56/59). In the play's first scene, set in 1809, Thomasina says of Fermat's theorem, 'There is no proof, Septimus. The thing that is perfectly obvious is that the note in the margin was a joke to make you all mad' (8/10). On the fateful last night of Thomasina's life, Septimus tells her that her conjecture 'will make me mad as you promised' (123/126). Is it, then, only an *imposed* 'Romantic' reading that has Septimus 'wasting away', losing his sanity to love and bereavement? On the contrary, the play's equivocations encourage such a 'Romantic' response. Resisting Thomasina's incipient seduction, Septimus passes from the topic of mathematics to love with telling confusion: 'It will make me mad as you promised. Sit over there. You will have us in disgrace' (123/126). Up to this point in the play, love has been treated as a game by Septimus, whose libertine wit – even in his devotion to Lady Croom – is one of the play's most entertaining features. In its cynical observance of social codes, Septimus's libertinism exhibits a degree of predictability that may be labelled 'classical'. But the 'Romantic' person 'wildly signalling' has long been surmised, the Romantic agony of his latter life foreshadowed. The play's first scene ends with Thomasina drawing the hermit whose character Septimus will later assume in a paradoxical instance of life imitating art, or fulfilling it. 'I have made him like the Baptist in the wilderness', she says ('How picturesque', he replies, 19/21). It is only posthumously that Septimus becomes Thomasina's (unheeded) prophet: this is one of the play's distinctive ironic reversals. Thomasina's hermit is a fantasy figure right out of Salvator Rosa, 'the very exemplar of the picturesque style' (14/17, compare 36/38), who painted several hermits, as well as Baptists in the wilderness. In Stoppard's figure of Septimus, who assumes the role of the hermit of Sidley Park by embodying an illustration modelled on paintings of John the Baptist (the number of removes is giddying), we also find traces of the dying lover, a tradition traceable to Virgil's Gallus. In the final words of Act 1, Valentine reflects on the possible motivation for carrying out a series of iterations to infinity 'with only a *pencil*'. Not only would you 'have to have a reason for doing it', he reasons, you would also 'have to be insane' (68/70). That the insanity of love – 'the whole catastrophe' – is the 'invention' of Roman love-elegy, is a main thesis of Stoppard's play about A. E. Housman, *The Invention of Love* (1997).[73] *Galle, quid insanis?*, Apollo demands in Eclogue 10.22: 'Gallus, what madness is this?' We ascribe Septimus's mathematical insanity to love all the more readily for being heirs to Shakespeare: 'The lunatic, the lover, and the poet | Are of imagination all compact' (*A Midsummer Night's Dream* 5.1.7–8). This text is recalled by Valentine, for whom the quality of visionary genius is 'only for lunatics and poets' (105/107). Stoppard reintroduces Valentine's suppressed term: the motivation for Septimus's genius is the bereavement of love.

If the formulaic character of Restoration-style sexual farce (associated in *Arcadia* with traditions derived from Restoration drama) may be compared to the predictability of love as a formal element in the archetypal pastoral scene (Tityrus playing 'Lovely Amaryllis') or the fatal passion of love–elegy (Gallus dying of love), then the *un*predictable may be said to occur in pastoral when the equally 'predetermined' traditions of pastoral and love-elegy are combined, as in Eclogues 2, 8, and 10. Might the confusion of the predetermined and the unpredictable in the figure of Septimus – the turbulence that can turn a Regency wit into a mathematical hermit – help us approach Virgil's experiments with generic mixture in the *Eclogues*? This need not insist on any retrofitted essentializing distinction between pastoral and love-elegy, but only acknowledge that the posthumous existence of these categories in the reception of Virgil is part of what makes Virgil legible to us in the first place, and therefore a necessary condition of interpretation.

The hermit *après la lettre*

Before she learns the hermit's identity, Hannah thinks of him in terms derived from John Dixon Hunt's book *The Figure in the Landscape* ('The hermit was *placed* in the landscape', 36/38) – that is, in terms about as hackneyed as the working title for her book, *The Genius of the Place* (37/40), which not only alludes to the Roman notion of the *genius loci* but nods to another book by Hunt of that title. Although Thomasina is arguably shown to be the true genius of the play (a genius glimpsed in her mute latter-day counterpart, the enigmatic Gus), it is Septimus whom Hannah takes to be 'the genius of Sidley Park' (88/90); one might consider him a prophet in reverse. (As Hannah gains more information, the question comes to seem less easy, and less urgent, to resolve. When Valentine proposes that Thomasina had a genius for her tutor, Hannah counters 'Or the other way round', and Valentine's apt rejoinder is 'Anything you like', 104/107.) Quite as much as Thomasina, the figure of Septimus serves to contradict Valentine's commonsense view that 'There is an order things can't happen in' (105/107), inasmuch as the play repeatedly shows life imitating art. The image of 'the Sidley park hermit' drawn by Thomasina in the landscape gardener's sketchbook is not the 'likeness' Hannah takes it to be (33/36). The image predates its real-life 'concretization' by Septimus, who assumes the identity after Thomasina's death, just as the figure of the poet *dying of love* both pre- and postdates its realization in Virgil's figure of Gallus (a poetic figure, not a 'likeness'). 'You can't open a door till there's a house', declares Valentine (105/107).[74] The play teasingly suggests otherwise. Yet the play does not positively argue that time is cyclical or that events recur exactly (though near-echoes come close to suggesting this, e.g., Thomasina: 'Septimus! Am I the first person to have thought of this?', 7/9; Chloë: 'Valentine, do you think I'm the first person to have thought of this?', 97/99).[75] What the play does imply is that in the process of time (the universe mixing irreversibly 'till there's no time left. That's what time means',

126/128, echoing Wilde's Miss Prism), the infinite number of unique trajectories
sometimes pass very close to each other, and that their courses, however
unpredictable, nonetheless exhibit traces of symmetrical or self-similar design.
(In chaos theory, the most celebrated image associated with this description is
the Lorenz attractor, a mathematical model of non-repeating yet recursive
behaviour in a deterministic system.) *Arcadia* also implies that the meaning of
events is both lost and revealed in time. The determining logic of drawing-room
comedy and farcical intrigue yields patterns that are often enigmatic yet also
unexpectedly moving. Perhaps something similar can be said about the
conventions of pastoral conventions that in their debased forms might chronicle
the loves of sportive satyrs and noodle nymphs, but that also have the power, at
their best, to irradiate and transcend the cliché of the visionary figure – the
lunatic, the lover, and the poet – at once exalted and laid low by love.

Error and apples, determinism and unpredictability

The reception-oriented approach to pastoral as a process *across time* rather than
a mere series of discrete departures from an exponentially distant (not to say
alien) point of origin entails an acceptance of reading Virgil anachronistically.
Consider this twentieth-century critic on Damon's elegiac lament in Eclogue 8,
focusing on a passage we have already mentioned:

> [T]here is one single compelling scene in Eclogue 8 that could by itself have
> generated much of the poetry of pastoral process.
>
> > saepibus in nostris parvam te roscida mala
> > (dux ego vester eram) vidi cum matre legentem.
> > alter ab undecimo tum me iam acceperat annus,
> > iam fragilis poteram a terra contingere ramos:
> > ut vidi, ut perii! ut me malus abstulit error!
> >
> > 37–41
>
> Within our garden-close I saw thee – I was guide for both – a little child,
> along with your mother, plucking dewy apples. My eleventh year finished,
> the next had just greeted me; from the ground I could now reach the frail
> boughs. As I saw, how I was lost! How a fatal frenzy swept me away!
>
> It is all there: the protected space (the enclosed garden, mother's guardian
> presence); the youth on the verge of sexual maturing, just able to reach the
> branches; the girl seen gathering apples with dew still on them; her instant,

devastating effect on him. He saw, and at once he was lost, gone astray from his true path. This deviation was *malus*, a term that hovers between ascribing his fall to some external ill fortune and acknowledging his own moral complicity. ('The woman whom thou gavest to be with me, she gave me of the fruit of the tree, and I ate.... The serpent beguiled me.') Even the resonance of the adjective *malus* with the noun *mala* a few lines above, conjoining apples with evil, falls in with the central Christian myth of pastoral process, in a way Virgil could not have anticipated. [...] Displaced and homeless, his own childhood suddenly dissipated by this alien child, Damon consigns the land to chaos and himself to death.[76]

It is not only Christianity that Virgil could not have anticipated; it is a safe bet that he could not have foreseen any part of Susan Snyder's sensitive and passionate reading of Damon's verses in Eclogue 8. Her reading – and perhaps especially the fact that she takes the song's speaker to be a fully characterized individual, Damon – owes everything to post-classical tradition. And yet this indebtedness is no mere liability; on the contrary, it is precisely the richness of post-Virgilian tradition that makes Snyder's reading not only possible but compelling. Even if we could hear with anything but post-Christian ears Virgil's conjunction of *malus error* ('an ill-fated turn') with *mala* ('apple'), it is not at all clear we should wish to. As Charles Martindale has argued, to ignore our own self-implication is not only futile but impoverishing.[77] The links we naturally perceive – or rather *culturally* perceive, through Genesis and *Paradise Lost* and other texts, regardless of how each of us may have encountered the Bible or Milton – these links between the garden, the awakening of sexuality, the passage from innocence to experience, love's bonds and limits, the relationship between happiness and knowledge, and the problem of free will: all these links may equally be considered paths leading to Virgil as diverging from him – though the 'Virgil' in question cannot then be considered a point of origin, but of destination.

Yet again it is important that reception should also serve to reveal ways in which the classical text may be said to resist our appropriating grasp. We should value what we come to perceive as traces of its alterity. The 'garden scene' of Eclogue 8 displays the tendency of pastoral to develop a series of self-conscious removes, and this very tendency to multiply perspectives may help us to acknowledge the inalienable 'otherness' of Virgil's text. Jenkyns observes of the 'garden scene' in Eclogue 8 that for all its vividness, it is presented at numerous removes:

Virgil introduces the poem in his own person [...]; he then invents the shepherd Damon; Damon then invents an imaginary lover; this imaginary lover then recalls an event long ago in his past. It is like looking though a telescope the wrong way round: we see the scene in the orchard with extreme precision, but far away and very small. It is thus important to the aesthetic effect that we should be aware of the separateness of Damon from the *persona* that he assumes in his song [...].[78]

The framing devices Jenkyns perceives here enable a perspective that may be said to be fundamentally ironic, promoting an aesthetic that sets precise value on degrees of distance and difference.[79] The conventions and traditions of pastoral literature characteristically work in similarly ironic or self-conscious ways. The motif of poetic investiture, for instance, describing how the pipes of an earlier shepherd or master-poet are handed down to the present singer, may be said to 'frame' the poet's relationship with his precursors.[80] It is this self-awareness that allows pastoral to engage with extraneous traditions even as it preserves its own sense of standing apart, untainted, and in a certain sense uncommitted. Take the motif of the apple in *Arcadia*. From its first appearance at the close of the second scene (45/46–7), the apple is perceived as a cliché. One might say that it is overdetermined – and there is rich irony in the fact that in one of the many things it represents, namely *eros*, it also serves to suggest the element of the unpredictable. Gus offers Hannah '*an apple, just picked, with a leaf or two still attached*' – the theatre's way of representing the freshness and apparent immediacy of Virgil's *roscida mala*. The gesture is a variant of the pupil presenting an apple to the teacher, and establishes that Gus is in love with Hannah. In the immediately following Romantic-era scene, the first stage direction specifies that '*There is also an apple on the table now, the same apple by all appearances*' (46/48). Septimus picks off the apple's twig and leaves, and his action of slicing it with a pocket knife suggests the values associated with the 'classical': precise division, symmetry, order, regularity. The classical geometry suggested by Septimus's neat apple sections is soon challenged by Thomasina, who, as we have seen, uses one of the apple leaves to illustrate the new fractal geometry she proposes (49/51–2). The apple evokes two fruits, Newton's and Eve's, wittily compared by Byron:

> When Newton saw an apple fall, he found
> In that slight startle from his contemplation –
> 'Tis *said* (for I'll not answer above ground
> For any sage's creed or calculation) –
> A mode of proving that the earth turned round
> In a most natural whirl called 'Gravitation',
> And this is the sole mortal who could grapple,
> Since Adam, with a fall, or with an apple.

Man fell with apples, and with apples rose,
If this be true; for we must deem the mode
In which Sir Isaac Newton could disclose
Through the then unpaved stars the turnpike road,
A thing to counterbalance human woes;
For ever since immortal man hath glowed
With all kind of mechanics, and full soon
Steam-engines will conduct him to the Moon.

Don Juan 10, stanzas 1–2

The apple is a figure of origins as well as of discovery – a moment commonly represented as originary in itself, as in the anecdote of Newton. The apple is also a figure of divergence, *error* (think of Atalanta), and Stoppard playfully depicts the deterministic pull of sex – a figure of turbulence, not to say chaos – as the yin against the yang of Newton's predictable gravity: 'Ah. The attraction that Newton left out. All the way back to the apple in the garden. Yes.' (97/100). Paradoxically, perhaps, the course implied by Valentine's phrasing ('all the way back to the apple in the garden') cannot be traced backward any more than the weather, or for that matter, the formation of genres. The apple is a double figure of determinism and unpredictability: a figure of one-way processes.

As Snyder observes, 'the entangling of sexuality with the primal sin goes very far back, perhaps to the Genesis narrative itself'.[81] The biblical narrative of the fall may be said to enter pastoral as a contamination of the classical tradition – and yet pastoral's typical form of accommodation, by adding perspectival removes, allows pastoral to acknowledge extraneous traditions while keeping them decorously at arm's length. Just so, in *Arcadia* the use of pastoral motifs proves hospitable to Stoppard's thinking about determinism and free will – themes that do not enter Virgil's *Eclogues.* Or . . . don't they? 'One look and I was lost.' Stoppard expands Virgil's focus on the determining instant of perdition (*ut vidi, ut perii*), and typically, approaches it from the opposite direction. Septimus and Thomasina's erotic attraction develops gradually over time, and the instant of perdition comes where it is least expected, in Septimus's unprecedentedly principled act of declining Thomasina's attempt to seduce him on the eve of her seventeenth birthday. (Compare Virgil's poignant particularity about the speaker's age in Eclogues 8.39, 'my eleventh year ended, the next had just greeted me'.)[82] It is this triply articulated refusal that leads, unpredictably, to Thomasina's death by fire, waiting up for Septimus by the candle he lit, warning her to 'be careful with the flame':

Thomasina   I will wait for you to come.

Septimus   I cannot.

Thomasina   You may.

Septimus   I may not.

Thomasina   You must.

Septimus   I will not.

129/132

The sheer economy of this stichomythic dialogue is part of what makes the exchange remarkably moving. The heightening trope of a thrice-occurring action or speech is familiar from epic (the thrice-attempted embrace of Achilles and Patroclus in *Iliad* 23; of Odysseus and Anticleia in *Odyssey* 11; of Aeneas and Creusa in *Aeneid* 2.792–3, then Aeneas and Anchises, 6.700–1) as well as the Bible (Peter denies Christ three times, as prophesied). Typically the trope signals the inevitability of the event it describes. It is not only the economy of Stoppard's exchange that seems distinctively pastoral, but also his adaptation of an epic trope, enriching the host mode (pastoral drama) without breaking its limits.[83] Septimus's threefold assertion of his freedom of will ironically seals his fate. It renders him a tragic figure. Yet it does so without rendering the *play* tragic: *Arcadia* retains its character as a version of pastoral tragicomedy.

Privilege as moral test

Septimus's tragic assertion of free will is framed by his privileged condition as a figure in a pastoral fiction, enjoying a moment or degree of freedom or *otium* from a demanding *negotium* or occupation. Pastoral *otium* is often treated as an escapist fantasy, but it is actually a moral test. *Otium* can be translated as freedom, leisure or ease. The word itself is used only twice in the *Eclogues* (1.6 and 5.61). Yet the shepherd's respite from work, however momentary, is essential to the notional situation of most of the Eclogues. Virgil's programmatic model here is the scene of noontime repose in Theocritus' first *Idyll*. It is the figure of contrast between work and leisure that defines the idea of *otium* as essentially contrastive, or relative in a radical sense. In the *Eclogues*, *otium* is not given an absolute value or purpose. Like work, *otium* can come to nothing, be misspent. Even lunchtime can be wasted. When Corydon pours out his heart to the woods during his midday break, his lament is pointedly described as *inanis* (5), an ambiguous, sonorous word that conveys not only futility but airy insubstantiality, a quality brought out by the contrast presented by the earthiness of the nearby reapers, with their commonsense and commonplace use of the noontime.[84] While they refresh themselves with their meal of pesto-like *moretum* in the noonday heat (10–11), the shepherd 'burns' (*ardet*, 1). *Otium* is intrinsically neutral, its value is determined by its use. It is the necessary condition for conversation, song, the arts.

Yes, and for love as well, from the moment Virgil's Tityrus uses the word *otium* to describe his own situation when Meliboeus finds him singing 'Lovely Amaryllis' (1.6). Yet Virgil's notion of *otium* balances playfulness and privilege against the harder realities by which such freedom is valued. We have seen that at the close of the *Georgics* Virgil contrasts his own artistic *otium* in Naples, where he presents himself as having written the *Eclogues* and *Georgics*, with Caesar's simultaneous military campaigns in the East. The effect is not to devalue the poet's sheltered art – Virgil's description of his own *otium* as *ignobilis* at *Georgics* 4.564 can be read as a display of modesty 'that conceals a conviction of superiority', to borrow a phrase from Philip Hardie – but rather to suggest that artistic privilege and military service must be understood to be mutually related if not actually connected.[85] Virgil typically presents *otium* as a figure of contrast or juxtaposition. At the beginning of the *Eclogues*, Tityrus' *otium* stands in the starkest possible contrast to Meliboeus' misfortune. At the climax of Eclogue 5, the *otium* that Daphnis is said to love [above all things?] (61) reflects a state of Epicurean enlightenment that is every bit as 'proved' by his death – realized, that is, by being tested – as this enlightened triumph of *otium* is celebrated by the whole enraptured universe in Daphnis' apotheosis. *Otium* may be translated simply as 'freedom', but there are several kinds: the artistic *otium* enjoyed by the single individual of Eclogue 1 is something quite different from the philosophical *otium* celebrated in Eclogue 5.

Virgilian *otium*, then – morally neutral, indispensable for art – is a remarkably capacious concept. The versions of *otium* we encounter in Stoppard's *Arcadia* – the various privileged existences sheltered by stately homes and modern academia – range from the trivial and frivolous (Chlöe, Bernard) to the commendable and even laudable (Valentine and Hannah; Thomasina and the hermit Septimus). *Otium*, it would seem, is not only an enabling condition, but also a touchstone in that it effectively 'proves' intellectual endeavour by distinguishing honest ambition from mere callowness or fraudulent careerism.

Nor has *otium* ever been a single thing, or a simple notion. The whole concept is mediated to us by its Renaissance and eighteenth-century traditions – in *Arcadia* perhaps most relevantly by the 'country house' tradition, especially the comic form it takes in one of Stoppard's literary models, Thomas Love Peacock's novel *Headlong Hall* (1815), a satire featuring the philosophical-scientific dialogues of caricature guests at a country house in Wales.[86] In fact the moment one starts to visualize *otium* in Virgil, one realizes that one cannot avoid thinking through reception. Brian Vickers' lengthy two-part article on Renaissance understandings of *otium* seems to me to inadvertently prove this point.[87] The more Vickers insists that Renaissance writers generally disapproved of *otium*, in stark contrast to the anachronistic self-indulgence of twentieth-century scholars, the more difficult it seems to suppress the positive gentlemanly conception of *otium* as the life of philosophical retreat on a country estate (the tradition reviewed in Maren-Sofie Røstvig's study *The Happy Man*, 1954–8). The *otium* of the Arcadian shepherds in the Louvre Poussin is a privileged state, despite their humble dress, which indeed serves only to dignify them: the gestures of all four figures suggest an unhurried, graceful, contemplative existence. Their curiosity is evident, too, even in the decorously disinterested inflection of their inquiry of the tomb. It is not that these shepherds are philosophers, but that their life is philosophical. It is this ideal of detached interest, which advertises its distinctness from self-interest, that prompted seventeenth-century gentlemen to identify themselves with such figures – an identification helped rather than hindered by the rustic figure's outward contrast with the gentleman. Now Poussin's scene is not drawn from any single scene in Virgil; nor does the serenity of the Louvre painting – the absence of pronounced contrasts, which are so plentiful in Virgil – really seem to correspond to the mood of any single *Eclogue*. Yet Poussin amplifies the concept of *otium* in a way that allows us to focus on its meanings in Virgil and relate these to Stoppard's handling of this pastoral trope. The privilege highlighted by the attitudes of unhurried inquiry struck by Poussin's Arcadians is the freedom to inquire at will – a privilege that depends on a degree of distance from immediate practical pressures.

This is the freedom celebrated at the beginning of Virgil's first Eclogue: under the protection of the godlike young man, Tityrus' cows graze freely (*errare*, 9), just as he himself is sanctioned to play whatever he wishes on his reed (*et ipsum | ludere quae vellem calamo permisit agresti*, 9–10). This is freedom in positive terms: freedom *to* range at will; it is but a step to say freedom of will. The *otium* Daphnis loves in Eclogue 5, on the other hand, is negatively defined: freedom *from* the fear of death, and other delusions from which Epicurean philosophy may be said to liberate people. In Poussin's Louvre painting, we may discern a kind of conflation of these *otia*: the freedom of inquiry guaranteed by leisure is also a condition of *philosophical* enlightenment. The concentration of subject matter endorsed by the pastoral tradition – here a concentration on the state or quality of *otium* – allows Poussin to *absorb* the theme of death. In the Chatsworth painting, death breaks in; it is a dramatic intrusion. In the Louvre painting, death is subsumed under the higher principles of a philosophical life. Pastoral's thematic concentration, then, allows Poussin to naturalize death within the limits of pastoral convention.

In Stoppard's *Arcadia*, we encounter the frivolous *otium* of vainglorious academics and pampered aristocrats – the equivalents, perhaps, of sportive satyrs and noodle nymphs – but we also encounter the serious possibilities of academic *otium*. In Hannah's pronouncement of scientific *ends* as 'trivial' (in the common sense of 'inconsequential', playing on the mathematical sense of ending up as a zero result), it is the freedom to lapse into vanity, as well as the freedom to range freely (*errare*), that gives *otium* a kind of dignity in the face of ultimate futility:

> **Hannah**   [. . .] It's *all* trivial – your grouse, my hermit, Bernard's Byron. Comparing what we're looking for misses the point. It's wanting to know that makes us matter. Otherwise we're going out the way we came in. That's why you can't believe in the afterlife, Valentine. Believe in the after, by all means, but not the life. Believe in God, the soul, the spirit, the infinite, believe in angels if you like, but not in the great celestial get-together for an exchange of views. If the answers are in the back of the book I can wait, but what a drag. Better to struggle on knowing that failure is final.
>
> 100/102–03

What Hannah is preaching is academic humility, identified as the only legitimate source of academic dignity. The freedom to err – to lapse as well as to range – is dignified by the certainty of error and the ultimate failure to redeem the losses of time. What Stoppard is doing here is to use the implications of chaos theory to reconfigure the Christian debate about determinism and free will in secular terms that reject the teleologies of providentialist ideas, especially the idea of an ultimate resolution of meaning as the revelation of a providential order. The only certainty, Hannah believes, is that the end of time is synonymous with reaching the point of maximum entropy – the point where the possibilities of ordering motion are finally exhausted, when 'failure is final'. Or as Septimus puts it, 'When we have found all the mysteries and lost all the meaning, we will be alone, on an empty shore' (126/128).

In the pastoral tradition, then, *otium* does at least two things. The freedom from business (*occupationes, officium, negotium*) provides a vantage point from which to view public affairs. The stability of this vantage point suggests the moral standard by which to value such pursuits. But *otium* is also the necessary precondition of intellectual or aesthetic achievements in contrast to worldly ones. Thus Virgil, as we have seen, presents his poetic career in contrastive juxtaposition with Augustus' military career.

Hannah's ethic of persevering in the knowledge 'that failure is final' would appear to takes us into the territory of georgic, where the ruling tendency of nature is presented as degenerative (*Georgics* 1.196–204). However, Hannah's ethic actually runs counter to such a view: her point is rather that the pursuit of meaning is itself the only source of meaning: 'It's wanting to know that makes us matter.' If Hannah's view recalls anything Virgilian, it may be the passage in the *Georgics* where pastoral and georgic are most strikingly juxtaposed, the so-called 'double *makarismos*' of *Georgics* 2.475–94, which will be discussed in Chapter 3 (on Wordsworth). Speaking for himself, Virgil identifies two alternative blessings – on the one hand, the glory of succeeding as a scientific poet, on the other, the piety of rural life – and voices two alternative prayers (2.475–89). The prayer form acknowledges that the dilemma here presented is not the poet's own to resolve, nor indeed a matter for his own choice, but instead uttered in deference to those who answer prayers. Virgil's first wish is to achieve Epicurean enlightenment through scientific poetry. In the event of intellectual failure, he prays to live in piety to the country gods, happy though unknown to fame (*inglorius*). The dilemma is left open: on the one hand, the love of knowledge – the fervour of scientific ambition, *wanting to know* – and on the other, the blessings of another kind of *otium*. But in Stoppard's *Arcadia*, the Virgilian dilemma between scientific glory and rural obscurity is recast as the elegaic theme of unfulfilled potential in the paradoxical story of Thomasina and Septimus.

The suspension of the normal flow of time in the final act of *Arcadia*, where the actions of both time periods run in parallel courses, is Stoppard's dramatic imitation of bifurcation, a figure of self-similar behaviour across scale that occurs at the onset of chaotic conditions. In fact the dramatic figure is a witty concretization of the mathematical term for a specific kind of bifurcation, a *period doubling* bifurcation.[88] But Stoppard's 'period doubling' seems to be enabled by a structural tendency of pastoral towards the kinds of sensitively poised, unstable states that Paul Alpers associates with the word *suspension*. He takes a passage by Charles Segal on Eclogue 1 as point of departure for his own explanation of pastoral 'suspension':

Despite the temporary effort toward calm and rest the tensions between sadness and peace, settledness and dispossession are unresolved. Rest is promised, it is true, but exile is no less pressing. The morrow still awaits. This atmosphere of suspension amid contraries, of rest amid disturbance, sets the tone for the *Eclogues*.

'Suspension' is the word that best conveys how the oppositions and disparities of Virgilian pastoral are related to each other and held in the mind. As opposed to words like 'resolve', reconcile', or 'transcend', 'suspend' implies no permanently achieved new relation, while at the same time it conveys absorption in the moment. It thus suggests a poised, even secure contemplation of things disparate or ironically related, and yet at the same time does not imply that disparities or conflicts are fully resolved. 'Suspension' is a modal term, in that it directly reflects the protagonist's strength relative to his world. The herdsman of pastoral poetry is conceived as the opposite of the hero: he is able to live with and sing out his dilemmas and pain, but he is unable to act so as to resolve or overcome them, or see them through to their end.[89]

If 'suspension is a modal term', this is because it says something about *how* something is, not *what* it is (an alternative title for Alpers's book would be the cryptic *How is Pastoral?*). The aptness of the approach outlined by Alpers to *Arcadia* as well as to Virgil should by now be clear. Not the least of its attractions is its understanding of genre in terms of process and relationship instead of progress, permanence and resolution. Can Alpers's passage suggest a way of reading Stoppard and Virgil in a mutual relationship that aims not to describe what pastoral *is* but rather to comprehend a variety (an 'eclogue') of ways in which the mode can be said to *behave*? 'Behaviour' is the favoured trope in chaos theory for describing dynamical systems – phenomena that exist at a remove of abstraction that makes it 'unnecessary', as Valentine says, 'to know the details'. As we have seen Valentine explain, chaos is 'not about the behaviour of fish. It's about the behaviour of numbers' (60/62). Literary scholars do not normally operate at a corresponding level of abstraction, and they should never lose sight of the behaviour of 'fish' (empirical detail). But when we engage with pastoral we should be conscious that the form is not mainly about the behaviour of shepherds, but rather about the behaviour of 'figures'. In other words, pastoral is more figurative than it is representational; it is mimetic at a remove. It is in this sense that *Arcadia* may help us to read the *Eclogues* in ways that are wholly determined by 'the point of reception' – without ever being wholly predictable.

Reception: no way back

Although motifs associated with pastoral traditions converge with problems of
determinism and free will in *Arcadia*, it might still be objected that the convergences,
however rich with regard to Stoppard's play, can only be said to touch on a few
isolated passages in Virgil's *Eclogues* – or more generously, that they have only been
shown to touch on Eclogues 2, 4, 5, 8 and 10. Such an objection need not imply that
all generalizing readings of the *Eclogues* should apply to each of the ten poems, for
after all 'there is no such thing as a "typical *Eclogue*".[90] But it is surely right to be
intrigued by the relationship between, one the one hand, the fragmentary aspects of
Virgil's *Eclogues* (the poems' remarkable variety, indeed 'eclecticism'; their obliqueness;
their extremely suggestive form of utterance, always demanding a supplement of
readerly inference to realize any aspect of their meaning) and on the other, the
universalizing, abstracting tendency of the pastoral mode.[91] In readings of the
Eclogues, this dynamic relationship between, on the one hand, the local, specific, and
fragmentary, and on the other, the universal, abstract, and unifying, generates the
processes by which the poems' meanings are realized, which is to say their reception.

Several pages ago I remarked that genres might be like the weather, or indeed
like any irreversible process. The idea is suggested to me by Tim Saunders's
analysis of the implications of treating Ovid's narrative of Marsyas
(*Metamorphoses* 6.382–400) as a fable of reception:

> The progression of events which leads up to the transformation of Marsyas from
> satyr to river involves a number of, often oblique, metamorphoses. First Marsyas
> is remembered; then flayed; then lamented; whereupon the tears of those
> lamenters are soaked up by the earth; until finally the earth transforms these
> tears into the river which now bears his name. The version of reception theory
> illustrated in the previous section [where Saunders argues that, since the river
> does not issue directly from the satyr's blood but, by an indirection, from the
> onlookers' tears, tracing the river to its source would lead to a *reception* of the
> Marsyas figure rather than to any original Marsyas] suggests that, while it may
> once have been possible to track Marsyas' transformation forwards from satyr to
> river, it is now no longer possible to make the same journey in the opposite
> direction. Each of his receptions has rendered the prospect of ever encountering
> an authentic or original Marsyas again utterly obsolete. Viewed from the point of
> reception, to remember Marsyas is to reconstruct rather than restore him.[92]

Saunders goes on to make the point that a reception-based hermeneutics not
only destroys any illusion of restoring the text to an original state, but that its
radical indirection also threatens to alienate the audience from the text, inasmuch

as readers' attention is entrapped by an endlessly proliferating series of receptions, diminishing occasions for any direct and authentic response. With regard, however, to the ironic reception implied by what has been termed 'the amused detachment of the *Eclogues*,'[93] this prospect might seem less alarming. I should like to focus on some positive implications of reception's indirection, and perhaps even its tendency to foster an ironic approach. For I began this chapter with a wish to investigate whether there is a route to be traced from Stoppard to Virgil, suggesting that if such a route should exist, it must also comprehend a plenitude of aspects of the intervening pastoral tradition. What should be clear by now (or perhaps it was obvious in the first place) is that the route cannot be traced backwards in the manner of Theseus retracing his passage through the labyrinth with Ariadne's ball of string. Perhaps the metaphor of a 'route' is ill advised, inasmuch as it suggests a single trajectory, however complex, that could be accurately retraced as a narrative. For although the causal web of historical events connecting Stoppard, Poussin and Virgil may be granted an ideal existence, it could not be mapped even by some avatar of Laplace's demon. History does not yield a 'lost algorithm' of the kind Stoppard's Valentine dreams of finding (61/63). Even if historians could 'put back the bits of glass', they cannot 'collect up the heat of the smash' (125/128). As with the weather, sensitivity to initial conditions entails inherent unpredictability. And yet it is also evident that such a network of real historical events has left traces of its passage, some of which we can discern, most of which we cannot. What is certain is that we cannot now read Virgil without awareness of Poussin – or to speak more practically, that we cannot contrive to do so for long. (The fact that the Louvre *Arcadian Shepherds* graces the dustjacket of Alpers's *What is Pastoral?* speaks more eloquently, one might argue, than the fact that the painting is not mentioned in the book itself.) We must read backwards, then, 'preposterously', without imagining that we are thereby retracing any real historical passage, while still remaining historically informed. If we cannot restore, we can reconstruct, provisionally.

The claim that Virgil would be unintelligible without his reception does not imply that all studies of Virgil must concentrate on his reception. One need not claim more for reception than its heuristic purpose. Yet if the ever-elusive 'true shape' of the *Eclogues* is thought of as a process, or rather as an infinite series of cognitive events in history, it is in the play of these interpretations that the process may be partially glimpsed.

Virgil's Shield of Aeneas through Auden's 'The Shield of Achilles'

Given that W. H. Auden's poem 'The Shield of Achilles' (1952) responds directly to Homer's famous description of the Shield in *Iliad* 18, it may seem beside the point to claim Virgil's relevance as well. To such an objection one might retort, echoing Persse McGarrigle, that neither we nor Auden can avoid reading Homer through the lens of Virgil. The argument I wish to develop, however, is that the Virgilian lens can help us to focus on precisely the main point of Auden's poem, namely its reworking of Homer.

Auden's recital of 'The Shield of Achilles' can be found on the web, and to listen would be an ideal preliminary to reading this chapter. Auden's poem contrastively rewrites Homer's famous description of the Shield in *Iliad* 18 by describing a series of thwarted anticipations. Three times, a trimeter stanza begins 'She looked over his shoulder'. Each time, the viewer's expectations are dashed. 'She', the viewer, is the sea goddess Thetis, mother of Achilles. She is overlooking the work of the armourer Hephaestus, the lame god of the smithy, who (as in Homer's epic) is busy finishing the shield for Achilles with elaborate metalwork scenes. Three times, Thetis expects to see scenes of orderly peace and prosperity: vines, olives, well-governed cities, athletic games, village dances. Each time she sees, by the flickering forge-light, 'quite another scene' (30). Auden's three-word trimeter line has a laconic finality reminiscent of Aeneas' *dis aliter visum*, 'the gods saw things differently', 2.428. Finally Thetis can only cry out 'in dismay | At what the god had wrought' (63–4). The scenes on the shield are utterly disorientating as well as distressing, to goddess and reader alike.

Auden's repetition of 'She looked over his shoulder' in the trimeter stanzas corresponds to the repetition of the epic reportive formula 'He made ('placed/ set/forged').[1] Auden's formula introduces the variation, 'she *expected* to see X, but *instead* he had made Y'. This opposition between hopeful expectation and disheartening revelation is mirrored by the contrast between the two kinds of stanza in Auden's poem. Whereas the four trimeter stanzas describe Thetis' expectations and her reaction to the shield, as well as Hephaestos' metalwork, the five rhyme-royal stanzas describe the scenes – or the world – represented on the shield.

The poem's back-and-forth movement from anticipation to disillusion emphasizes the fact that Thetis has expectations. In this she is like us, the reader. We share her perspective of looking over Hephaestus' shoulder at the artwork on the shield. But we also stand at a further remove. We look over the shoulder of Thetis as well as Hephaestus. Auden's goddess expects to see scenes as though out of Homer. In a manner of speaking, she is already familiar with the *Iliad*. So are we – and we know, besides, a good deal more than Auden's Thetis of what comes after the *Iliad*, not just in history, but also in literary history. To us, the making of an illustrated shield is an epic trope par excellence, thanks of course to Homer but also to his successors, foremost of whom is Virgil, whose reworking of Homer's Shield is the famous ekphrasis of the Shield of Aeneas in *Aeneid* 8.619–728.[2]

So for all that Auden's poem explicitly responds to Homer's Shield of Achilles, he is placing us in a position from which we look back to Homer not only across literary history, but through it. Our knowledge that we are reading a modern version of Homer's ekphrastic passage broadens into awareness that such reworkings have been composed before, most notably by Virgil, the great precursor of all subsequent poets who rewrite Homer. (After Homer, all epic is secondary, notwithstanding the fact that Homer too inherited an epic tradition, however lost this oral tradition is to us – except as mediated by Homer.) With his Greek predecessors such as Apollonius, Virgil stands at the head of secondary epic, a tradition distinguished by its perennial anxieties of belatedness. We can say that the problems posed by epic that Auden confronts in 'The Shield of Achilles' were defined for posterity by Virgil. It is our awareness of these problems, and the literature by which they are mediated, that can make Auden's poem feel as appalling to us as the scenes on the poem's shield appear to Auden's figure of Thetis.

Auden was troubled by the temporal perspective of the *Aeneid*, particularly by the fact that Virgil, having set his epic in a mythic past at the very threshold of historical time, implants into his narrative proleptic scenes such as the Parade of Heroes in Book 6 and the Shield of Aeneas in Book 8, representing much later historical figures and events that Virgil knew would be familiar to his own contemporaries. Virgil is counting on his readers to understand these scenes as early prophecies that have since been fulfilled by the course of Roman history. Auden's poem 'Secondary Epic' (1959) remonstrates directly with the prophetic and didactic poet of *Aeneid* 6 and 8:

No, Virgil, no:
Not even the first of the Romans can learn
His Roman history in the future tense,
Not even to serve your political turn;
Hindsight as foresight makes no sense.

1–5[3]

Auden is perturbed mainly by the fact that Virgilian epic is ideological and didactic – that it serves a 'political turn', as he accuses, obeying a civic and religious purpose. Auden's objection that 'hindsight as foresight makes no sense' acknowledges, first of all, that Virgilian epic tries to make sense of things, to explain. It is 'aetiological' (from Greek *aitía*, 'cause' or 'explanation') in that it traces Roman customs, rites, beliefs, political practices and institutions, historical events – in short, all kinds of historical circumstances – to sources in the past that may explain them (as if) by their origins.[4] Virgil's great innovation, it is often observed, is the vast temporal scope of his aetiological narrative, which grounds Augustan Rome in a capacious myth of origins set in a primeval epic world that, unlike Homer's world, is ancient in a historical and even archaeological sense. This is not to say that Homer lacks awareness of earlier ages, only that his awareness of the distant past lacks a dimension of chronological continuity.[5]

Virgil's poem is suggestively prophetic of future history even beyond his own time: this is what Auden considers no trivial vulnerability but a flaw betrayed by the unintended consequences of its own bad faith. The teleological pageant displayed on Virgil's Shield culminates in Augustus' victory at Actium. But Virgil's prophecy, Auden insists, is undermined by its own forced closure: a closure Auden finds not only arbitrary and opportunistic, but also ineffectual. Virgil is brought to book by historical events that happened after his lifetime. Auden protests that Virgil's rhetorical 'device' of anticipating the political present by projecting it from the vantage-point of a mythical past exposes the Roman's prophetic stance as an imposture.[6] 'It lets us imagine a continuation' to the historical pageant of Aeneas' shield *beyond* Actium and Augustus: a historical narrative of the Decline and Fall of Rome that is available to us but not to Virgil – except, perhaps, as foreboding. Virgil's pretence of foresight, Auden thinks, is beggared by the historical ironies revealed by our hindsight.

No, Virgil, no:
Behind your verse so masterfully made
We hear the weeping of a Muse betrayed.

47–9

The Muse betrayed is Clio, the Muse of History. (The collection in which 'Secondary Epic' appeared is *Homage to Clio*, 1960.) Virgil's poem, Auden chides, simply cannot contain the actual Fall of Rome. This view of course is open to debate. One may argue that, on the contrary, Virgil does indeed invite us to imagine a time and place beyond Rome's eventual demise. In my Introduction, I observed that the well-known lines in which Virgil describes the site of Rome's future Capitol at Pallanteum (8.347–8) are temporally ambiguous: either the site is golden now where the ground was once densely wooded, or golden now where the ground will (again) be densely wooded – or if we wish, both. Even Virgil's 'now', *nunc*, stimulates our awareness of transience as well as of our own situatedness. We realize how differently from us Virgil's contemporaries would have visualized the golden roof of the temple to Jupiter Capitolinus, which was ruined with the fall of Rome – or how differently from Gibbon, who first conceived of writing *The Decline and Fall* as he heard vespers sung in the church of Santa Maria in Aracoeli, amid ruins on what he took to be the site of the Temple of Jupiter. And isn't the transience of *every* age precisely what Virgil acknowledges when he furnishes even the primeval Pallanteum with *ruins* (8.355–6)? When Aeneas sees cattle lowing in what will be, yet also seems already, the Roman Forum and the posh neighbourhood of the Carinae (*armenta . . . Romanoque foro et lautis mugire Carinis*, 8.360–1), Virgil is challenging the reader to imagine a time not just before, but also *long after* Augustan Rome, a scene recognized by countless tourists to eighteenth-century Rome, including Gibbon, when they saw cattle grazing among the ruins of the Forum.[7] For the Auden of 'Secondary Epic', however, Virgil's Shield is simply vitiated by Gibbon's story of decline.

But in Auden's 'The Shield of Achilles', the problem of secondary epic is even more basic. How can 'the poetry of explanation' confront the horrors of the twentieth century? Warfare and suffering call out for epic, despite all literary inhibitions, today as in Virgil's day. But epic demands a sense of personal dignity that the peculiarly dehumanizing and alienating horrors of the twentieth century – specifically, the bureaucratic, depersonalizing dimension that finds its grotesque extreme in Auschwitz – were widely felt to have blighted. ('If Priam today were to think of entreating Achilles', wrote the philosopher Rachel Bespaloff during the Second World War, 'he would find Achilles no longer there. [. . .] Humiliation, poisoned by the lie that the fact of force is wrapped in, has never before so eroded the inwardness of existence.')[8] The chief epic device for making sense of things, moreover, is repetition, which in turn is incoherent without recognition. In 'Secondary Epic', for instance, the grim historical irony

Auden relishes in the figure of the last of the Roman emperors depends on our first remembering his name, Romulus Augustus, and then recognizing in each of the two names a pregnant recurrence. Epic should ideally be equal to such historical ironies, though in Auden's eyes Virgil's epic falls short of anticipating them. But how can the challenge of epic be met in a twentieth-century world that militates against recognition itself, and so also against meaningful repetition?

Auden's 'The Shield of Achilles' can be said to turn on the problems of repetition and recognition. As we have seen, the poem's structuring conceit is the repeated frustration of Thetis' expectations, in the description of which we recognize traces of scenic formulas from the world of classical epic, before finding ourselves wrong-footed by the shield's actual scenes. The final scene presents a feral boy:

> A ragged urchin, aimless and alone,
> Loitered about that vacancy; a bird
> Flew up to safety from his well-aimed stone:
> That girls are raped, that two boys knife a third,
> Were axioms to him, who'd never heard
> Of any world where promises were kept,
> Or one could weep because another wept.
>
> 53–9

Auden's nightmare vision of the future is premonitory of a modern return to barbarism, a modernity stripped of the traditional features of civilization, a condition in which the traces of civilization are no longer even recognizable. The 'ragged urchin' to whom rape and violence are axiomatic has 'never heard | Of any world where promises were kept, | Or one could weep because another wept' (57–9). These lines evoke the end of *Iliad* 24, the climactic conciliatory meeting of Priam and Achilles, where Achilles weeps 'because another wept'. Homer's Achilles weeps from recognition, since Priam reminds him of his own father (a restorative masculine influence, the *Iliad* suggests). Yet Auden is not merely lamenting the demise of universal humane values in an imminent future, but also the disappearance of literature itself. If Auden's ragged urchin prompts us to recall a very different youngster in Theocritus' ekphrastic portrait of the boy with the cricket trap (see Theocritus' description of carvings on a wooden cup in Idyll 1),[9] then this is precisely the kind of literary recognition that will no longer be possible in the future Auden imagines. Auden's ragged urchin has *never heard of* any world where promises were kept. Auden is not just imagining a modern world where trust and sympathy are unknown, but also a world in which the stories that transmit those values have died from memory. In other words, he is imagining a world bereft of the occasions for recognition provided by art, such as the famous occasion experienced by Aeneas as, entering Carthage, he comes to gaze on the murals there in the temple of Juno, depicting episodes from the Trojan War:

> constitit et lacrimans, 'quis iam locus', inquit, 'Achate,
> quae regio in terris nostri non plena laboris?
> en Priamus! sunt hic etiam sua praemia laudi;
> sunt lacrimae rerum et mentem mortalia tangunt.
> solve metus; feret haec aliquam tibi fama salutem.'

1.459–63

> He stopped and weeping cried: 'Is there any place, Achates, any land on earth not full of our sorrow?[10] See, there is Priam! Here, too, virtue finds its due reward; here, too, are tears for misfortune and human sorrows pierce the heart. Dispel your fears; this fame will bring you some salvation.'

Virgil's ekphrasis of the temple's depictions of Troy (1.456–93) includes allusions to the Homeric scene of the suppliant Priam and the relenting Achilles (1.461–3 and esp. 1.487). As R. G. Austin comments, 'Aeneas had expected to find himself among barbarians; he now finds that they too have the ordinary emotions of humanity'.[11] What is more, the Carthaginians know the story of Troy and evidently appreciate its significance, though of course their own understanding must differ from Aeneas', and must be imagined to differ from ours. Auden's poem, by contrast, imagines a world that is dead to Virgil's identification of two cornerstones of civilized life: artistic sensibility itself, and more specifically, the tradition of Homeric narrative. What Auden mourns, then, is not the loss of Trojan or Greek civilization, not the loss of the Homeric world, but the loss of Homer (and all he represents), the literary standard that Virgil inherited and passed on, the cultural tradition by which to register the meaningful continuities that are implied by recognition across time.

Auden's final stanza brings the poem's meditation on the problems of literary recognition to an emotional climax in a way that brings into sharp focus the relationship between Homer and Virgil:

> The thin-lipped armorer,
> Hephaestos, hobbled away,
> Thetis of the shining breasts
> Cried out in dismay

At what the god had wrought
To please her son, the strong
Iron-hearted man-slaying Achilles
Who would not live long.

60–7

Auden's final lines orchestrate a powerful tonal contrast between the speaker's unsparingly dispassionate appraisal of Thetis' murderous son – 'the strong | Iron-hearted man-slaying Achilles' – and an unexpectedly sympathetic, reflective voice of poignant paradox, 'Who would not live long'. Auden's spondaic tricolon of Homeric epithets (*strong, iron-hearted, man-slaying*) presents the violence of Achilles with maximum starkness and insistence, until the pathos of the completing final line, a counterbalancing trimeter with strong pauses ('Who would not live long'), utterly transforms the effect, compounding the note of dry-eyed objective horror with an answering climactic surge of pity.[12] This seems close to a device that Gian Biagio Conte observes in the *Aeneid*, namely the coupling of a Homeric 'impersonal, objective' voice with a 'new voice' that is 'modern, sentimental, and reflective'. (As Conte himself explains, his vocabulary draws on Schiller's seminal essay 'On Naïve and Sentimental Poetry', 1795).[13] Conte illustrates this Virgilian combination of voices with a line from Virgil's description of Priam's palace at the moment that Achilles' avenging son Neoptolemus (Pyrrhus) enters in search of the old Trojan king. Virgil's line describes *quinquaginta illi thalami, spes tanta nepotum*, 'those fifty bridal-chambers, such hopes of grandchildren' (2.503, my translation).[14] The Homeric-sounding *quinquaginta illi thalami* ('those fifty bridal-chambers'), Conte observes – 'where *illi* ['those'] is the mark of memory' – recalls the relatively dispassionate description of Priam's palace at *Iliad* 6.244. The second half of Virgil's line, Conte argues, introduces a note of pathos that is new and distinctive of the Roman's sensibility:

> Over the descriptive objectivity and materiality of Homer's model is superimposed, in strong contrast, the sympathetic and reflective – 'sentimental' that is – intrusion of Virgil's *spes tanta nepotum*, 'such great hope of grandchildren'.[15]

Describing the way in which Virgil recalls Homeric language only to suffuse the literary memory with powerfully subjective feeling, Conte observes that it is often 'appositions which complete the utterance with an intense note of pathos, just as in *spes tanta nepotum*'.[16] This comes close to describing what happens in Auden's final lines, even though 'would not live long' reworks a Homeric epithet ('short-lived') quite as surely as 'iron-hearted', which reworks Homer's 'lion-hearted Achilles'. Auden's grimly formulaic description of Achilles – a form of Homeric pastiche – is completed, and transformed, by the acutely poignant apposition or supplement of the poem's final line, 'Who would not live long'. The line can be read as resembling free indirect style, for it is meted out in the measured, laconic voice of the poem's third-person speaker, yet also strikes a note of pathos that echoes the plangent, 'sentimental' voice of Homer's Thetis as she beseeches Hephaestus: 'Therefore now I come to your knees; so might you be willing | to give me for my short-lived son a shield and a helmet | and two beautiful greaves fitted with clasps for the ankles | and a corselet' (*Iliad* 18.457–60; trans. Lattimore, 18.535–7).[17] 'My *short-lived* son' (the Homeric epithet is *okumoros*, compare 1.417, 505; 18.95): Auden's final line not only draws out the pathos in the Homeric phrase, but marries the perspective of Thetis with the more 'objective' perspective of the Homeric narrator. One could argue that 'Virgil' (or, the *Aeneid* with its reception) has enabled Auden to join together two 'voices' in Homer, the 'objective' and the 'subjective' or pathetic. One could also argue that Virgil's reception has made it possible for us to distinguish a 'Virgilian' note in Homer, for instance the note of pathos in Thetis' reference to her son's doom. But it seems truer to say that Virgil's example and reception enable us to perceive Auden's combination of two 'Homeric' registers as the hallmark of a style that is, to use one of Conte's epithets, 'reflective' – a style in which the complexities of literary history may be taken as an index of emotional complexity. Auden's final line may even enable us to pose a question about Virgil's imitation of Homer that it might otherwise not occur to us to ask. Does Virgil ever, like Auden, evoke two tonally contrastive Homeric passages or hallmarks of Homeric style simultaneously, orchestrating a contrast out of two Homeric elements? The question might draw us further into Virgil scholarship, and finding an analogue, perhaps, in Alessandro Barchiesi's discussion of the moment at the end of the *Aeneid* where Aeneas hesitates between sparing the suppliant Turnus and killing him. Here Barchiesi finds Virgil combining traces of two alternative Homeric models, that of the vindictive Achilles of *Iliad* 22 and that of the merciful Achilles of *Iliad* 24. 'With a genuine imitative tour de force Vergil invites us to read, in Aeneas's hesitation, two contrasting traces – two tracks mixed – both signed by Homer.'[18] Perhaps, then, Auden's final lines show us something distinctive about Virgil that is not entirely new, but not entirely familiar, either.

In Auden's poem, the complexities of literary history serve as a correlative for the complexities of human feeling and morality. Both are undermined by the traumas of the twentieth century. To repeat, it is not merely the ethical values of the *Iliad* that Auden fears losing, and certainly not the values that underpin ancient responses to war. Auden believed that since the Napoleonic Wars at least, it had been 'impossible to think of war in terms of individuals and choice', much less 'to "sing" of war'. He believed that the Great War revealed modern warfare to be 'not merely irrational, but an obscene inexcusable nightmare'.[19] But Auden harboured no illusions about ancient warfare. 'The assumption of the *Iliad*', he wrote, 'as of all early epics, which is so strange to us, is that war is the normal condition of mankind and peace an accidental breathing space'.[20] Contrary to Oliver Taplin, who argues explicitly against Auden that Homer's set-piece of the shield of Achilles serves to place the poem's martial action within the wider context of the peaceful world that war disturbs, Auden seems to have considered the peaceful scenes on Homer's shield as something of an anomaly in the *Iliad*.[21] In the ancient tradition of allegorical readings of Homer, the two cities represented on Homer's shield, one at peace and one at war (18.490–540), correspond to the two cosmological principles of Love and Strife.[22] In striking contrast to views that might reconcile war and peace within a philosophical framework, Auden's poem makes the claim that the very distinction between war and peace 'had become in his era almost meaningless'.[23]

The fact that the post-epic totalitarian world Auden describes in his poem is distinguished precisely by the absence of any clear boundaries between war and peace, between warriors and civilians, needn't imply a contrast with the ancient world. Indeed it may be taken to align Auden's vision of the modern world either with his own view of Homer's world, which he found 'unbearably sad because it never transcends the immediate moment',[24] or else with the militarized peace of Anchises' vision of Roman *imperium* (*Aeneid* 6.851–3).[25] On Claude Summers's reading, Auden may be suggesting 'not that the Homeric idealization of war contrasts with contemporary militarism, but that the heroic age contained in it the seeds of modern dehumanization'.[26]

'The Shield of Achilles' may be read, then, as a criticism of the martial values of classical epic, and of Greek culture itself, as well as a criticism of the modern totalitarian state. For Auden, the really great watershed in history is Christianity, dividing ancient pagan from modern Christian, yet also mediating classical culture. Christianity, he wrote, 'raised western literature from the dead'.[27]

The central event in 'The Shield of Achilles' is indeed the Crucifixion:

> A crowd of ordinary decent folk
> Watched from without and neither moved nor spoke
> As three pale figures were led forth and bound
> To three posts driven upright in the ground.

34–7

'Is' this the Crucifixion? To most critics, 'the reference to the Crucifixion [in lines 36–7] – why else "three"? – is obvious'.[28] The Gospel narratives' Roman soldiery is discernible in Auden's sweating sentries and lounging 'bored officials' in lines 32–3 ('one cracked a joke'). The allusion to the Crucifixion powerfully informs this central scene. The scene is 'central' literally in that it occupies the poem's central lines. Yet there is a paradox in its figurative centrality, for here what may be recognized by its barest contours as a momentous historical event is presented obliquely, marginalized and defamiliarized by a context that insists on the scene's anonymity. The irony in that historical catastrophes and suffering are always upstaged by their contemporary setting in everyday life is one of Auden's most distinctive themes, most famously in 'Musée des Beaux Arts' (1938), which praises Bruegel's painting 'Landscape with the Fall of Icarus' for ironically displacing its mythic catastrophe from the traditional foreground. The Old Masters 'never forgot | That even the dreadful martyrdom must run its course | Anyhow in a corner', while 'the torturer's horse | Scratches its innocent behind on a tree' ('Musée des Beaux Arts', 9–13). With a similar observance of history's blind irony, Auden places his Crucifixion scene (if so we take it) at the dead centre of 'The Shield of Achilles'. We may contrast this to Virgil's placement of the sea battle of Actium at the centre of Aeneas' shield, and of the figure of Augustus at the centre of his ekphrasis.[29] Auden places his Crucifixion scene in the middle only to offset or displace the event from this traditionally central position. His very description of the scene's setting poses an initial challenge to any expectations of deliberate placement or significant location: 'Barbed wire enclosed an arbitrary spot' (31). 'The Shield of Achilles' runs to sixty-seven lines, and given the thematic importance of the Crucifixion and the fact that its allusive evocation occupies the poem's central stanza (the fifth of nine), one might expect the poem to turn on its central line (34) to suggest a symbolic scheme of 33+1+33. In fact line 34 – 'A crowd of ordinary decent folk' – is dead centre in more than one sense, for it stages one of the poem's great ironic anticlimaxes, namely the poignant non-recognition of a Crucifixion scene by its inert, uncomprehending onlookers. (If they even realize that they are observing a crucifixion, these bystanders certainly do not recognize the Crucifixion. Whereas they can do no more than look on blankly, only Auden's readers can be witnesses, inasmuch as bearing witness requires recognition.) In the spirit of 'Musée des Beaux Arts', 'The Shield of Achilles' appears to mark out a place at its centre in ostensible deference to the 'centrist' expectations implied by Virgil's centre-positioning in his rewriting of Homer's Shield – only to offset that centre and frustrate those expectations. Auden is not only rewriting Homer *and* Virgil, but also playing against his Roman intermediary in a way that the Virgilian tradition itself has taught him to do.

I have noted that Auden's poem is *about* expectations, and that Thetis' expectations are conspicuously those of someone familiar with Homeric epic:

> She looked over his shoulder
> For vines and olive trees,
> Marble well-governed cities
> And ships upon untamed seas

1–4

Taken together, lines 2–4 form a pastiche of details one might expect from ekphrastic vignettes of an nonspecific version of classical antiquity (the kind, if not the quality, we find in Keats's 'Ode on a Grecian Urn'). What we experience, however, is not a sense of perfect recognition of familiar tropes, but a less comfortable, more haunting and dim sense of half-recognition, of commonplaces put together in a slightly odd, unfamiliar way. Auden's mixture is not quite homogenized. The epithet 'untamed seas' is odd. It may conceivably derive from Chapman's *Odyssey* (7.118, 'th' untamed sea'; 17.396, 'th'untamed seas'). It gives a wrench to the classical trope in which ships are said to 'plough' the seas (*arare*, *Aeneid* 2.780, 3.495; *secare*, 5.218–19, 10.166; *sulcare*, 5.158), since ploughing is precisely an act of 'taming'.[30] 'Marble well-governed cities', by contrast, with its awkward cadence, catches the tin-eared tone of prose paraphrase or bureaucratic speech.

There is a semantic dissonance, too, in the contrast between 'well-governed' and 'untamed' in otherwise parallel constructions. This sense of half-recognition introduces an element of the uncanny that is further developed in the paradoxical description of what Hephaestos instead places on the shield: 'An artificial wilderness, and a sky like lead' (7–8). The poem seems to be at once goading and frustrating the spectator's efforts to visualize metalwork images on a shield. 'An artificial wilderness' is not only oxymoronic, but challenges a distinction between art and nature we normally take for granted.[31] In the context of metalwork 'a sky like lead' subverts, too, the normally assumed dichotomy between the represented object and the medium of its representation. James Heffernan discusses a similar 'representational friction' in Homer, 'when the metal of the signifier approximates or even matches the substance of the signified' – for instance in Homer's detail of soldiers depicted on the shield covering themselves 'in the fiery bronze' of their shields (18.522), an ambiguous phrase since it can also be read as a description of the Shield itself.[32] Heffernan discusses at length how Virgil too achieves subtle effects of this kind, for instance in all his references to golden objects and aureate effects in the scenes depicted on the partly golden shield. In Virgil's representation of Actium, the waves are said to be 'ablaze with gold' (*auroque effulgere fluctus*, 677). The visual effects of different metals are also contrasted in ambiguous ways, for instance in Virgil's description of the shield's silver goose flying through the Capitol's gilded colonnades (655–6). Virgil's ambiguous phrasing allows us to read the goose either as the shield's representation of a live goose, or else as the shield's representation of the silver statue of a goose that stood outside the Capitol, commemorating the famous geese that alerted the Romans to the approach of the invading Gauls in 390 BC. Virgil's silver goose and golden Capitol can be read as real objects in Rome that are (respectively) sculpted in silver and gilded with leaf, or else/as well as figures represented with these metals on the shield.[33] We see that Auden's attention to the shield's material capabilities as a medium of representation is anticipated by Virgil as well as Homer. Auden's 'sky like lead', which contrasts so sharply with Virgil's aureate touches, nevertheless allows us to discern Auden's affinity with Virgil's intriguing description of his shield's *non enarrabile textum*, its 'ineffable fabric' (625).[34]

This figure of aporia – a touch that distinguishes Virgil's ekphrastic passage from Homer's – is related to a pronounced feature of Auden's poem, namely its resistance to the conventions and preconditions of material or physical representation. The 'plain without a feature, bare and brown' of Auden's first rhyme-royal stanza is as inhospitable to the metalworker's art as to the figures that could conceivably inhabit its scene:

> No blade of grass, no sign of neighborhood,
> Nothing to eat and nowhere to sit down,
>
>   10–11

The shield seems to resist the figures described on it:

> Yet, congregated on its blankness, stood
> An unintelligible multitude,
> A million eyes, a million boots in line,
> Without expression, waiting for a sign.
>
>   12–15

Congregated on its *blankness*: the oxymoronic tension between these words leads towards an aporia, teases us out of thought. How can a 'multitude' be imagined as represented in metalwork, yet also be 'unintelligible'? 'An unintelligible multitude': the agglutination of syllables thickens the line to a remarkable opacity. 'A million eyes, a million boots in line': Auden's vivid metonymy simultaneously invites and resists visualization.

Another central feature of Auden's poem highlights a fundamental distinction between Homer's and Virgil's Shields. As many have observed, Homer describes the shield in the process of being made by Hephaestus, whereas Virgil first portrays Vulcan's Cyclopes forging the shield itself (8.445–53) and later describes as finished work the scenes Vulcan set, or caused to have set, on the shield (625ff.).[35] Whereas Homer's description of scenes on Achilles' shield unfolds concurrently with his narrative of Hephaestus' artistry, Virgil's description of the shield's already executed scenes focuses instead on the viewer's processes of perception. 'In Virgil the pluperfects take us into the mind and eyes' of the beholder.[36] So too throughout Auden's poem, where it is the pluperfects that explain Thetis' dismay ('His hands *had put* instead', 6; 'his hands *had set* no dancing-floor', 51; and a modal past pluperfect, 'where the altar *should have been*', 28 – my emphases).

Since having specific expectations of pictures set on an epic shield identifies the viewer as a reader, we might say that this Thetis has already 'read' Homer and Virgil (and for that matter, Keats) in the sense that her expectations imply prior knowledge of the epic genre, and specifically the conventions of ekphrastic art. Auden's Thetis can be contrasted with Virgil's Venus, who at 8.383–4 seems to be knowledgeable about epic: the differences highlight what is distinctive about each poem. Venus beseeches her husband Vulcan to make the armour by reminding him of two previous occasions on which he was persuaded by a weeping goddess to undertake that very task. This is a moment of remarkably complex allusion. Venus first reminds Vulcan of the time when, as Homer's Hephaestus, he was persuaded by Thetis to make armour for Achilles in *Iliad* 18, then of the time he was persuaded by Aurora to make armour for Aurora's son, Memnon. Virgil has mentioned this armour twice before, in his ekphrasis of depicted scenes of the Trojan war on the wall of Juno's temple at Carthage (1.489), where Aeneas recognizes Memnon's armour in the picture, and later when we are told that Dido asks about its story (751). Whereas Aeneas recognizes the armour from having himself encountered Memnon on the battlefield, Dido knows it by its fame, and well-read Romans would have recognized the armour from the now lost ancient Greek epic *Aethiopis*, Virgil's source for the story of Eos (Aurora) begging Hephaestus to make armour for her son Memnon (who was later killed by Achilles). Various kinds of recognition accumulate with dizzying speed. The chief contrast to be drawn between Virgil's Venus at 8.383–4 and the expectant Thetis of Auden's poem is that whereas the knowledge showed by Venus is supported by the fiction she inhabits, the knowledge betrayed by the expectations of Auden's Thetis is not. That is to say, whereas the *Aeneid* is a fiction sufficiently developed and coherent for a goddess to conceivably be aware of the literary precursors on whom she is modelled, the fiction of Auden's poem is deliberately made to be inchoate. Auden's poem is not an epic but a fragment haunted by distorted recollections of epic. Thetis' expectations of olive trees and dancing floors are like fragments of a remembered dream, dashed by the shock of horrified non-recognition. Auden's Thetis herself is scarcely a character, more like a shade from ancient epic displaced into a nightmare scenario. In her disappointment she presents a striking contrast to Virgil's Aeneas, who not only admires the images on his shield (617–20, 730) but whose wonderment (Virgil uses the verb *mirare*, 619 and 730) does not imply any particular expectations. Besides his admiration of Vulcan's craft, Aeneas' rejoicing wonderment is linked to the fact that he does not – indeed he *cannot* – recognize the future events represented on the shield. He is described as *ignarus*, incognizant of the future (730).[37]

But Auden's Thetis is not only different from Aeneas, she is also like him in that she too is unable to recognize the scenes set on the shield. Her dismay, like Aeneas' joy (cf. *laetus*, 617; *gaudet*, 730), is independent of specific recognition. Thetis only realizes that the scenes she views are distressing, but she does not know what they mean. In fact Auden's word *dismay* – the 'utter loss of moral courage or resolution in prospect of danger or difficulty' (*OED* s.v. 'dismay', n., a.) – suggests that Auden's Shield of Achilles has taken on something of the baleful character of Athena's Medusan aegis (Ovid, *Met.* 4.802–03). Virgil's Venus, by contrast, is only dismayed, *exterrita* (8.370), by the real and quite unmysterious dangers faced by her son with armies gathering against him – and that is *before* she begs her husband to arm Aeneas. The comparison between Virgil's Aeneas and Auden's Thetis reinforces our sense that Aeneas' 'joy' is not an informed anticipation of a certain kind of good things in store, but rather a fortifying of the heart, a rekindling of 'moral courage or resolution in prospect of danger or difficulty'. Indeed, the historical scenes Aeneas cannot recognize are not unambiguous even to hindsight, but open to interpretation. As Stephen Harrison has argued, the historical scenes on Aeneas' shield need not be construed as inevitable triumphs, but rather a series of narrow escapes.[38]

Whereas these historical scenes would at least be instantly familiar to Virgil's contemporaries, the scenes that Auden's Thetis views are only partly and *uncannily* familiar given our hindsight. Auden orchestrates a series of disjunctions between, on the one hand, Thetis' repeatedly stymied expectations, and on the other, the apparent 'hindsight' that enables the reader to dimly recognize aspects of the scenes Thetis presumably cannot, for instance, the traces of the Crucifixion in the vignette of 'three pale figures ... led forth and bound | To three posts driven upright in the ground'. But do we imagine this travesty of the Crucifixion to be in our past or in our future? In Auden's poem, the horizons of past and future are disturbingly confused. Once more, this awareness of historical time, if not its utter confusion, derives from Virgil, not from Homer (except, of course, insofar as Homer is always implicated in Virgil).

Given that the poem is governed by the opposition between its two stanza forms, what might these forms themselves be taken to imply? Joseph Brodsky identifies Auden's trimeter stanzas as hexameters,[39] in other words English rhymed approximations of the unrhymed epic metre. One might, then, read Auden's trimeters as Alexandrines in couplet rhyme:

> She looked over his shoulder ∧ for vines and olive trees,
> Marble well-governed cities ∧ and ships upon untamed seas,
> But there on the shining metal ∧ his hands had put instead
> An artificial wilderness ∧ and a sky like lead.
>
> 1–8

As Brodsky observes, the distinctiveness of these 'hexameters' lies in the domination of their medial caesura, which utterly controls the rhythm: 'It's a situation where you [i.e., the poet] can't really put accents.'[40] The rhyme-royal stanzas allow greater flexibility, with much variation of the pause: although many of the lines in these stanzas are end-stopped, enjambment is also frequent and often expressive.

Auden's contrast between the two kinds of stanza does not correspond, however, to any opposition between characteristics associated with, respectively, classical and English measures, but rather to two distinct aspects of ekphrasis: on the one hand its tendency to arrest time – to freeze one moment in the scene represented on the artwork, as well as to suspend the narrative – and on the other, the capacity of ekphrastic scenes to function as inset *dramatic* vignettes, presenting a living, breathing, ever-unfolding scene. Keats has captured this double character of ekphrasis more poignantly than anyone in his juxtaposition of eternal arrest and eternal deferral in 'Ode on A Grecian Urn', where the urn's lover 'winning near the goal' will never kiss his beloved, but then neither will she ever 'fade' (17–20). In this arrested scene, love is 'for ever warm and still to be enjoyed' (26), its pastoral accompanist 'for ever piping songs for ever new' (24).

If the distinctive rhetorical figure of Keats's ekphrasis in the 'Grecian Urn' is apostrophe ('Thou still unravish'd bride of quietness'), Virgil's description of the epic shield adopts the deictic rhetoric of a guide, painstakingly indicating the position of each figure on the shield and pointing out the order of each scene:

illic, 'there' (626, 628), *hic*, 'here' (*passim*), *nec procul hinc/haud procul*, 'not far from here' (635,642, 646), *post idem*, 'next' (639), *aspiceres*, 'you could see (there)' (650), *in summo*, 'at the top' (653), *in medio*, 'in the middle' (675). As David West has argued, Virgil's ekphrastic technique fosters the illusion of pointing out the features of a metal shield.[41] Auden's rhyme-royal stanzas, by contrast, follow Homer in describing scenes that are implausible as illustrations on a metal artefact, but instead appear convincing as vivid observations of things in the world, drawing the reader into the sphere of 'the things themselves'.[42] Homer's description of ploughmen (18.541–9) presents a bravura example of this general effect, 'the verbs in the imperfect and the suggestion of repeated action in 543–46' conveying the impression of a completely living scene, even as Homer draws attention, in closing, to the artfulness – and artifice – of the metalwork:[43]

> He made upon it a soft field, the pride of the tilled land,
> wide and triple-ploughed, with many ploughmen upon it
> who wheeled their teams at the turn and drove them in either direction.
> And as these making their turn would reach the end-strip of the field,
> a man would come up to them at this point and hand them a flagon
> of honey-sweet wine, and they would turn again to the furrows
> in their haste to come again to the end-strip of the deep field.
> The earth darkened behind them and looked like earth that has been ploughed
> though it was gold. Such was the wonder of the shield's forging.
>
> trans. Lattimore

It is not that there are no verbs denoting process in Virgil's Shield of Aeneas, but rather that his moments of focus on unfinished processes (as when 'Neptune's fields *redden*' with blood – *rubescunt*, 695) tend rather to heighten the vividness of a tableau – an arrested moment – than to describe an ongoing activity. Auden's scenes suspend historical time and place, but like Homer's they draw the reader into a world of 'the things themselves' – with the crucial difference that Auden's world is a surreal (yet uncannily familiar) nightmare. The scenes in Auden's 'Shield of Achilles' may be described as 'Modernist' in their tendency to distance themselves from the situations they allusively parody or evoke. They disorientate the reader. In this respect Auden's reader is quite unlike Virgil's privileged contemporaries, whose historical knowledge presumably made them confident of recognizing the scenes that Aeneas cannot possibly know.

Our experience of reading Auden's poem is in many ways like that of Aeneas 'reading' the Shield, and indeed not unlike our own experience of reading the *Aeneid*. As K. W. Gransden has observed:

the modern reader, unlike Virgil's implied Augustan reader, may well be nearly as ignorant as Aeneas of the historical significance of events, people and places displayed in book VIII. The modern reader, then, must make that implied Augustan reader's response a part of his own reading experience. To some extent, I suppose, this process forms part of the reading of any ancient text, but I think it belongs to readings of the *Aeneid* in a special way. The poet's manipulation of disparate temporalities (those of Aeneas and the implied reader) becomes for the modern reader a paradigm of his own temporal dislocation. In Aeneas Virgil has created a hero who is only partially able to relate to the things he sees and learns. He is thus a figure of every reader.[44]

In Auden, the figure of modern alienation, a radical disability to 'relate to' things, may be traced in the expressionlessness of the faceless troops who are 'waiting for a sign'. This last phrase, with its military context, may be taken to evoke the famous patristic accounts of the Roman emperor Constantine hearing the words *In hoc signo vinces* ('By this sign you will conquer') before the pivotal civil war battle of the Milvian Bridge in 312, and of his army seeing in the sky the sign of the cross. If we catch an echo of this ancient episode – or indeed if we instead picture a modern scene, such as Flanders in the Great War – either way, Auden's version will be a chilling mockery of any historical scene that we remember, because we remember historical events on the assumption that they were and remain meaningful:

> Out of the air a voice without a face
> Proved by statistics that some cause was just
> In tones as dry and level as the place:
> No one was cheered and nothing was discussed;
> Column by column in a cloud of dust
> They marched away enduring a belief
> Whose logic brought them, somewhere else, to grief.
>
> 16–22

More generally, it is the teleological and prophetic dimensions of Virgilian epic that Auden is playing against, denying their relevance for the modern world. Against this stanza (16–22) one may contrast signs of divine will in the *Aeneid*, such as Venus' lightning and thunder sent from a clear sky (8.524ff.), and the tragic dignity of scenes such as the mustering of Evander's horsemen with Pallas in the centre (8.588) as they ride off, column by column, in a cloud of dust (8.592–6). But there are similarities between the worlds of Auden's poem and Virgil's, as well as differences. Auden's haunting phrase 'enduring a belief' may not seem specifically reminiscent of Virgil on stylistic grounds,[45] but the grimness of the paradox and the pessimistic underpinning of the phrase may strike some as 'Virgilian' in flavour. Aeneas and his followers have to endure much for the idea of Rome, even when they are not labouring under their own misapprehensions, especially through the misreading of prophecies. In *Aeneid* 3, for instance, the 'voice without a face' belongs to Apollo (93) as he bids the Trojan fugitives to 'seek their ancient mother' (96) in response to Aeneas' prayer for a sign (*augurium*, 89). Anchises misinterprets the message to mean Crete (103–17), and for this inauspicious belief the Trojans must endure all the trouble (*laborum*, 145) of another false start. Indeed, even when the Penates reveal to Aeneas that Apollo was referring to Italy (154–71), the Trojans' corrected course proves full of unexpected troubles. If ever there were a poem where beliefs must be endured, that poem is surely the *Aeneid*.

But Auden's poem differs from Virgil as well as from Homer in the degree to which it foregrounds the passive suffering of helpless civilians in modern warfare. In the stanza that describes the helplessness of victims in war, an almost savage authorial severity in the handling of ironic rhetorical surprises serves to counterpoise the overwhelming pathos of powerlessness:

> The mass and majesty of this world, all
> That carries weight and always weighs the same
> Lay in the hands of others; they were small
> And could not hope for help and no help came:
> What their foes liked to do was done, their shame
> Was all the worst could wish; they lost their pride
> And died as men before their bodies died.
>
> 38–44

The stanza is a tour de force of the expressive handling of enjambment and pause, arts in which Virgil was a master. 'The mass and majesty of this world, all | That carries weight and always weighs the same' – the severe magnificence of phrasing, the force of the hendiadys 'mass and majesty', might strike one as Virgilian; so too the use of enjambment in the following line that so desolatingly reverses the charge of that magnificence, giving and taking with one hand. Virgilian too, perhaps, is Auden's profound empathy with helpless victims. As critics have suggested, the stanza's final line about dying 'as men before their bodies died' may well owe something to Simone Weil's description of death-before-death on the Homeric battlefield in her famous essay 'The *Iliad*, or the Poem of Force' (1940).[46] But whereas Weil analyzes Homer's accounts of warriors' actions in the heat of battle, Auden's stanza does not seem to describe the experiences of combatants but rather of civilians, or more accurately of all passive sufferers of the distinctly modern kind of warfare that overwhelms and blurs the distinction between soldier and civilian, denying the focus of epic on the heroic individual. In fact, Auden's poem is open to interpretations that reach beyond literal warfare and include victims' experience of any kind of totalitarian régime. To Joseph Brodsky, Auden's 'they lost their pride | And died as men before their bodies died' sounded 'a bit like a Dantesque epitaph to a handful of East European nations'.[47]

Such interpretations depend on the reading, standard among commentators, that takes Auden's 'they were small' (line 40) to refer to victims,[48] so that 'they', together with the stanza's subsequent pronouns, are seen in contrast to those malignant 'others' mentioned in line 40, in whose hands 'the mass and majesty of this world' is said to lie.[49] 'Others' are the 'foes' (42) of the helpless victims. To my ear, the statement 'they were small | And could not hope for help' only makes sense with reference to the victims of violence, not to its perpetrators. However, Auden's equivocal or non-specific manner of representation works precisely to blur the lines between aggressor and victim. The extreme anonymity of Auden's phrasing may be said to generate uncertainty on the part of the reader as a form of instructive entrapment. Auden uses impersonal or passive constructions ('no help came', 'what their foes liked to do was done') to avoid identifying the perpetrators as well as the victims of suffering. The overwhelming impression is of an absolute impersonality that denies the sense of reciprocal relationship that necessarily underpins the notion of moral responsibility. This depersonalizing effect could hardly be more different from the profoundly empathetic impersonality of Virgil's famous line, *mens immota manet, lacrimae volvuntur inanes* (*Aeneid* 4.449), which C. S. Lewis translates as 'the mind remains unshaken while the vain tears fall'.[50] To the question 'Whose tears?', Virgil's line remains ambiguous: the unspecified *lacrimae* must be Aeneas', but the phrase may well suggest Dido's too (and even her sister Anna's), and is arguably designed to do so.[51] The world of Auden's shield, by contrast, denies a face to agent and to object alike, depersonalizing the human figures it depicts, effacing the traces of responsibility. One answer to the question 'Who are 'they'?', could be 'Precisely'.

'They lost their pride | And died as men before their bodies died.' On the Homeric battlefield, Weil argues, the rejected suppliant becomes a corpse even before his bodily death. But if taken in a modern setting, Auden's description of victims' 'shame' (42) and loss of 'pride' (43) suggests the experience of routine torture rather than martial engagement. Though torture certainly occurs in ancient epic (consider Melanthius' fate in *Odyssey* 22 and Mezentius' grisly customs, *Aeneid* 8.485–8), it is not a salient feature of epic warfare. Auden's concentration on the vulnerability of the weak before the impersonal force of violence summons a pathos that invites comparison with Virgil as well as Homer.

I began by asking why, if the primary reference of Auden's 'The Shield of Achilles' is so obviously to Homer's ekphrasis in *Iliad* 18, it should seem necessary to look beyond the Homeric model to a secondary or intermediary one. I hope it now seems plausible that as an irritant as well as an inspiration, Virgil's mediation of the Homeric episode partly informs and perhaps motivates Auden's confrontation of the Homeric model with his own dystopic vision of modernity. Comparing 'The Shield of Achilles' to Auden's elliptical treatment in 'Musée des Beaux Arts' of the Icarus myth – a story known chiefly though Ovid – Robert DeMaria and Robert Brown remark that 'The Shield of Achilles' 'similarly focuses on what is not there in the classical model'.[52] Yet one could also say that Auden's poem focuses on what was *once* 'not there' in the Homeric model, but must be said to be 'there' *now*.[53] 'Presence' should not be taken as something immutable: what 'is there' in a situated 'now' may be lost on another occasion in the future.[54] A great deal of what has been perceived to have 'presence' in Homer is perceived via secondary epic, especially Virgil.

It is virtually a truism that the receptions of Homer and Virgil are implicated in each other. Yet inasmuch as modern scholarship has tended to concentrate on establishing chronological relations of 'influence', Virgil has often been neglected in close readings of Homer. It was not ever thus: Alexander Pope's extensive commentary of his own translation of the *Iliad* (1715–20), for instance, constantly draws attention to Virgil's readings of Homer as a source of critical insight on specific passages. (Pope is heeding his own advice on how to read Homer in *An Essay on Criticism*: 'Still with itself compar'd, his text peruse; | And let your comment be the Mantuan Muse', 128–9.) Another reason why Virgil has faded from view in many modern receptions of Homer is that since the early eighteenth century – Pope himself provides an important example – the tendency to compare the Greek with the Roman has been increasingly at the latter's expense. In an influential stereotype, a Dionysian figure of Homer is seen to pulse with the heat of invention, while the corresponding Virgil, an altogether cooler genius, appears to imitate (or 'invent', in the rhetorical sense of composing his gathered materials) in the manner of his patron Augustus' patron deity, the archer Apollo – with consummate aim, from a great distance.[55] In this account, Homer is the great original while Virgil is the arch-inheritor, the first great epic poet (saving Apollonius) after the flood that separates Homer from posterity – or from modernity, one might say with W. H. Auden, who in 1945, surveying the ruins of Europe in 'Memorial for the City', calls the contemporary world, *our* world, 'the Post-Virgilian City', in contrast to the world of Homer, which is *not* ours.[56] It is Virgil who reconfigures epic to respond to the pressures of modernity, and to reflect or rather promote an ideological argument. Virgil, then, is the first of the moderns, and as a father figure he has duly been resented as well as revered. As the paradigmatic epic of empire, the *Aeneid* has endured many damning judgments on the terms of Virgil's compromise with power. Virgil's epic has been perceived as *compromised by* its political balancing act in heralding an imperial age of settlement (always in the future), even while it also emphasizes the necessary precariousness of such an achievement, and the necessity – the positive need as well as the inevitability – of its painful cost. Auden's criticism in 'Secondary Epic' of Virgil's 'betrayal' of History's Muse in order to serve his 'political turn' should not impede our view of the ways in which Auden's response to Homer in 'The Shield of Achilles' is mediated and enabled by Virgil, or indeed of the ways in which our own reading of Homer *and* of 'Auden-reading-Homer' are mediated – enabled, facilitated and perhaps distorted – by Virgil (or 'Virgil', the quotation marks acknowledging his inseparableness from his reception). In brief, Auden responds to Homer *through* Virgil; and inevitably, so do we.

The chain of receptions, of course, is endless. We needn't stop with Virgil, and perhaps we shouldn't, for the great mediator between Auden and the classical epics is Milton, and it is Milton's reworking of Homer's and Virgil's ekphrastic scenes that poses in its specific form the perennial problem Auden too has to face, namely 'the impossibility of writing modern epic'. In Milton's tutelary Christian epic, the archangel Michael offers the fallen Adam a scene-by-scene prospect of postlapsarian history up to the Crucifixion (11.423–12.330), and then outlines a more general narrative of Christianity until the Second Coming as a series of trials endured by conscientious individualists (12.485–551). Adam is initially 'dismayed' (11.449) by these revelations (11.500–14, 754–86), and must even suffer his first, tentative and naïvely optimistic interpretations to be dashed by Michael (11.598–630). But under Michael's dry-eyed instruction Adam's responses are tempered to a 'dexterous' understanding of God's benevolent purposes (11.870ff.) that finds expression, properly, in joy and wonder (12.372ff., 12.469ff.). It is the Christian epic's pedagogical cast itself that most strikingly separates Milton's world from Virgil's – and from Auden's. Michael's lessons may be delivered sternly (the occasion for Raphael's affability is past), but they are still lessons offered by a caring and solicitous God. Adam finds that he still can 'have [his] fill | Of knowledge' (12.558–9), as he had before the fall. This is a satisfaction quite unknown to Aeneas, whose virtue is ever to make do with insufficient or at best ambiguous information about his own future and that of his descendants. The Homeric Achilles' bitter foreknowledge of his own fate, lamented in the final line of Auden's poem, makes a striking contrast with Adam's privileged assurance of the ultimate salvation of his own descendants. In Auden's poem, the exact frustration of readerly expectations creates a sense of miscarried prophecy that is not merely equivocal, as in Virgil, but sinister. Terrifyingly, Auden represents as readily recognizable something Milton would only have imagined for his fallen angels: a post-Christian existence in a timeless present, cast in the uncannily familiar image of a pre-Christian world.

The relationship between Milton and Virgil can of course be configured differently. David Quint, for instance, has argued that that the 'the triumphant Virgilian endpoint' of *Paradise Lost* that corresponds to Virgil's Actium is the final victory of the Son, which is 'outside of human history', and that, since the perspectives of Adam and Eve (as well as our own, and Milton's) are located within an unfolding story that has yet to reach its end, neither author nor reader of *Paradise Lost* has

> the advantage of historical retrospect from the achieved political end of Augustus enjoyed by the author and reader of the *Aeneid*. But in this condition of faith, [Milton and his readers] are much like Virgil's hero Aeneas himself, who, saved from drowning, soldiers on for the sake of a city he will never see founded and for a scene of triumph on a shield he does not understand.[57]

This makes a good point, but it also ignores what seems to me a crucial difference between Aeneas and Adam, and so between Virgil's world and Milton's, namely that Adam – and with him, Milton's reader – has his 'shield' intelligibly explained. Michael Putnam proposes that Milton's key Virgilian intertext in this connexion is the moment in *Aeneid* 2 when in the chaos of burning Troy, Venus appears to her son Aeneas just as he prepares to vengefully kill Helen. Venus explains that it is neither Helen nor any mortal but the gods who are responsible for Troy's destruction, and she tears away the cloud that shrouds his vision so he may see his surroundings clearly (2.602–07). The corresponding moment in *Paradise Lost* is Michael's removal of the film from Adam's eyes, purging Adam's vision 'Even to the inmost seat of mental sight' (11.418).[58] Venus delivers Aeneas to his father's house (2.620), but Michael delivers Adam to a greater father. The clarity of 'mental sight' that Milton imagines for Adam is beyond even the divinely assisted acuity of Virgil's Aeneas. Auden's 'Shield of Achilles' refocuses our imaginative sympathy with the limited visibility of the *Aeneid*, even at the most visionary moments of Virgil's epic.

Equivocal Blessings: *Georgics* 2 through Wordsworth's 'Tintern Abbey'

A favourite passage of Wordsworth's in the *Georgics* is that in which Virgil describes his own love of rivers and woods – and implicitly, the ideals they represent – concluding *flumina amem silvasque inglorius*:[1]

> sin, has ne possim naturae accedere partis,
> frigidus obstiterit circum praecordia sanguis,
> rura mihi et rigui placeant in vallibus amnes,
> flumina amem silvasque inglorius.

2.483–6

> But if the chill blood about my heart bar me from reaching those realms of nature, let my delight be the country, and the running streams amid the dells – may I love the waters and the woods, though I be unknown to fame.[2]

Rhetorically the passage is a prayer framed as a conditional statement (*But if the chill blood bar me ... [then] let my delight be ...*). Virgil contrasts alternative possibilities to consider their respective blessings. Those 'realms of nature' (*naturae partis*) are the intellectual province of the scientific poet, a far ampler expanse than the landscape of secluded streams and dells by which Virgil represents the delights of the countryside. Should he fail to gain entry into those higher expanses, Virgil prays that his devotion may become itself in the rustic recesses of their homelier alternative. Virgil's figure of juxtaposing hypothetical outcomes to consider their respective blessings is discernible in the rhetorical pattern that drives the argument of Wordsworth's 'Lines written a few miles above Tintern Abbey, on revisiting the banks of the Wye during a tour. 13 July 1798'. This chapter will consider what may be gained from reading Virgil at the point of this particular Wordsworthian reception.

What Wordsworth may be said to develop from Virgil is the language of provisionality and deferral, at once *putting off* a response that must attend a future outcome, and deferentially *holding off* from any premature response, yet nonetheless anticipating with full imaginative engagement and emotional urgency the possibilities and contingencies involved. Wordsworth's main concerns differ substantially from Virgil's: indeed Wordsworth does not even consider the question of intellectual achievement or literary *gloria*, and his wishes do not depend, as Virgil's prayers do, on the outcome of alternative fates. Like Virgil, Wordsworth faces the threat of having to 'suffer' his 'genial spirits to decay' (114), but whereas Virgil is facing up to the possible failure of his highest ambitions as a poet, Wordsworth countenances what he takes to be, eventually, the inevitable experience of every person. And although Wordsworth contemplates this condition with a mixture of restraint and passion that may be compared to Virgil's uttering his most heartfelt prayers with a decorous gesture of attending his fate, the differences between them are equally plain. Nor am I suggesting that Wordsworth actually imitates or alludes to the Virgilian double prayer or *makarismos* at *Georgics* 2.490–4.[3] Wordsworth's argument articulates a statement of faith ('ejaculated as it were fortuitously in the musical succession of preconceived feelings') about the developing value of experience through time, and it bears repeating that the continuum he perceives between the sublime and the everyday is not presented as either a privileged or even a specifically literary insight.[4] As 'a worshipper of Nature [...] Unwearied in that service' (153–4), Wordsworth does not aspire beyond Virgil's second alternative of remaining *inglorius*: indeed, few poets have written with a more rooted indifference than Wordsworth to literary fame. Wordsworth seems authentically alive to the Epicurean precept *lathe biosas*, 'live unknown', which informs Virgil's *inglorius* as well as his nearly synonymous epithet *ignobile* (in *ignobile otium*, 'inglorious ease', *Georgics* 4.564).[5] It is true, as Michael Putnam observes, that when Virgil echoes *De Rerum Natura* 1.922–5 in *Georgics* 2.475–6, he does not adapt Lucretius' explicit mention of 'the sharp spur of fame': Virgil 'makes no mention of goading ambition but sees himself, as Lucretius could not, as a priest, instilled with love alone'.[6] In this respect Virgil might be considered closer to Wordsworth than to Lucretius. But the *gloria* Virgil is prepared to forgo, if forced to by his own shortcomings, is still the object of his 'primary' intellectual ambition (*primum*, 2.475). Nevertheless, many critics have felt, with Putnam, that Virgil's second alternative, to live in the obscurity of devotion to the river and the woods, shows (however we take this figurative wish) that his 'true interests lie elsewhere'.[7]

We cannot assume that Wordsworth shared Putnam's view of Virgil's passage, though it would not be surprising. But for his own part, Wordsworth goes further than even Putnam's Virgil, since literary ambition and intellectual achievement are never alluded to in 'Tintern Abbey', and indeed have no bearing on the various possibilities considered in the poem. This is precisely what allows Wordsworth to anticipate his sister sharing the experience he describes.[8] So whereas Lucretius does not draw contrastive distinctions between his sense of fame's sharp spur and his hedonistic love of the Muses (in Lucretius the sharpness, *acritas*, and the delight, *suavitas*, seem two sides of the same coin, however paradoxically), and while Virgil does distinguish between two ways of serving his single 'mighty love' (*ingens amor*, 2.476), one through intellectual ambition and the other through 'inglorious' devotion and delight,[9] Wordsworth does not even consider intellectual ambition, concentrating exclusively on what may be taken to correspond to Virgil's 'inglorious' option, which Wordsworth refigures as common experience. Here Wordsworth diverges sharply from his English model, Thomas Warton's 'Sonnet: To the River Lodon' (1777), which establishes the late-eighteenth-century tradition of poems in which the speaker revisits his 'native stream'.[10] It has been observed that 'Tintern Abbey' 'expands the characteristic structure' of Warton's sonnet ("Since first . . . interval between . . . Yet still")'.[11] Yet Wordsworth develops the Wartonian pattern in order to reach a completely different conclusion. In contrast to Warton, who concludes with the consoling reflection that all his 'vacant days' have flowed neither 'obscure, | Nor useless . . . Nor with the Muse's laurel unbestow'd' (11–14), and equally in contrast to Virgil, who prays for poetic illumination, Wordsworth concentrates exclusively on the conditions for being fully content with an experience that does not depend on poetic success.

Wordsworth can nevertheless be said to be reworking the main elements of Virgil's double prayer. These are, first, the acknowledgment that blessings are relative to *other* blessings (which may differ to the point of contradiction). Second, Virgil's prayer involves the suspension or deferral of judgment before unresolved or yet unrealized possibilities: at this point Virgil seems to be cultivating an awareness of what must remain provisional before alternatives that relate to future outcomes. (The distinctive quality of this awareness, we might say, is *conditional* or *modal*.) And third, Virgil's prayer observes the contrast, or at least a strong distinction, between the experience of the sublime and what we may call common experience.

Virgil contrasts the scientific or Lucretian poet's philosophical devotion, which aims to enter the realm of the sublime, with that of the 'inglorious' worshipper of the countryside (though Virgil's evocative use of Greek place-names – the Thessalian river Spercheus, the mountain range of Taygetus in the Peloponnese, land of Spartan bacchantes – also suggests that this idealized countryside actually stands for a literary ideal). These vocations, the scientific and the bucolic, each associated with Dionysian rapture (Lucretius represents himself as touched by the *thyrsus*, while Virgil's Spartan women perform Bacchic rites), are two separate modes of experience.[12] Yet Virgil's juxtaposition also implies that they are complementary. A kind of parity is implied between the sublime and the common forms of devotion. If post-Christian and post-Romantic readers are disposed to seek a connection between the sublime and the humble polarities of Virgil's strictly poised juxtaposition, it is partly Christianity that enables them to imagine such a link – I am thinking of the Christian *sermo humilis* described by Erich Auerbach – and partly Wordsworth.[13] It is Wordsworth who insists radically that the experience of the high sublime proceeds from the most common experiences, and feeds back into them as well.

The notion that height is a measure of profundity – a notion that needn't depend on knowing that *altum* means either height or depth in Latin – is introduced early in Wordsworth's Wye Valley 'Lines':

> – Once again
> Do I behold these steep and lofty cliffs,
> Which on a wild secluded scene impress
> Thoughts of more deep seclusion; and connect
> The landscape with the quiet of the sky.
>
> 　　　　　　　　　　　　　　　　　　　　4–8

Not only do the 'steep and lofty cliffs' inspire thoughts of an even 'more deep' seclusion than the densely wooded valley floor itself suggests, but they 'connect' the valley bottom with 'the quiet of the sky' – as, similarly, in Virgil's famous passage in paise of Italy (*Georgics* 2.136–76), the 'rocky crags' on which hilltop towns are perched (*praeruptis . . . saxis*) rise from the quiescent depths of rivers that glide beneath the ancient walls (2.155–7).[14] Whereas, in Virgil's *makarismos* passage, the 'realms of nature' (*naturae partis*) associated with the stars and planets (2.477–82) are contrasted with river valley landscapes (2.485–9), Wordsworth's poem describes his progressive realization of the ways in which the 'sweet inland murmur' of the Wye (4) and the 'the quiet of the sky' are connected – a 'harmony', it seems, with its own 'power', allied with that of joy, to make the eye 'quiet' and so enable us to 'see into the life of things' (48–50). Michael Mason observes that the connection between river and sky 'prepares for the sense of "something" which "rolls through all things" at ll. 97–103 (picking up also the "rolling" Wye of l. 3)'.[15] The phrasing of Wordsworth's description of *rolling waters* seems significant because 'rolling' normally describes the motion of a river as a single entity, and here 'waters' is no mere poeticism for 'river' because Wordsworth traces *them*, plural, to their several headwaters, 'their mountain-springs' (3). He is preparing us for the point he will make about the landscape in which green orchards 'lose themselves | Among the woods and copses', about 'these hedgerows, hardly hedgerows, little lines | Of sportive wood run wild (13–17), namely that it is the commingling of innumerable, unidentifiable small things that makes up the 'something' that rolls through all things. This is what allows us to accord value even to feelings of 'unremembered pleasure' (32), as part of the mass of sensations that together influence 'that best portion of a good man's life, | His little, nameless, unremembered acts | Of kindness and of love' (34–6). Wordsworth is the poet of memory, but also of *deep* memory, and here he is appreciating the feelings of *unremembered* pleasures and the *unremembered* acts of kindness and of love that lose themselves yet are not quite lost as they become commingled. His language is not, however, positive, but on the contrary, strikingly tentative and provisional: 'such [feelings], *perhaps* | As *may have had* no trivial influence (32–3)'; 'Nor less, *I trust*, | To them I *may have* owed another gift' (36–7) – a tentativeness of phrasing prepared by Wordsworth's opening description of the woodland scene, notably in the notoriously vague line, 'With some uncertain notice, as might seem' (20; my emphases).[16] The contrast here is between, on the one hand, a secondary activity of consciousness – the poet's deliberative process of articulation (Wordsworth's 'qualification, "hardly hedge-rows", calls attention to the act of the mind picking its way towards the right word or phrase')[17] – and on the other, a primary phenomenon in the quickness of all smaller originary bursts of life: the spontaneous, automatic and self-guided vitality of 'little lines | Of sportive wood run wild' (a quality Wordsworth will recognize in 'the shooting lights' of Dorothy's 'wild eyes', 118–20). Wordsworth's assertion that these primary, originative 'forms of beauty have not been to me | As is a landscape to a blind man's eye' (24–5) is slightly obscure, but if Wordsworth is assuming that a blind man may imaginatively construct some of the particulars of a scene from what he can learn about the general composition of the landscape, then Wordsworth's point is that in his own case, by contrast, it is all his original sensory impressions of the minute particulars themselves that have assumed a continuing life of their own, though in ways too myriad to be individually remembered.

These 'sensations sweet' that pass from Wordsworth's blood and heart into his 'purer mind', together with his feelings of 'unremembered pleasure' (the subject of 28–36), may be taken as analogous to Virgil's love of woods and waters – the *inglorius* alternative – just as 'that serene and blessed mood', that other 'gift | Of aspect more sublime' (the subject of 37–50) may be taken to correspond to

Virgil's longing evocation of the cosmic sublime.[18] Each of these sensations or moods in Wordsworth – on the one hand, the primary or 'lower' sensations and feelings 'felt in the blood' that are 'felt along the heart' on their passage to the 'purer mind' (29–30), and on the other, that exalted mood that *quiets* the blood and allows the mind to penetrate inward and within so that 'We see into the life of things' (50) – derives from the same source, each is 'owed' (27, 37) to the original 'forms of beauty' (24) that Wordsworth has observed in the Wye Valley landscape. These alternative modes of perception represent the ends of a scale of cognition that ascends from lower to higher, but only to allow the deepest penetration into origins when 'We see into the life of things' (50).

The phrasing of the latter line is strikingly Lucretian, recalling the Roman poet's self-description at work through the tranquil nights, writing to enable his patron Memmius 'to see into the heart of hidden things' (*res quibus occultas penitus convisere possis*, *DRN* 1.145). In contrast to another Lucretian trope of scientific vision in which the all-penetrating eye travels outward though creation to the furthest reaches of the universe (*DRN* 1.62–79), Wordsworth's eye is 'made quiet by the power | Of harmony, and the deep power of joy' (48–9). This 'deep power of joy' too has a Lucretian flavour, though principally in the phrasing, for Wordsworth's joy is something altogether gentler than either the divine delight (*divina voluptas*) that grips Lucretius as he trembles before the intellectual power (*vis*) of Epicurus (*DRN* 3.28–30), or else the mighty love by which Virgil says he is struck (*ingenti percussus amore*) in his Lucretian description of scientific rapture (*Georgics* 2.475–82). It is the *quiet* of 'the power of harmony' and the *depth* of Wordsworth's 'power of joy' that seem most Wordsworthian, evoking a state of intense concentration. To 'see into the life of things' (a phrase that might even recall Lucretius' name for the atoms, *semina rerum*, 1.59) is made possible by the invisible, quiet, fathomless traffic Wordsworth intimates between the common and the sublime.

For Wordsworth this is a matter of 'trust' ('Nor less, I trust', 36), and it is important not to lose sight of the premise of uncertainty than underlies his entire poem's rhetorical movement towards affirmative statement by stages of conditional argument. It is in this un-Lucretian condition of fundamental uncertainty that Wordworth owes most to Virgil, whose double *makarismos* hinges on mutually unreconciled alternatives: '*But if* the chill blood about my heart bar me from reaching those realms of nature, let my delight be the country...'. Wordsworth goes a step beyond this agnostic position and anticipates as a certainty that he must 'suffer [his] genial spirits to decay' (114): it is the various possibilities for solace he intimates in Dorothy's companionship that teach him to 'suffer' this acceptance, reassured by the knowledge that blessings too are transient and, given the crucial faith that they will be superseded by other blessings, that they are therefore relative – as well as contingent on future events.

Like Virgil's passage, Wordsworth's poem is about forms of love or worship. Distinctively, Wordsworth ('*so long* | A worshipper of Nature') presents his love as a process in time: 'Therefore *I am still* | A lover of the meadows and the woods | And mountains' (152–3 and 103–05, my emphases). The poem is an attempt to explain how and why the river valley landscape has become 'dear' to him *over time*. In this poem 'On revisiting', Wordsworth's refrain is 'again' and 'once again' (2, 4, 9, 15, 62). While the poem continually registers discontinuities in time, distinguishing the speaker's present self from earlier selves, its many temporal markers establish a sense of continuity across these gaps (e.g., 'oft', 'often', 'oftentimes': 26, 51, 56, 58, 91).[19] Virgil's temporal perspective seems different, not only in that in his *makarismos* passage he is not explicitly concerned with earlier versions of himself, but also in that the whole question of the mutual impact of the future and the past seems relatively unpronounced. Readers accustomed to interpreting Virgil metapoetically, however, mindful of Virgil's proleptic references in the *Eclogues* and *Georgics* to the progress of his own career through the poetic genres, will identify his frame of reference as precisely this progress through the genres, which does imply the question of how the present and the future impinge upon the past. If Virgil succeeds as a scientific poet, he will win *gloria*; if he fails, he prays to remain the *inglorius* poet of the *Eclogues*, the poet as whom he self-identifies at the close of the *Georgics*. But if Virgil does eventually succeed in his Lucretian ambition – how then will things stand with his devotion to the arts of *ignobile otium* (4.564), a phrase we may take to imply the Hellenistic aesthetics as well as the ethics of his whole poetic life thus far in Naples? The double *makarismos* of *Georgics* 2.490–94, compressing and restating the problem of Virgil's preceding passage (475ff.), juxtaposes the blessings of the Lucretian ideal and the blessings of rural piety without saying how or even whether they can be attained together:

> Felix, qui potuit rerum cognoscere causas,
> atque metus omnis et inexorabile fatum
> subiecit pedibus strepitumque Acherontis avari.
> fortunatus et ille, deos qui novit agrestis,
> Panaque Silvanumque senem Nymphasque sorores.

> Blessed is he who has succeeded in learning the laws of nature's working, has cast beneath his feet all fear and fate's implacable decree, and the howl of insatiable

Death. But happy, too, is he who knows the rural gods, Pan and aged Silvanus
and the sisterhood of the Nymphs.

Perhaps there is no real conflict here, not least since Epicurean philosophy is
precisely what Virgil is thought to have studied in Naples (*Parthenope*, 4.564).
Poised against each other, the alternatives also sustain each other like archstones.
The Lucretian first alternative is superior because its success brings absolute
independence from the workings of fate, though this success is itself dependent
on fate (i.e., on whether or not the poet's intellect allows him to achieve
enlightenment). Whereas the successful Lucretian is called *felix*, 'blessed', the
votary of the rural gods is, less superbly, *fortunatus*, 'honored by and yet subject
to *Fortuna*'.[20] The humbler second alternative too, albeit in its less secure way,
preserves its 'happy' or fortunate beneficiaries, specifically from the evils of
Roman civic life, which are lengthily detailed in the passage that immediately
follows (495–512). What is less clear is how either of these blessings is compatible
with Roman civic life. In Virgil's 'seal' or *sphragis* at the end of the *Georgics*, which
I discuss in my Introduction, we have seen that Virgil represents himself in
striking contrast to Caesar, who thundered Jove-like on the Euphrates while the
poet sang in the heartland of Greek Italy. Virgil's closing retreat to Naples – his
revisitation of the *Eclogues* and his younger self who flourished in the arts of
inglorious ease – draws attention to yet further similarities and differences
between the Italian poet and the Cumbrian. While both poets staged retreats
from the life of the metropolis, the hub of empire, Virgil's imagination is always
nourished by his literary longing for Greece. Wordsworth's closest equivalent to
Virgil's Greece is the rural world of his own childhood and adolescence.[21]

The mighty love of the Muses that smites Virgil, then, is one, but he imagines
two ways in which this love may manifest itself: as a rapturous form of scientific
enlightenment or as a more quiescent and habitual (but not therefore less
powerful) delight in the countryside. Whereas Virgil holds up his two forms of
love as distinctive of two quite alternative biographical outcomes – one associated
with intellectual ambition and the sublime, the other with a self-effacing devotion
to simplicity (the purity of the commonplace) – Wordsworth is concerned to
trace both kinds of experience to a single source. Wordsworth links 'the joy of
elevated thoughts' with an *inward* recognition of 'a motion and a spirit, that
impels | All thinking things', but also 'all objects of all thought' (94–103).
Wordsworth, then, is trying to locate the transcendent and the immanent within
a single dynamic of cognitive experience: he is trying to combine experiences
corresponding to the two mental states juxtaposed by Virgil – the aspiration to

the sublime and the devotion to the commonplace – within a single account of his own experiences (and with anticipation, of Dorothy's) in time. The 'presence' that disturbs Wordsworth 'with the joy | Of elevated thoughts' (95–6) is sensed within the poet's mind rather than in any outward manifestation; the sense is 'sublime' and so conventionally, it concerns *height* ('elevated thoughts'), yet it also perceives 'something far more deeply interfused' (96–7). Empson famously criticized this uncompleted comparison, but Wordsworth seems to be suggesting that height and depth, the outward and the inward, reflect the dimensions of the same motivating principle that 'rolls through all things'. Commentators have identified a debt to *Aeneid* 6.724–7: Wordsworth appears to be echoing Anchises' pantheistic description of an all-infusing spirit *within* that sustains all things (*spiritus intus alit, totamque infusa*, 726). In *Georgics* 4.219–27, a similar passage concerning the divinity of bees, Virgil calls this world spirit 'the divine intelligence' (*divinae mentis*, 220) and explicitly identifies it with God (*deus*, 221), but he also preserves an agnostic stance by pointing out that he is merely reporting what 'has been said' (*dixere*, 221).[22] The tentativeness of Wordsworth's sense of 'something', then, should not be taken in contrast to Virgil, but rather, perhaps, as a sign of affinity with the agnostic Italian.[23]

Wordsworth's urgent preoccupation with time itself is his most distinctive trait. By comparison, Virgil's attendance on blessings and fate seems relatively unpreoccupied with the passage and impact of time. But Virgil's concern with *modality* in the framing of his prayer, his preoccupation with potentiality, his pains to establish the provisional and conditional aspect of an utterance as, paradoxically, the very foundation for a sense of faith: these may be seen as providing a skeleton for the logic of Wordsworth's argument.

I have suggested that Virgil's suspension of judgment before the outcome of his fate may be taken as an implicit *deferral* of judgment, pending the verdict of time itself. This appeal to a future outcome or disclosure identifies the language of prayer that Wordsworth develops from Virgil. It is important to recognize that it is not only Wordsworth's peroration to Dorothy (112ff.) that takes the form of prayer, but the whole poem. The first part of the poem is uttered in thanksgiving for blessings experienced in the past (1–50), the second in confirmation of those blessings as they have since evolved and now appear (differently) in the present (50–112), the final in anticipation of future events. Wordsworth's language is permeated with qualifiers ('perhaps', 'perchance', 'I trust', 'I dare to hope', 'no doubt', 'I would believe') modal auxiliaries (may, would, should), and all manner of conditional statements ('If this | Be but a vain belief', 'If I were not thus taught', 'If I should be where I no more can hear | Thy voice'). Yet these qualifying expressions do not compromise or undermine Wordsworth's authority or the truthfulness of his statements. Instead they impel his assertions: rhetorically, they drive his argument.

It is this modal suspension between alternatives or possibilities that facilitates the poem's distinctive 'backward- and forward-looking formula',[24] the constant oscillation of temporal perspectives. Wordsworth's description of the Wye's rolling waters, which I have already touched on, contains this pattern in miniature. Isobel Armstrong finely observes how, when Wordsworth imaginatively traces the waters of the Wye to their sources in 'mountain-springs' (3),

> a curious spatial displacement occurs as the mind is drawn away from the as yet undescribed, unitemized prospect and penetrates backwards and inwards to origins. And, because the words 'inland murmur' negatively imply the sea, the mind reaches forwards to comprehend endings, without ever quite reaching them (the sea is out of the poem).[25]

Time and again in this poem, Wordsworth builds up an argument based on a description of an experience in the past (an experience that is lost and cannot be fully reconstructed, yet nonetheless informs and nourishes the present), the meaning of which depends on something else being true that can only be known in the future. 'If this | Be but a vain belief, yet, oh! How oft, . . . How oft, in spirit, have I turned to thee, | O sylvan Wye!' (50–7). Whether the belief be 'vain' cannot yet be known – hence the subjunctive mood – yet experience itself is grounds for faith: Wordsworth's argument looks back to the origins of his experience, though these origins cannnot be recaptured ('I cannot paint | What then I was', 76–7), as well as forwards to an expected realization of this experience somewhere beyond the horizon. (It is tempting here to invoke Derrida's *différance* and *supplémentarité*.)[26] The object of Wordsworth's faith is, to put it simply, the plenitude (that is to say, the infinity) of Nature's blessings; blessings that are common in every sense. Nature's 'privilege' is 'Through all the years of this our life, to lead | From joy to joy' (124–6), and it is this long succession of joys that shapes and nourishes the mind – not just the poet's but Dorothy's too – so as to safeguard 'Our cheerful faith that all which we behold | Is full of blessings' (134–5).

The middle section of the poem (59–112) is concerned with Wordsworth's daring, anxious hope that the changes that have taken place in him since his visit to the Wye Valley five years previously will not prevent but rather ensure 'That in this moment there is life and food | For future years' (65–6). Wordsworth's contrast between his past and his present experiences of the natural scene is strikingly suggestive of Locke's distinction between the primary and the secondary pleasures of the imagination as presented in Addison's famous series of *Spectator* essays (nos. 411–21). The younger Wordsworth's joys were exclusively immediate and appetitive, but 'that time is past' (84). Wordsworth frankly acknowledges this 'loss' (88): the mental picture that 'revives again' (62) on revisiting the Wye, with its 'gleams of half-extinguished thought, | With many recognitions dim and faint, | And somewhat of a sad perplexity' (59–61), hardly matches the vividness and appetitive urgency of his earlier impressions. Yet since that earlier phase, compensatory gifts have followed (87–8): the ability to hear in nature, or rather in what eye and ear not only perceive but also 'half create' (107), 'the still sad music of humanity' (92), as well as to perceive the 'presence' of that 'something far more deeply interfused' which inhabits the cosmos as well as the mind of man (94–103). Wordsworth is no longer dependent on the eye or on the senses. Instead, he is able to recognize 'in nature and the language of the sense' (109) an abiding principle that promises to serve as a kind of security (his metaphors are 'anchor', 'nurse', 'guide', 'guardian', 'soul') for his unfolding inward or 'moral' being (110–12). 'The language of the sense' must mean something distinct from the language of poetry: by 'language', Wordsworth seems to mean a kind of consciousness articulated over time, which is precisely the 'secondary' kind of experience he has been describing. *Therefore*, he concludes – because compensatory gifts have followed the earlier vivid ones, now lost – '*am I still* a lover of the meadows and the woods, | And mountains' (103–05, my emphases), in expectation that other blessings yet unknown will eventually succeed those of the present as well.

This, then, is what enables Wordsworth to maintain hope, albeit daringly, with a sense of precariousness, in the face of the certain 'decay' of his own 'genial spirits' (114) as well as universal processes of diminishment and loss. Mason is right to identify 'the threat of a loss of vitality and happiness' as the poem's 'groundwork ... from which the two unequal parts of its double structure both spring by way of antidotes'.[27] Wordsworth's alternative 'antidote' is Dorothy, to whom he suddenly turns to address at line 115, revealing her as his companion all along:

> Nor, perchance,
> If I were not thus taught, should I the more
> Suffer my genial spirits to decay:
> For thou art with me, here, upon the banks
> Of this fair river: thou, my dearest friend,
> My dear, dear friend, [...]

112–17

Even if nature had not taught Wordsworth what he has thus far been articulating in the poem, he might still have managed to resist allowing his genial spirits to decay, for Dorothy is with him, and from her company an analogous lesson is to be learned. Wordsworth's recognition of the Wye Valley scene allowed him to consider a series of possible continuities across the intervening chasm of five years' removal, distance and growth, despite the fact that his former self is now inaccessible to him. Turning to Dorothy, he now recognizes his past self in her voice and 'wild eyes' (117–20). He knows this recognition can only be possible for 'yet a little while' (120), for Dorothy too will change similarly to the change he has described within himself in the first 112 lines of the poem. 'The shooting lights' (119) of her eyes too will be 'made quiet' (48), her 'wild ecstasies' be 'matured | Into a sober pleasure' (139–40). In short, her primary sensations too will pass into secondary pleasures. And the faith his own experience has given him that 'Nature never did betray | The heart that loved her', but leads instead 'from joy to joy' (123–6), will serve as a buttress against all future threats, griefs and losses – his own as well as hers. Dorothy's mind too 'shall be a mansion for all lovely forms', her memory will be 'as a dwelling-place | For all sweet sounds and harmonies' (140–3). If misfortune should then befall her, as it necessarily must in some degree, her memory of her brother (mirroring his present recognition of his former self in her), and even the very lines of 'these my exhortations', will provide her with 'healing thoughts' (143–7). And if she outlives her brother, then her memory of their Wye Valley journey together will bear witness to the fact that Wordsworth, 'so long | A worshipper of Nature' (152–3), came to return, despite the fading of his youthful joys and impressions, 'With warmer love, oh! with far deeper zeal | Of holier love' (154–6). Wordsworth's love of Nature, he entreatingly argues ('rather say', 154), has paradoxically *gained* warmth and depth, both by the passing of time *and* by Dorothy's companionship. It is as though Wordsworth is now reversing Virgil's *makarismos* passage to trace it back to its origin and present this as an intensifying process. Whereas Virgil began by describing himself as struck by a mighty love of the Muses (*ingens amor Musae*) and then considered two alternative manifestations of this love, Wordsworth is proposing that the two alternative compensatory blessings he describes are not compensatory only, but also feed back to intensify their common origin in the love of Nature.

When Wordsworth as a Cambridge undergraduate translated part of Virgil's *makarismos* passage into rhyming couplets, he seems only to have translated 2.485–9, lines from Virgil's 'second' alternative:

Ah let me inglorious court the shade
And stream[s] soft-murmuring through the opening glade.
Oh that my feet might tread the holy grove
Where oft the frantic bacchanalians rove!
There let the deepening forest still and dead
Hang in dim solemn twilight o'er my head.
What God in that cool vale [my form will hide]
Where Hæmus spreads her darkening umbrage wide![28]

Bruce Graver has commented on this passage:

> Virgil's speaker has turned to a landscape, a Hellenic landscape steeped in literary associations, as a retreat where he can gain imaginative restoration. But his doing so is fraught with ambiguity: to go there is to make himself vulnerable to the destructive power of bacchic frenzy. In translating, Wordsworth deepens this sense of ambiguity: to tread there is to violate a 'holy grove' – rather than 'campi' (plains); and the forest that in Virgil protects ('protegat') here hangs 'still and dead'. The retreat to idyllic landscape is not without risk. At age eighteen Wordsworth is developing the complex attitude toward rural retreat that so deeply imbues poems like *Home at Grasmere* and 'Tintern Abbey'.[29]

To this, one might add that Wordsworth seems to be translating with yet another Virgilian passage in mind. If Wordsworth's ominously 'deepening' forest 'hangs', perhaps this is because he is remembering the quiet natural harbour near Carthage where Aeneas and his crew disembark on reaching the North African shore. Specifically, Wordsworth's impending forest recalls the overhanging gloomy grove of *Aeneid* 1.164–5 that casts its shade over steep woods that shimmer eerily like a theatre curtain:

> tum silvis scaena coruscis
> desuper, horrentique atrum nemus imminet umbra;
>
> Glancing aloft in bright theatric show
> Woods wave, and gloomily impend below;
>
> Wordsworth's translation[30]

It might be objected that the forest of Wordsworth's *Georgics* translation simply hangs 'still and dead', whereas in the *Aeneid*'s chiaroscuro forest the curtainlike shimmering is foregrounded against the surrounding backdrop gloom – an effect Wordsworth's heroic couplet translation conveys with a distinctly Augustan relish for antithesis. But Wordsworth's darkly numinous forest in the *Georgics* translation may still appear to catch that sense of suspense and foreboding in

Virgil's famous description of the African forest, the sense of an unknown outcome. What Wordsworth's fragmentary renderings of the *Georgics* suggest in any case is that the undergraduate translator was mainly trying his hand at short passages to convey local effects, not to present Virgil's longer discursive material in full. As a translator, the early Wordsworth seems like the young man he recalled a decade later in 'Tintern Abbey' who bounded like a roe over the mountains with an appetitive, picturesque sensibility.[31] It is only the later poet revisiting the Wye who, by contrast, reponds to Virgil's articulated logic in the *Georgics*.

We may take it as axiomatic that we cannot now read Virgil free of the traces Wordsworth has left in the reception through which the *Georgics* is mediated. But can Wordsworth's Wye Valley 'Lines' actually teach us to read Virgil's *makarismos* passage differently than we could without a willingness to put this reception to active use?

Yes, if we take instruction from the contrasts. We have observed Wordsworth's efforts to trace back his own set of bifurcating alternatives to a common source in the past, as well as project them towards a common goal in the future. This common source is 'common' in three senses: 1) common to both alternatives; 2) held *in common* by William and Dorothy; and 3) universally common, as in 'common experience'. What is distinctive in Wordsworth is his drive toward unity: unity as a coherence of shared experience, and unity in his posited single origin of experience. Wordsworth's impulse toward unity helps us to see ever more clearly, by contrast, the radical binarism and ambiguity of Virgil's *makarismos* passage, with its sustained and unresolved tension between mutually opposed alternatives. Similarly, Wordsworth's search for a common source of human experience can help us to appreciate – once more, by contrast – Virgil's distinction between the solitude of the great poet (when Virgil names himself in the *sphragis*, it is in pointed juxtaposition to his singular counterpart, Caesar) and the common piety of Virgil's 'second alternative' figure, the anonymous votary of the rustic gods, an anonymous figure among the many.

Virgil's alternative blessings in the 'double *makarismos*' have traditionally been seen as two *literary* ideals, one corresponding to the Lucretian sublime (visionary, illuminated, scientific, explicitly didactic) and the other to the Hellenistic aesthetic associated with the *Eclogues*, in which the rustic world serves as the enabling fiction for a sophisticated coterie poetry.[32] The *Georgics* may indeed be seen as the means by which Virgil combines these mutually contrastive literary models. The mighty love that smites the poet seems specifically literary-philosophical in its origin, as Virgil seems to acknowledge by reworking the passage in which Lucretius represents himself as struck by the Dionysian *thyrsus (DRN* 1.922–5),[33] and this love seeks, fittingly, a literary-philosophical expression. It is hard to decide whether Virgil considers the possibility that an originary love of Nature might be pre-literate, or that it may not need literature *at all* for its full realization. This could be what Virgil's Spartan bacchantes serve to acknowledge (if so, the obliqueness of Virgil's gesture, and its literariness, are characteristic). But it is Wordsworth who, distinctively, gives this possibility his full and explicit attention.

And yet there also exists an emphatically *literary* Wordsworth of the Wye Valley 'Lines', the poet described by David Fairer as 'Approaching Tintern Abbey' in implicit conversation with a group of late-eighteenth-century poets whose lyric revisitings of 'native streams' draw inspiration from Warton's 'Sonnet: To the River Lodon'. Fairer traces a 'textual interplay' between Wordsworth's poem and a 'Wartonian' tradition of poems that use the 'riparian revisiting' as a trope of engagement with a specifically native literary tradition.[34] Fairer's main argument about 'Tintern Abbey' is that 'alongside the individual recollected history (so easily mistaken for egotism [suggested by Keats's remark about 'the wordsworthian or egotistical sublime']) there is what might be termed a bio-history in its literary relations'.[35] In Fairer's analysis, intertextuality is presented as a figure of community in a critical discourse in which the organizing metaphors are biological. Can this 'intertextual' Wordsworth throw Virgil into relief, or else keep him company?

The question is rather whether this 'intertextual' Wordsworth can help us appreciate anything *new* in Virgil, who is already familiar as the most profoundly intertextual of poets. On Wordsworth's engagement with his 'riparian' precursors in 'Tintern Abbey', Fairer concludes that 'the sounds to which Wordsworth is attuned (and we as readers only barely overhear) are elusive ones'.[36] Like the orchard-tufts that 'lose themselves' in woods and copses (11–13), Wordsworth's figure of the 'sweet inland murmur' of the Wye waters 'rolling from their mountain springs' (3–4) represents the way in which individual elements lose distinctness through intermixture or confluence, even as they may gain power in the process. As classical scholars are perhaps most acutely aware, the sounds to which Latin poets are attuned are similarly elusive, 'barely overheard' – if heard at all – since a great amount of the literature Virgil knew and echoed is now either partly or wholly lost. Perhaps some (precisely, Romantic) consolation may be found in the possibility that the traces of countless lost Virgilian intertexts may nonetheless occasion some resonance, albeit by being not actually perceived but instead taken on trust, akin to the feelings of 'unremembered pleasure' and the 'little, nameless, unremembered acts | Of kindness and of love' that Wordsworth celebrates.

In 'Resolution and Independence', Wordsworth's description of the morning air all 'filled with pleasant noise of waters' (7) sets the scene for his meditation on the contrast between, on the one hand, young poets who typically fall prey to 'despondency and madness', and on the other, the old Leech-gatherer who maintains his cheerfulness and firmness of mind.[37] Does Virgil meditate on the vicissitudes of poetic vocation and the challenge of sustaining personal integrity in any comparable way? Virgil's self-presentation, his ideas about poetic aspiration in general and his own vocation in particular, are so oblique and so mediated by literary convention and scholarly tradition that we cannot have even the illusion of access to the poet as a private individual. Virgil the person is elusive in a way that Wordsworth is not. What we have to work with are, precisely, the mediating recourses of reception. Virgil's running streams and rivers (*rigui amnes ... flumina*) may be taken metapoetically to represent, with the woods that contain them, the ideal of poetic freedom (*otium*) celebrated in the *Georgics* as well as in the *Eclogues*.[38] They may also be understood as generic tokens, representing a literary tradition. Or they may also be understood more literally. What we do not have in Virgil is any explicitness of statement about his feelings for rivers, let alone about his own self-understanding.

Although Virgil writes feelingly about rivers – surpassingly, perhaps, in his representation of the Tiber in the *Aeneid*, but also in his description of Italian rivers winding beneath the ancient walls of hilltop cities in the *Georgics* (2.155–7) – he does not quite revisit them. Even his own native Mincio, which he mentions four times and is understood to deploy as a marker of his own origins and identity (*Eclogues* 1.51 and 7.12–13; *Georgics* 2.199, 3.15), cannot be said to be 'revisited' in that Virgil's references to it do not seem to recall previous events or occasions. The main place in which Virgil revisits a localized figure of his former self is the famous *sphragis* or 'seal' with which he ends the *Georgics*, where he identifies himself by alluding to the first lines of the *Eclogues*. Virgil portrays himself as writing both the *Eclogues* and the *Georgics* in the Greek-Italian city of Naples, which he calls by its Greek name, 'Parthenope': both works spring from the culture of this city. Virgil's self-portrait is explicitly paired against that of Augustus, contrastively portrayed as thundering in war on the banks of the Euphrates, the threshold of Asia.

Now the Euphrates is a generic marker of epic: Callimachus, whom Virgil is imitating by the exact placement of his reference (six lines from the end of the poem), has Apollo dismiss contemporary epic as 'the Assyrian river' whose massive stream is turbid with silt and trash, in contrast to the purity of springs associated with Demeter (end of *Hymn to Apollo*).[39] At the heart of the *Eclogues* (the beginning of Eclogue 6), Virgil makes a programmatic gesture of holding his poetry off from epic: an identifying gesture of Callimachean or neoteric poetics in general, and of pastoral poetry in particular. At the close of the *Georgics* Virgil positions himself once more against epic, as he did in Eclogue 6, and against Augustus, as he did in the opening verses of his first Eclogue, in which the shepherd-poet Tityrus presents himself in contrastive relation to his saviour in Rome. The protective figure of Augustus, then, is antithetical to that of the protected poet. Indeed if there is any revisiting of a river in Virgil, it is an intertextual revisiting (and revaluation) of Callimachus' rejected Euphrates. But Virgil's recollection of his earlier self composing poetry in Naples nevertheless bears comparison with Wordsworth, in that Virgil's juxtaposition of past and present selves registers a continuity that mediates personal and poetic identity.[40]

The understanding of identity not as a stable constant but as an articulated process always mediated across discontinuities in time and dislocations in space is one that David Fairer has identified as a defining aspect of Wordsworth's poetry and of 'the Coleridge circle' in the 1790s. It is tempting to bring to bear this notion of identity, with its attendant critical vocabulary, on our understanding of Virgil's self-presentation, despite the obvious fact that, unlike Wordsworth, Virgil offers very little in the way of biographical information, let alone narrative. In Virgil, the biographical hints we are offered must be read together with markers relating to affinities of genre and intertextual relationships. The *makarismos* passage proves this point, as we have seen. I have discussed the passage in relation to Wordsworth, but what can we now say about its significance in Virgil's work as a whole, and what might this tell us about Virgil's sense of identity or coherence as a poet?

The alternative blessings of the *makarismos* passage are those of scientific enlightenment, on the one hand, and on the other, the ideals associated with the pastoral landscape. Lucretius is the literary representative of the first ideal, and pastoral poetry of the second. The Lucretian ideal is philosophical in the broadest sense, as well as specifically Epicurean. In this context, the main value of scientific knowledge about the causes of eclipses and tides and earthquakes is ethical, for he who truly understands the laws of nature will also master his own fear of fate and death (2.490–2). This philosophical mastery is implicitly compared to man's precarious mastery over his environment. The figure in Virgil who comes closest to representing this ideal is the frugal old Corycian or Cilician of Tarentum in *Georgics* 4.114–48. As commentators have observed, this digressive passage seems placed to correspond to Virgil's stern theodicy of labour in *Georgics* 1.125–59, suggesting that an ideally ingenious and frugal husbandry may triumph even over the most limiting conditions.[41] Read metapoetically, the passage may also be taken as a suggestion of how the ideals of the husbandman and the poet might converge.[42] The old Corycian, a settler from Asia Minor, manages to produce a truly beautiful livelihood from a corner of unclaimed land unfit for either ploughing, pasture, or viticulture. The location seems significant: Tarentum was originally a Spartan colony; according to Strabo it was, like Naples, still linguistically and culturally Greek in Virgil's day.[43] The old Corycian lives where the city and the country meet: Virgil remembers seeing this suburban dweller beneath the towers of Tarentum's citadel, where the river Galaesus irrigates the cornfields (4.125–7). The Corycian may perhaps be taken as a counterpart of the Neapolitan Virgil who 'ingloriously' produced the *Eclogues* and the *Georgics*. (Propertius' representation of Virgil singing verses from his *Eclogues* by the Galaesus, 2.34.67–8, has been taken to suggest that some of the Eclogues may have actually been composed near Tarentum.)[44] The old Corycian may also be taken as a concretization of the Epicurean ideal of self-sufficiency, his know-how and practical flair corresponding to the philosopher's ideal mastery of the unrelenting certainties of mortality. If the Corycian is taken as an Epicurean paragon, he represents a path that appears to have been Virgil's lifelong ideal. While the Corycian's way of life suggests a topic that is formally beyond the purview of the *Georgics* – Virgil breaks off, excusing himself from writing more extensively on gardening, but only after having accomplished his purpose – the Corycian's ethical relevance to georgic values seems clear.

Yet the old Corycian is also held off from the world of the *Georgics*. He is a solitary figure, as are all Virgil's figures that may be taken to represent the poet. (While the old Corycian may be taken as a figure of the poet as philosopher, it somehow seems difficult to imagine him free of poetic implications, or existing independently of his poetic context. He seems essentially a reflection of poetic needs or aspirations, not an alternative to them.) The set-piece on the old Corycian seems to reinforce the sense we have from the *makarismos* passage that Virgil's highest ideals are aspired to in solitude. Virgil may rhetorically invite the participation of Maecenas and the support of Augustus, but when he speaks of his own hopes a poet, he speaks alone. In the epyllion of *Georgics* 4, Aristaeus and Orpheus – Virgil's mythic figures of the georgic hero and the bard, respectively – are essentially (in Orpheus' case, quintessentially) solitary figures. There is an isolated, distanced quality about the Virgil of the double *makarismos*. The alternative to visionary beatitude and scientific enlightenment is a kind of poetic oblivion, not something separate from poetry itself. Virgil does not turn to a Dorothy.

A strong sense of community and even companionship is nonetheless palpable in Virgil, namely the fellowship of allusion which issues from the network of poetic relationships implied by literary intertextuality. One may even say that the figure of Virgil in his own verse – the *Vergilium* projected exclusively in the *Georgics* – could not or would not (or at any rate does not) exist without the specific intertextualities, the allusive poetic decorum, of the *Georgics*. It is Hesiod and Lucretius who enable the georgic poet to speak in his own voice. By their example – the Greek poet exhorting his brother Perses, the Roman enlightening his patron Memmius – it is Hesiod and Lucretius who, presenting themselves in the first person, underwrite what Addison calls the *address* of the georgic poet. If one asks why Virgil does not speak in his own voice (i.e., as an identifiable individual) either in the *Eclogues* or in the *Aeneid*, the main answer must be that his models, Theocritus and Homer, do not license him to do so. It is the allusive poetics governing all three of Virgil's canonical works that allows him to speak in his own voice in one of them, the *Georgics*, where his defining choice of literary models makes it decorous to do so.

When Virgil does speak in his own voice in the *Georgics*, his authority is not undermined by his ceremonious hesitation in framing his double prayer, but on the contrary, derives much of its force from that gesture. In contrast to Virgil's predecessors Hesiod and Lucretius, whose assertions are upheld by the conviction of an inspired seer, Virgil's statements gain power by their deliberate ambivalence. Here Virgil is more comparable to his far-off successor, Wordsworth. We have seen how Wordsworth's assertions seem to be impelled by hesitations. It is by his repeated assertions of trust, by his elaborate progress through provisional conditions articulated by modal expressions, that Wordsworth underwrites the 'cheerful faith' he shares with his sister. It is not that trust becomes faith in Wordsworth, or vice versa, for the distinction is sustained; but rather that each counterpoises the other – an achievement inspired, 'as might seem', by Virgil's deferential hesitation between *felix* and *fortunatus*.[45]

I argued that the young Wordsworth of 'Tintern Abbey' may help us appreciate the 'modal faith' of Virgil's *makarismos*. Virgil's deferential form of prayer was to remain a rhetorical model for Wordsworth in his later works, notably in *The Excursion*, where the Wanderer prays that 'if the time must come' when his physical faculties should fail, his mind may then remain 'unimprisoned', and his memory retain the 'visionary powers of heart and soul' he possessed in his youth (4.103–22). In the same book of *The Excursion*, the Wanderer describes the truly sublime blessing of philosophical understanding, to comprehend the entire scale of Creation, not merely the human ('Happy is He who lives to understand! | Not human Nature only, but explores | All Natures . . .', 4.332ff.).[46] But in Wordsworth's own 'Preface to *The Excursion*: the Prospectus to *The Recluse*', he mainly invokes *Paradise Lost* as his epic model, the work that represents Milton's fruition as a poet. What Wordsworth's Wye Valley 'Lines' can finally help us to appreciate in Virgil is the extent to which the *Georgics* is the work of a relatively young man who, offering his incomplete experience as a pledge for the future, is chastened as well as exhilarated by the distinctly undetermined character of his fate.

Mantua via Mossbawn: Virgil via Heaney

In a conference paper published shortly before his death, Seamus Heaney identified the 'five main European starting points' that gave him 'short cuts back into Irish destinations'. He surveyed, in other words, the main sources of poetic influence that had fed into his own work, grouping these into five categories:

1. the 'classical', i.e., the whole Graeco-Roman-Judaic inheritance in European culture;
2. the 'barbarian', or, as Heaney explains, 'all that is symbolised by the runic Germanic letter or the Irish ogham stone rather than the lines of Roman script';
3. the 'Hyperborean', represented by 'twentieth-century poets of Russia and Eastern Europe';
4. the 'province ... invigilated by' Dante Alighieri, 'the poet whom Yeats called "the chief imagination of Christendom"', and
5. a 'fifth zone of European operations', namely 'more or less direct translation ... mainly carried out in three of the four provinces already mentioned'. (In this last point, Heaney acknowledges the fact that he did not translate directly from the Slavic languages).[1]

One inference we may draw from Heaney's auto-survey is that his own poetic engagement with Virgil should be viewed as part of a many-stranded enterprise, for all that one may choose to focus on one strand or category at a time. As Heaney explains, his paper's title 'Mossbawn via Mantua' alludes to the remark of Joyce's Stephen Dedalus who, when challenged about his decision to leave Ireland, explains that the shortest way to Tara is via Holyhead.[2] Years earlier, Heaney had explained his appropriation of Stephen's 'enigmatic declaration' in his 1986 essay on the impact of Slavic-language poetry in translation on contemporary Anglophone poets: 'Might we not say, analogously, that the shortest way to Whitby, the monastery where Caedmon sang the first Anglo-Saxon verses, is via Warsaw and Prague?'[3] If Heaney's conference paper is to be credited and the route to his own birthplace, the farm at Mossbawn, may be traced by way of Virgil's Mantua, then our own way to Heaney's Virgil is likely to pass through several Holyheads, including the respective birthplaces of Dante, Wordsworth, Eliot and Miłosz.

Responses to Virgil

As is happens, Heaney's fullest description of the overall shape of Virgil's career appears in a tribute to Czesław Miłosz ('Secular and Millennial Miłosz', 1999), in which Heaney develops a 'parallel' between the Polish and the Latin poet to find 'something Virgilian about the curve of Miłosz's whole destiny':

> Like the Latin poet, [Miłosz] is a child of the countryside, starting at eye level with the ripening grain and the grazing beasts and ending up at the twentieth-century equivalent of the emperor's court. Both poets have left early work that is confidently lyrical and 'gives glory for things just because they are', but then in their maturity both proceeded to give plangent and abundant expression to their sense of 'lacrimae rerum', in longer and more elaborated works. In these, the subject was 'arms and the man', and the intonation of the poetry became increasingly grievous.[4]

As Brian Donnelly has remarked, 'This might serve as a description of Heaney's own career'.[5] We notice too how Heaney's view of Virgil cleaves to the traditional notion of the Roman poet's poetic progression as the steadily amplifying expression of a sensibility that is instinctively responsive to beauty and increasingly troubled by harsher circumstances. ('There is something Virgilian', writes Heaney, 'in [Miłosz's] combination of tenderminded susceptibility and melancholy understanding.')[6] It is worth noticing that Heaney's description of Virgil's 'early work' does not explicitly distinguish between pastoral and georgic, though he does observe the distinction in other critical writings. If one paused to consider whether the work Heaney describes as 'confidently lyrical' might refer to the *Eclogues,* and the work that '"gives glory for things just because they are"' to the *Georgics,* one would surely struggle to draw any line between poetic lyricism and thanksgiving.[7] As Heaney's inverted commas indicate, he is quoting the final line of Miłosz's poem 'Blacksmith Shop' (1991), 'To glorify things just because they are'.[8] Like Heaney's own early poem 'The Forge' (*Door into the Dark,* 1969), 'Blacksmith Shop' is a lyric poem about poetic vocation. In the case of either poem, the agricultural subject matter does not itself identify the poem as 'georgic' any more than its lyric character identifies it as 'pastoral'. The question of distinguishing between elements of pastoral and georgic in Heaney's work is complex, and will be one of my preoccupations in this chapter.

The parallel that Heaney develops between Virgil and Miłosz centers on Heaney's idea of Miłosz as an exemplary figure who is 'secular' in the sense of bearing witness to the entire twentieth century, implying an analogous sense in which Virgil is taken to bear witness to the political events of the closing century of his own millennium (BC).[9] By analogy with Virgil, Miłosz is said to be 'millennial' also in the sense that he 'culturally [...] spans the millennium'.[10] Virgil is presented as a figure of maximum fetch and summation, the poet from the periphery who masters all genres, including the master genre, epic, and becomes world poet. Miłosz makes his first appearance in Heaney's oeuvre as 'The Master' in the poem of that title from *Station Island* (1984), which refers to Miłosz's own poem 'The Master' and also evokes *maestro*, the title by which Dante the pilgrim characteristically addresses Virgil.[11] Heaney's prose tribute to Miłosz praises the master poet above all for his 'magnificent' handling of the traditionally ideal balance between instruction and delight:

> The needle is constantly atremble between the reality principle and the pleasure principle: Prospero and Ariel keep adding their weight to either side of the argument. Miłosz dwells in the middle, at times tragically, at times deliciously, for he will renege neither on his glimpses of heaven upon earth nor on his knowledge that the world is a vale of tears.[12]

The parallel with Virgil is thus sustained, and once more the conventional ideal of balancing extremes, or finding one's own balance between them, may be easily – perhaps too easily? – applied to Heaney himself.

Heaney's avowedly superficial comparison between Miłosz and Virgil rests on fairly conventional ideas about the Latin poet. Indeed there is nothing *recherché* about Heaney's approach to Virgil. This does not mean that Heaney's allusions to Virgil are easy to interpret, or even to identify. One of Heaney's most intriguing poems, 'Aisling' in *North* (1975, p. 42), at one point recalls Aeneas' strange meeting with his mother Venus at the beginning of the *Aeneid* (1.314–410), but then immediately refers to the figure of Actaeon, whose story is best known from Ovid's *Metamorphoses* (3.138–252). The aisling is the traditional Irish vision poem in which the poet encounters a female figure (Ireland), who typically delivers a lament or prophecy and an entreaty.[13] In Heaney's 'Aisling', the unidentified male figure ('he') encounters a woman whose identity is never established. We are told that 'He courted her | With a decadent sweet art | Like the wind's vowel | Blowing through the hazels'. Because in *North* 'Aisling' follows immediately after 'Ocean's Love to Ireland', which features the figure of Sir Walter Raleigh, it may be tempting to suppose that in 'Aisling' too, 'he' refers to Raleigh, in which case the 'decadent sweet art' might refer to the Elizabethan lyric. Alternatively, Neil Corcoran proposes Edmund Spenser as the poem's male subject.[14] We simply do not know, any more than we can be sure that the poem's female figure represents Ireland. (Is she 'the ruined maid' from the collection's previous poem?) We come to realize, I think, that this uncertainty about identity is precisely what Heaney's poem is about. In the absence of any geographical reference, the poem's setting must be inferred from genre. The poem's hazels recall the 'hazel wood' of Yeats's 'Song of Wandering Aengus', inspired by the medieval *Aisling Oengus*. Yet when Heaney's male figure speaks, asking '"Are you Diana ...?"', it is tempting to recall Aeneas asking that very question, *an Phoebi soror?* (1.329), when in a very aisling-like scene, his mother Venus epiphanically appears to him disguised as the huntress Diana on his coming ashore at Carthage.[15] Heaney's poem does not allow us to linger on the allusion, passing immediately to a follow-up question: if she is Diana, does that make him Actaeon? 'And was he Actaeon, | His high lament | The stag's exhausted belling?' The swift deflatory metamorphosis from 'high lament' to 'belling' (the cry of the stag at rutting time) seems very Ovidian.[16] When Ovid's Actaeon tries to lament, *me miserum!*, he finds all he can do is groan, *ingemere* (3.201–02). Yet it is not Ovid's Actaeon who asks 'Are you Diana?'. It is Virgil Aeneas who asks that question. Moreover, whereas Heaney's word 'belling' is starkly sexual, Actaeon's error is not really erotic. In Ovid, Actaeon comes upon Diana not through lust but by mistake. Virgil's scene, by contrast, has a very powerful erotic charge. Aeneas utters *his* 'high lament' of disappointment (*quid ... crudelis tu quoque ...*, 1.407–09) when he realizes, just as the huntress-figure turns to flee, that he has been speaking with his mother in disguise. If we entertain the parallel between Heaney's 'Aisling' and Virgil's scene, we observe that Aeneas, a traveller exploring a strange country, encounters a goddess whose appearance is not only deceptive, not merely a disguise, but an erotic disguise. Venus is dressed as the virginal Diana, but being Venus, her attractiveness is palpable in Virgil's description. *And* she is Aeneas' mother.[17] For that reason too the erotic situation in 'Aisling' ('He courted her') may seem more apposite to Virgil's scene of Aeneas meeting Venus than to Ovid's story of Actaeon – though of course Aeneas never actually 'courts' the Diana-like figure, for all his hardwired gallantry in immediately addressing her as a goddess, as Odysseus first addresses Nausicaa in the scene on which Virgil modelled his passage (*Odyssey* 6). Finally, neither of the classical scenes offers a detailed analogue to the courtship in 'Aisling', which Heanery only sketches in thumbnail outline. Heaney's poem moves swiftly from a brief 'Virgilian' possibility ('Are you Diana ...?') to its closing trope of Ovidian metamorphosis ('And was he Actaeon [...]?'). The effect is perhaps deliberately confusing, as vision-encounters often are. One question that Heaney's 'Aisling' poses to readers of Virgil is how far we might go in allowing our awareness of the conventions of an Irish genre, the aisling, to frame and shape a reading of Aeneas' first encounter with his mother in *Aeneid* 1. There are not only similarities to consider, but differences too. Aeneas does not dream the encounter, as would normally be the case in an aisling. Which arguments will a comparative reading support?

I leave the question open, since an even clearer allusion to Virgil occurs in the poem that immediately follows 'Aisling' in *North*, namely 'Act of Union' (1975, p. 43–4). Here the allusion seems quite pointed.[18] Heaney's poem casts the speaker and his expecting wife as the male and female archetypes in a political allegory of the sexual act of union. 'No treaty | I foresee', the speaker concludes, 'will salve completely your tracked | And stretchmarked body, the big pain | That leaves you raw, like opened ground, again'. As Jasper Griffin has observed, the younger Pitt famously quoted Aeneas' prophetic prayer at *Aeneid* 12.191–2, *Paribus se legibus ambae | invictae gentes aeterna in foedera mittant* ('Let the two nations, unconquered, unite in endless union and shared laws') when proposing the Union of Britain and Ireland to the House of Commons in 1799. Not only was the quotation a 'transparent sophistry', since Ireland was a conquered nation, but the Virgilian quotation became a venerable cliché of Unionist politicians and continued to set Irish teeth on edge long after Daniel O'Connell 'begged that the odious verse might no longer be repeated about Ireland'.[19] Heaney's negating allusion to the Virgilian 'act of union' will appear grimly ironic. The 'opened ground' of the wife's tracked and stretchmarked body is a strikingly violent and vivid realization of an ancient agricultural metaphor. Heaney's speaker can foresee no treaty that will 'salve' this wound 'completely'. (In the *Aeneid*, even the eventual treaty between Virgil's Juno and Jupiter at 12.818–42 may prove inconclusive: perhaps their conflict is fundamentally enduring.) Heaney's allusion plays not only against the *Aeneid*, giving the lie to conquest and anticipating the renewal of civil war, but develops the imagery of ploughing in ways that draw out elements of violence and pain in Virgil's descriptions of farming in the *Georgics*.[20] This early allusion to Virgil (if so taken) reflects the conventional aspect of Virgilian allusion as a commonplace of political rhetoric. I take this to confirm my sense that Heaney tends to think of Virgil as part of a common patrimony.

Heaney's most focused and sustained academic response to Virgil is in his 2002 Royal Irish Academy lecture, 'Eclogues *in extremis*: On the Staying Power of Pastoral'. Heaney's main verdict on pastoral is that 'the human value of the perfectly made-up thing [...] depends on the seriousness of what is at stake beyond the attainment of artistic finish, and on the depth of the poet's engagement with considerations other than the technical and the aesthetic'.²¹ Unsurprisingly, then, it is Virgil's Eclogues 1 and 9, both poems set against the roughly contemporary evictions that followed the redistributive land confiscations of the civil wars, that Heaney closely considers as Virgil's 'testing [of] the genre he inherited from Theocritus' in order to prove 'that it is fit for life in his own deadly Roman times'.²² But Heaney also describes the *Eclogues* as 'a kind of Crystal Palace, beautifully structured and strong because of inner relationships and symmetries; the author in late Republican Rome, like the engineer in Victorian England, was fully aware that artificial conditions were being created, but he was also proud of his extraordinary ability to contrive the transparent tegument'.²³ Taking his lead from Paul Alpers's study *What Is Pastoral?* (1996) on Schiller's distinction between naïve and sentimental poetry, Heaney discusses Miłosz's 'The World' as a 'sentimental' poem in Schiller's sense (i.e., self-aware and complex), notwithstanding its subtitle 'A Naïve Poem', inasmuch as its deliberately 'naïve' qualities are actually 'sentimental' in being 'the result of imagination pressing back against the pressure of reality'.²⁴ This is the sense in which Heaney reads the *Eclogues* and 'The World' as mutually comparable examples of 'sentimental' poetry. 'There is something bulletproof about Miłosz's crystal palace'.²⁵ In Heaney's typically balanced pronouncement, the ideal literary artifice is not only poised against historical and political actualities, but held in place by that balance.²⁶

One aspect of Alpers's analysis on which Heaney does not explicitly remark is Alpers's scepticism about the survival beyond the eighteenth century of pastoral 'as an intertextual genre', by which he means an intramural genre, as distinct from its persistence, with other genres, within the wider operative context of 'the writer's works and endeavors as a whole (in which intertextual relations of various sorts may of course be important)'.²⁷ But then Alpers does not deny the persistence of the pastoral tradition in modern literature, or indeed contradict anything Heaney says about pastoral. As early as 1975, reviewing the *Penguin Book of English Pastoral Verse* (1974), Heaney took a critical view of its editors' attempts to foreclose on the viability of twentieth-century pastoral.²⁸ The value of using genre as a critical tool might be tested with reference to the Heaney poem that most exquisitely comprehends the conventions of Virgilian and

Renaissance pastoral, 'The Harvest Bow' (*Field Work*, 1979, pp. 55–6).[29] The poem exhibits several of the classic tropes of pastoral: let me list three. We recognize the first in the poem's representation of the rustic work of art as an emblem of poetry ('this frail device'), demonstrating the ideal virtues of succinctness, intricacy, and completeness (cf. *Eclogues* 10.70–1). We recognize a second pastoral trope in the poem's use of quotation as multiple echo. (Commenting of the poem's proposed motto for the harvest bow, '*the end of art is peace*', Heaney remarked, 'I enjoy the triple take of it because Coventry Patmore said it, Yeats used it and I used Yeats using it'.)[30] A third feature of pastoral is exhibited in the poem's entertainment of a wide range of themes by artful implication, some of which would also be at home in epic, such as filiation and investiture. (In fact, the riverbank tableau of Heaney father and son on 'an evening of long grass and midges' in 'The Harvest Bow' would be revisited much later, with explicit reference to epic, in *Human Chain*'s 'The Riverbank Field' and 'Route 110'.) But to say that 'The Harvest Bow' is pastoral may be little more than an academic way of praising it as a lyric that is close to perfect, not only in its tightness but also in its springy give. Heaney's poems are lyric, certainly in a broad sense;[31] they operate in a tradition of modern lyric that is capable of drawing a huge variety of poetic kinds within its compass, including pastoral, georgic, and epic.[32]

What we see in Heaney's *oeuvre*, then, is a reconfiguration of the Virgilian generic repertoire within the compass of lyric. Virgil is part of Heaney's educational patrimony, a 'corroborative' presence in his work from the beginning, and an increasingly palpable presence from the late 1970s until his death. In the 1980s Virgil begins to assume the shape that distinguishes him in Heaney's work: the poet of the underworld and the afterlife, the poet of *Aeneid* VI and guide of Dante.

Corroborative figures, ghosts and allusion

The phrase 'corroborative' is Heaney's own, given critical currency first by Fiona Stafford and then by Neil Corcoran, who both use it in opposition, or by way of alternative, to Harold Bloom's agonistic model of poetic influence.[33] Heaney's early 'corroborators' include Patrick Kavanagh, Yeats and Wordsworth. (In Corcoran's estimation, Wordsworth 'is probably the most deeply and originally informing presence in Heaney, despite his far more extensive critical engagement with Yeats'.[34] Interestingly, given Milton's influence on Wordsworth as well as Milton's centrality as mediator of Virgil, Milton is conspicuously absent from

Heaney's pantheon.[35]) It is not mainly through these 'exemplary' poets that Virgil becomes either a monitory or a corroborative figure in Heaney's work, but Virgil becomes both kinds of figure through Dante, who was most influentially mediated to poets of Heaney's generation by T. S. Eliot, as Heaney himself observes in his 1985 essay 'Envies and Identifications: Dante and the Modern Poet'.[36]

Yet as 'Envies and Identifications' explains, it was not Eliot but the Russian poet Osip Mandelstam who came to corroborate Heaney's embrace of Dante in the 1980s. In Mandelstam's essay 'Conversation about Dante', written in the 1930s, Heaney discovered a Russian alternative to Eliot as an exemplary reader of the Florentine poet. Mandelstam appeared to rescue Dante 'from the pantheon' in which Eliot had unhelpfully enshrined him. For Heaney, Mandelstam brings Dante 'from the pantheon back to the palate'. Unlike Eliot's philosophical Dante, the sensuous Dante of Mandelstam's essay 'makes our mouth water to read him'.[37] Whereas Eliot's famous 1929 essay describes Dante's poetic language as an idiom that is austere, limpid, supra-regional and universalizing, Heaney compares the 'mouth-watering' Italian of Mandelstam's Dante with precisely the example that Eliot's essay offers as a *contrast* to Dante, namely the 'erotic' and demotic English of Shakespeare, illustrated by Duncan and Banquo's dialogue about Macbeth's castle and the temple-haunting martlet (*Macbeth* 1.6.1–10).[38] As Heaney explains, he found the revelation of Mandelstam's Dante 'indispensable'.[39] 'This Dante', he discovers, 'is essentially lyric'.[40] As Michael Parker has observed,

> Heaney's emphasis [in 'Envies and Identifications'] on Dante the *lyric* poet illustrates his own contention that 'when poets turn to the great masters of the past, they turn to an image of their own creation, one which is likely to be a reflection of their own imaginative needs, their own artistic inclinations and procedures'.[41]

In 'Envies and Identifications', Heaney explains how his discovery of Mandelstam's 'essentially lyric' Dante helped him, too, to wrest the Italian master free from the mortmain of Eliot's grip.[42] Heaney needed that freedom precisely to encounter the aspect of Dante that had also gripped Eliot: Dante's power to haunt, and to be haunted by, the living and the dead, including poets as well as family members. 'T. S. Eliot's work', Heaney says, 'is haunted by the shade of Dante'.[43] In an earlier lecture from 1998, he shows how intimate he takes this 'haunting' to be:

> [...] Eliot's dream processes fed upon the phantasmagoria of *The Divine Comedy* constantly, so the matter of Dante's poem was present to him, and Dante had thereby become *second nature* to him. Dante, in fact, belonged in the rag-and-

bone shop of Eliot's middle-ageing heart, and it was from that sad organ, we might say, that all his lyric ladders started.[44]

It is in the 1980s, when Heaney not only continues to meditate on the victims of political violence in Ireland but must also confront the natural deaths of his own parents, that Heaney turns to Eliot, Mandelstam and Dante, and through them to Virgil, for various kinds of corroboration, finding himself haunted by, and needing himself to haunt, the dead.

But Heaney's engagement with Virgil really begins on the first page of his first collection, in the poem he would continue to treat as programmatic throughout his life, namely 'Digging'. Heaney's emblematic juxtaposition of the spade and the pen sets up at least three paradigms that would be sustained throughout his oeuvre. The first may be called quintessentially georgic, namely the parallel between the agricultural and the poetic vocation. (The incidental archaeological implications of digging would ramify further in Heaney's work: his 1974 essay 'Feeling into Words' describes the ideal poetry as 'a dig for finds that end up being plants'.)[45] The second paradigm is the Hesiodic motif of vocational inheritance and investiture. (The Muses hand Hesiod a laurel staff at the beginning of the *Theogony*.) In 'Digging', it is not the Muses on Mount Helicon we encounter presenting the shepherd-poet with the laurel staff, but the poet taking up his pen as the emblem of his forefathers' work with the spade. The third paradigm might be called epic: the theme of filial succession and piety, memorable too in the same collection's poem 'Follower'.

None of this counts as an 'allusion' or a deliberate reference to Virgil. It is certainly true that in the middle and final stages of his career, Heaney developed an increasingly allusive dialogue with Virgil, specifically with the *Eclogues* (notably 1, 4 and 9) and the *Aeneid* (especially Books 2 and 6) – a dialogue mediated particularly by the figure of Dante and the tradition of the *Commedia*. But before *Field Work* (1979), by which time Heaney had achieved his foundational body of work, I find only two allusions to Virgil.[46] The one in 'Act of Union' I have already discussed. The other, in 'Bog Oak' from *Wintering Out* (1972), positively disavows Virgilian allusion. As Colin Burrow observes, 'Bog Oak' 'presents the Irish landscape as one from which groves where a golden bough might grow have been uprooted – "The softening ruts | lead back to no | 'oak groves', no | cutters of mistletoe | in the green clearings" – before it goes on to imagine Edmund Spenser dreaming of suppressing the Irish.' Burrow's 'uprooted' entails some exaggeration if taken to imply some actual deforestation in historical time: Irish bog oak is prehistoric. But that is not his main point, and he is surely right that 'Heaney's earlier verse [...] tends to be much more edgy about imperial rule than his later writing'.[47] Heaney's quotation marks round the phrase 'oak groves' are superbly dismissive.

Earthings

More strikingly still, perhaps, Heaney never seems to have alluded to or imitated the *Georgics* in any of his poems, early or late. Bernard O'Donoghue's chapter on Heaney as a poet of country life is entitled 'Heaney's Classics and the Bucolic' (2009), preferring 'bucolic' to 'pastoral' not because the figure of the herdsman is more appropriate than the shepherd to Heaney, the son of a cattle dealer, but avowedly because *bucolic* 'in modern usage is also a wider term, to embrace country concerns in all senses'.[48] O'Donoghue immediately observes that with reference to Virgil's *oeuvre*, the poetry of 'tadpoles and blackberries and digging and thatching [...] is more the matter of the *Georgics*' than the *Eclogues*, concluding that the *Georgics* 'remains to be treated by Heaney and [...] might indeed be even more in his element'.[49] This raises the question of how one understands the phrase 'to treat'. O'Donoghue sidesteps the term 'georgic' as pastoral's traditional counterpart by preferring the all-purpose term 'anti-pastoral'.[50] However, by the time O'Donoghue singles out Heaney's characteristically precise distinction of soil types in 'The Loose Box' ('Sandy, glarry, | Mossy, heavy, cold . . .', *Electric Light*, p. 14) as emblematic of 'the early *pastoral* volumes' (my emphasis), the pressure to acknowledge georgic has grown overwhelming.[51] O'Donoghue's 2019 chapter 'Heaney, Yeats, and the Language of Pastoral' concludes by quoting in full Heaney's 'Quitting Time', a late poem in *District and Circle* about a pig farmer's routine of 'redding up the work' at day's end, without mentioning georgic.[52] While it is important to observe that Heaney never self-consciously presents himself as a georgic poet, this need not prevent readers from recognizing georgic motifs or tropes or characteristics in Heaney's poetry, or from bringing back such recognitions to a fresh re-reading of Virgil's *Georgics*.

For illustration, let us take another glance at 'The Loose Box'. Heaney's string of adjectives – 'Sandy, glarry, | Mossy, heavy, cold' – is a propos of something he remembers Parick Kavanagh saying 'on an old recording', namely 'That there's health and worth in any talk about | The properties of land'. Yet 'the actual soil', says Heaney's poem, 'almost doesn't matter'. As Bernard O'Donoghue observes in his reading of the poem, Heaney says the importance of talking about the properties of land lies in the way it suggests 'of treating a subject':

> the main thing is
> An inner restitution, a purchase come by
> By pacing it in words that make you feel
> You've found your feet in what 'surefooted' means
> And in the ground of your own understanding –
> Like Heracles stepping in and standing under
> Atlas's sky-lintel, as earthed and heady
> As I am when I talk about the loose box.
>
> *Electric Light*, p.14[53]

Heracles is a key figure in Heaney's early poetry as the antagonist of Antaeus, the giant who was invulnerable so long as he stayed in contact with the maternal source of his power, the earth, but whom Hercules finally managed to defeat by lifting into the air. The first part of *North* is bookended by the poems 'Antaeus' (p. 3) and 'Hercules and Antaeus' (pp. 46–7), both of which explore the myth of Antaeus' paradoxical fall by elevation.[54] It was Yeats who introduced the figure of Antaeus into modern Irish poetry in 'The Municipal Gallery Revisited' (1938). Speaking of himself, John Synge and Augusta Gregory in their effort to build an Irish national theatre, Yeats writes of their shared belief that 'All that we did, all that we said or sang | Must come from contact with the soil, from that | Contact everything Antaeus-like grew strong' (42–4). For Heaney, too, Antaeus represents the imperative to stay rooted in the values of the earth. But whereas his early Antaeus poems focus on the clear and present dangers of defeat by uprooting, in his middle and later poetry the ideal of staying rooted in the earth is expressed as the greater ideal to serve as a conduit between the earth and sky, which is the latent idea in Yeats's poem. Heaney's favoured adjective to describe this ideal is 'earthed'. In 'The Loosed Box', Hercules – no longer as antagonist to Antaeus, but reliever of Atlas – is 'earthed and heady'. As Wes Davis observes, Heaney now 'appears comfortable with the idea that a poem may be both grounded *and* heady, in touch as much with native soul as native soil'.[55] Electricity provided the redemptive sense of 'earthed'. 'To earth' is to provide a grounding channel for an electric charge. In 'The Stone Verdict', we encounter 'a tumbled wallstead where hogweed earths the silence' (*The Haw Lantern* [1987], p. 19). In 'Lightenings' iv, Heaney describes an ideal mental state (initially associated with something intimated by the audiences in Roman theatres): 'How airy and how earthed it felt up there' (*Seeing Things* [1991], p. 58). And beautifully, in 'Postscript', the final poem in *The Spirit Level* (1996), 'The surface of a slate-grey lake is lit | By the earthed lightning of a flock of swans' (p. 70).[56] By the time Heaney uses 'earthed' in 'The Loose Box', he has transformed the idea of connection to the earth into an idea of connection between earth and air.[57]

The connection between earth and sky is an idea we encounter in the first lines of the *Georgics*, when Virgil introduces the task of identifying the right time for ploughing, 'beneath what star to turn the soil' (*quo sidere terram | vertere . . . conveniat*, 1–3). Besides the figurative meaning of 'star', signifying time or season, Virgil is introducing an idea that will be vital in his poem, namely that there is a connection between matters of the earth and matters of the stars. The first four lines of the *Georgics* announce its thematic ascent from earth through plants and animals to aerial creatures, bees, linked to Jupiter in a passage that encapsulates the chain of being at 4.219–27.[58] The idea of elemental ascent is fundamental in Heaney's work as well, and we do not need allusions to Virgil in his poetry to sanction reading the *Georgics* with a sense of the effort involved in Heaney's long quest to find fitting emblems for the charge connecting earth and air.

The *Georgics* as a model?

One might pause momentarily and ask oneself what a *self-conscious* imitation of the *Georgics* by Heaney might have been like, had it existed. It if were anything like Heaney's 'Glanmore Eclogue', which presents an elaborate compliment to a friend and patron, it might be arch, occasional and allusive. (O'Donoghue observes in 'Glanmore Eclogue' 'a strong element of the affectionate pastiche').[59] If Heaney's hypothetical imitation of the *Georgics* had been like 'Bann Valley Eclogue' in the same collection, it would once more be occasional, though self-consciously cast in a higher mood. Each of these imitations of Virgil's *Eclogues* in *Electric Light* showcases two distinctive aspects of pastoral: its awareness of its own element of artifice, and its self-awareness of operating within what Alpers calls 'an intertextual genre'. For Heaney to be writing georgic in this manner, he would presumably be in the vein of Thomson's *Seasons* and other eighteenth-century georgics, because georgic 'as an intertextual genre' in English poetry is almost exclusively restricted to that century. It is hard to imagine Heaney doing this, unless for a joke.[60] The ironies of georgic and pastoral are not identical. True, the authorial figure of Virgil's *Georgics* is every bit as self-conscious as the implied poet of the *Eclogues*. But although the georgic poet presents himself as analogous to the farmer in his resourcefulness and skill, he does not present himself *as* playing a literary game. Nor does georgic typically feature the figure of a tutelary (and semi-mythical) master-poet, as in Dante. These seem to me good reasons why it would be unreasonable to expect Heaney's engagement with the *Georgics* to be allusive.

But there is little need to speculate so hypothetically when there are simpler reasons to hand. The simplest is that Heaney, especially in his earliest work, had no need to invoke a classical model when writing about the scene of his childhood, especially when he was aiming for imaginative immediacy. Heaney may well have found it invidious to assume that writing about forges, pitchforks, threshers and turnip-snedders necessarily implies a field of figurative reference beyond the poet's own lived experience.[61] One might protest that after Virgil it is impossible to read about agriculture in verse without consciousness of the *Georgics*, but I suspect Heaney would reply that this can only be true for people whose experience of farming is mainly academic. His constant aim was the imaginative transcendence of fact. Of Frost's work, Heaney said that 'the oversound' – the poetic imagination's transcendence of mere fact – was more rewarding than 'the data', and that he therefore preferred 'the extravagance of "The Witch of Cöos"' to 'the pastoral of "The Axe-Helve"'.[62] Heaney needed Virgil neither to assist 'oversound' nor to achieve aesthetic distance.[63] Heaney's poem 'Sweetpea' in *Station Island*, for instance, describes the way in which the 'pain' caused to the plant by the act of pruning creates the physical space for its heart to sing 'without caution or embarrassment, once or twice' (p. 46). The poet's commitment to standard gardening practice, combined with his imaginative empathy with inanimate things, may well be described as 'Virgilian'. But Heaney does not seem to be drawing on classical inspiration. It is significant that Heaney, who was always happy to discuss his own work and background, is silent on this subject in 'Eclogues *in extremis*' and instead discusses work by Radnóti, Miłosz, MacNeice and Longley. For all that Heaney calls Virgil his 'hedge-schoolmaster' in 'Bann Valley Eclogue', his own poetic impulse is fundamentally different from Virgil's, in that it is not only subjectively inflected but profoundly introspective. Heaney's work has been described as 'Wordsworthian' in the sense that it examines private memory and personal experience mainly as means of *poetic* discovery. While the *Georgics* is distinguished by the very fact that Virgil speaks 'in his own voice', as Addison puts it, and while it is uniquely in the *Georgics* that Virgil identifies and even names himself, nevertheless Virgil does not present himself as exploring *private* (as distinct from personal or subjective) experience. When Virgil introduces the old gardener of Tarentum in *Georgics* 4.125–48, he says 'I remember seeing him' (*memini videre*). But this still seems more a case of personal testimony than of private or intimate revelation, if such a distinction is allowed.[64] Even at what might be taken as the most heartfelt moment in the *Georgics*, the so-called *makarismos* passage of Book II (475–94), Virgil does not represent sharply individualized experience or perception, what one might call lyric expression. Heaney's poetic impulse, like Wordsworth's but unlike Virgil's in the *Georgics*, is not merely 'first-personal', but specifically lyric as well as autobiographical.[65] Even Heaney's habitual allusiveness seems invariably and fundamentally to serve a lyrical purpose. The young poet of 'Personal Helicon', the closing poem of Heaney's first collection, declares himself an adult who, unlike Narcissus, looks in wells *to discover himself* in the reflection. This is 'poetry as divination, poetry as revelation of the self to the self'.[66] The operative word of the poem's title is 'personal'. When Heaney says he rhymes 'to set the darkness echoing', his figure of allusion is pointedly introspective as well as outwardly radiating. Contrastively, while the *Georgics* does imitate and allude to earlier didactic poets such as Hesiod, Aratus, Nicander, and Lucretius, Virgil's allusiveness does not seem self-exploratory in a *lyrical* sense.[67] Heaney is like Virgil insofar as both are profoundly allusive and intertextual poets, but Heaney seems never to have felt that alluding to the *Georgics* might serve his own distinctively lyrical aims.

Nonetheless, in many respects Heaney's poetic aims may be considered intimately congenial with key aspects of Virgil's ambition in the *Georgics*. We see this in the question of poetic language. Historically, critical debate about the *Georgics* has tended to arise from the practical problems of translation. The main problem that underlies and typically vexes all imitation and emulation of the *Georgics* is how to follow Virgil's example and transpose the mundane onto the highest plane of universality (represented by the realms of religion, philosophy and science) as well as the most familiar plane of common experience (rural life), and to endow this poetic achievement with normative force. That is a tall order, to say the least. As Heaney describes Wordsworth's achievement, the poet's task is 'to bridge the gap between the quotidian and the visionary worlds'.[68] Heaney's whole oeuvre may be taken as a transposition of the mundane into a register that aspires to the highest order of poetic universality – a matter not merely of factual fidelity or literal correspondence to real experiences and things, but of poetic composition and language. Once more, the parallel with the *Georgics* seems closer than mere verbal imitation.

'The Pitchfork' in *Seeing Things* (1991), for instance, describes a farm implement emblematically, unfolding a parable about a poet's development from initially idealizing poetic *aim* to latterly idealizing poetic *receptivity* ('Where perfection – or nearness to it – is imagined | Not in the aiming but the opening hand').[69] The poem presents, in two parts, a narrative of the development of a poetics. The first three stanzas describe the qualities of the physical pitchfork in the poet's imagination, qualities taken as a metaphor for 'an imagined perfection'.

The final two stanzas describe how the poet further extends the qualities of the pitchfork in his imagination, projecting its flight into the outer cosmos, and even beyond the trajectory described by 'its own aim, out to an other side', where a complementary idea of perfection is imagined ('not in the aiming but the opening hand'). Now, the continuity imagined between the farm world and the interstellar spaces may well be perceived as 'Virgilian', as indeed may the journey traced by the Lucretian mind that penetrates the universe through. The poetic description of agricultural implements too has a georgic pedigree that reaches back to Hesiod. And Heaney's description of the pitchfork's action as a javelin takes us straight to Virgil's description of farming implements as *arma* (*Georgics* 1.160).[70] As William Batstone observes, 'Virgil's military metaphors for farming' begin almost immediately in the *Georgics*. 'The language of violence and control', he argues, is not only 'part of the poem's diction' but 'was there all along [...] since the poem began, since before the poem began, and the poem catches the reader within the developing force of the metaphor. Military language and metaphors, just like many military virtues (and vices), grew out of the Roman experience with the land and their ideology of that experience'.[71] Here is a condition that Heaney shares with Virgil: metaphors inhabit the common language before they enter into poetry.

But the differences between Heaney's treatment of the pitchfork and Virgil's description of the farmer's arms, with instructions for building a plough (1.160–8), are quite as significant as the similarities. Heaney summons the pitchfork to our senses as an object of meditation, and as the meditation intensifies, Heaney develops it as a metaphor in its own right, leaving the concrete for the abstract. Virgil's georgic descriptions and precepts, by contrast, accumulate metaphors in ways that do not tend towards further abstraction, but are organized by a principle of contiguity such as that which governs metonymy. Passing on from the description of farmers' tackle using the martial metaphor of *arma*, carts and baskets are next described with imagery evoking the religious festivals at Eleusis. The harvest wagons appear as 'the slow-rolling wains of the Mother of Eleusis [i.e., Demeter]' (*tardaque Eleusinae matris volventia plaustra*, 1.163) and basketwork is associated with Celeus (1.165), king of Eleusis when Demeter came there in search of Persephone and taught men agriculture, and with Iacchus, a deity associated with the Eleusinian mysteries.[72] The effect of this juxtaposition of imagery is not only to suggest that agriculture has a martial dimension as well as a religious one, but that all three spheres – warfare, farming and religious ritual – are parts of a single civic and cosmic order. Heaney naturally has a more modern sense of the separation of spheres. Warfare,

athletics, and farmwork are presented contrastively as alternatives ('whether ...
or ... or'), but only farmwork is entertained 'in earnest':

> So whether he played the warrior or the athlete
> Or worked in earnest in the chaff and sweat,
> He loved its grain of tapering, dark-flecked ash
> Grown satiny from its own natural polish.

True, the ensuing stanza makes us feel the completeness of the pitchfork's
repertoire as a javelin as well as a farm instrument, an epic spear as well as a
georgic tool:

> Riveted steel, turned timber, burnish, grain,
> Smoothness, straightness, roundness, length and sheen.
> Sweat-cured, sharpened, balanced, tested, fitted.
> The springiness, the clip and dart of it.[73]

A line that begins with 'riveted steel' and ends with 'grain' certainly works to erase
the boundaries between the martial and the agricultural. Nevertheless, 'The
Pitchfork' is unlike Virgil's description of farming implements in that Heaney's
aim is not primarily to describe a concrete artefact in a way that relates it to
several areas of common experience in the physical world, but instead to describe
an instrument and its action so that they represent a state approximating that of
a pure sign. First the thing is described so that its concreteness is evoked with
maximum sensory vividness. Then that impression of concreteness is shed, and
the idea of the pitchfork is refigured by the poetic imagination as a bipolar ideal
of perfection, which is to say, as an abstraction.[74]

Georgic diction

The affinity of Virgil and Heaney is seen most importantly in the matter of
diction. The common complaint against translators and imitators of the *Georgics*
is that they do not achieve Virgil's dignity of diction, perceived as a striking an
ideal balance between the mundane and the universal. By its very relationship
with the original, translation is always and of necessity open to comparative
criticism. In the Irish poet Peter Fallon's translation of the *Georgics* (2004), for
instance, which Heaney reviewed with praise, Virgil's reference to *mystica vannus
Iacchi* (1.166) is rendered 'Iacchus' marvellous riddle' (by comparison, the Loeb
translation gives 'the mystic fan of Iacchus').[75] Fallon's rhythmic sprightliness

here, which approximates Virgil's dactylic metre, contrasts pointedly with the deliberate drag in his translation of Virgil's earlier lines about 'hefty carts' and the 'heavy-weighted' mattock. But there is also the question of lexical choice. A riddle is a coarse-meshed sieve: the word's register is agricultural and regional. But Fallon's lexical choice might also make a sophisticated point, whether fortuitously or by design, since 'turning the riddle' is an old form of divination in Britain and Ireland, and therefore aptly suggests analogies, from however great a distance, with the Eleusinian mysteries as well as harvest festivals.[76] Ever since Servius, the *vannus* of Iacchus or Bacchus has proved something of a mystery to commentators – some would have it a winnowing basket, others a winnowing fan – so there is also some wit in calling it a riddle. There is an element of exuberance and flourish in Fallon's lexical choice that either confirms or jibs against a reader's sense of 'the Virgilian'. Is 'Iacchus' marvellous riddle' too rustic, too regional, too demotic, too arcane, too fanciful or playful?[77] Or are all these qualities held in (an appropriate) balance? These are questions that the translator or close imitator of Virgil must naturally confront, but which would prove a distraction to Heaney in poems that are not concerned with Virgil, however congenial they may be with some of Virgil's achievements in the *Georgics*. The balance achieved in 'The Pitchfork' between the artisanal and the cosmic, the immanent and transcendent, measures up to Virgil but does not measure itself against him.

As Hugh Haughton has observed in an essay on Heaney's affinity with Wordsworth, 'As a poet and critic, Heaney is never happier than when he is acknowledging debts and influences'.[78] Heaney's above-quoted formulation about the task of poetry being 'to bridge the gap between the quotidian and the visionary worlds' avowedly paraphrases Wordsworth's famous passage from the 1800 Preface to *Lyrical Ballads* about his aim to present scenes from common life in common language, irradiated by the poetic imagination ('a selection of the real language of men in a state of vivid sensation'). It is striking how fully Wordsworth's project also describes Heaney's own poetics. Throughout his career, Heaney's critical essays drew on examples from Wordsworth to illustrate the impulses of his own poetry. I mention this for two reasons. First, it illustrates the active role Heaney typically played in identifying his own affinities, which may serve as a point of reference when considering influences that are less openly acknowledged or less clear. Second, it serves to remind us once more that Heaney's Virgil is modified in the guts of his mediators, especially Dante, Wordsworth and Eliot.[79] When Heaney recalls the boat 'that wafts into | The first lines of the *Purgatorio*' ('The Biretta', in *Seeing Things*, 1991), he is recalling

Dante's 'la navicella del mio ingegnio' ('the little ship of my imagination'), but of course Heaney does not invite us to trace Dante's use of the commonplace back to its many classical sources, which include *Georgics* 2.39–46 and 4.116.[80]

Archetypes and points of origin: Virgil in Heaney's early work, 1966–75

Setting aside the fact that Heaney's early poems, including *North* (1975) but especially in the three earlier collections, are characteristically concerned with rendering the perspective of the poet's younger self – an autobiographical preoccupation, I have argued, that is not matched in Virgil – Heaney's poems about the farm world are certainly hospitable to comparisons with Virgil. After the programmatic 'Digging' in *Death of a Naturalist*, the collection's title poem introduces the theme of brooding menace in natural processes observed in the environment of a farming community: the sense of latent or gathering violence, never vanquished but only ever held at bay. In 'The Barn', the child's imaginative perceptions of the barn and farmyard are developed into a kind of phantasmagoria composed on the principle of *chiaroscuro*. The most important poems in the collection have an emblematic force, each representing a particular kind of experience: as in the *Eclogues*, the sense of deliberate selection is strong. A key theme is the juxtaposition of sensations of delight and disgust, in the 'stink' of the house 'long after churning day' in the poem of that title, 'acrid as a sulphur mine', or when in 'Blackberry-Picking' the 'rat-grey fungus' is discovered 'glutting' on the hoard of berries. The aesthetic of minutely balanced contrast is perhaps too general and essentially 'classical' to be considered specifically Virgilian, though Viktor Pöschl describes Virgil's technique throughout his works as 'a model for a composition by contrasts'.[81] Still, 'a composition by contrasts' describes Heaney's technique too. Since the earliest reviews of Heaney's work, critics have been observing that Heaney's verse (again, 'classically') strives to exhibit the aesthetic qualities it celebrates: as Christopher Ricks wrote in his review of *Death of a Naturalist*, 'What he praises is to be praised in his own work'.[82] In Heaney's 'Follower', the reversal of roles between father and son recalls Virgil's concern with filial piety, and the verse itself describes the figure of reversal in the enjambment of the lines that describe the turn of the plough at the end of a furrow: 'the sweating team turned round | And back into the land' (p. 12). As Heaney explains in his 1978 lecture 'The Makings of a Music', '"verse" comes from the Latin *versus* which could mean a line of poetry but could also mean the turn that a ploughman made at the head of the field as he finished one furrow and faced back into another'.[83] Further analogies between farming and poetry may be traced in Heaney's early work, converging on Virgilian themes or tropes. The question is, does this lead us to Virgil – and if so, how?

I think there is relatively little more to be gained from eking out parallels between Heaney's early work and Virgil from thematic convergences between them, particularly regarding rustic occupations. The critic who has gone furthest in this direction, Sidney Burris, works with a very broad notion of pastoral/'anti-pastoral' tradition that does not yield very close links between Virgil and Heaney.[84] I would like instead to consider a different quality of Heaney's early work that I think has something fundamental in common with Virgil, albeit *without being influenced by Virgil*, namely Heaney's mythologizing of place. This takes us directly to the grounds on which Heaney was most acutely criticized in Ciaran Carson's review of *North*, which described Heaney as a 'mystifier' of political violence, and in the process, a mystifier of place. In Carson's contemporary analysis of *North*, illustrated by his reading of 'Kinship (III)', the collection was generally marred by Heaney's attempt to obey two mutually incompatible imperatives, the laudable 'need to be precise' and the deplorable 'desire to abstract'.[85] While some critics have expressed similar reservations, the majority have applauded Heaney's combination of observational fidelity with mythic allusiveness and abstraction.[86] One reason for this critical success is that *North* was widely seen to be continuous with his earlier work. As Edna Longley observes, Heaney himself regarded *North* as a culmination rather than a new departure, and considered his first four collections as 'one book'.[87] Heaney's characteristic commitment to tracing continuities, especially at points of boundary, is fundamental to what I have so far called his mythologizing of place, but 'aetiologizing' might be more accurate, since Heaney is characteristically drawn to myths of origin.[88] This disposition to trace continuities backward to a point of origin, whether real, ideal or imagined, is evident in Heaney's criticism too. In the review of *The Penguin Book of English Pastoral Verse* (written while composing *North*), Heaney revealingly describes the classical tradition as 'the ancient hinterland', and as the context makes clear, Heaney considers the 'hinterland' to be integral to the sense of any landscape. Heaney explains that in poetry 'the hinterland' means 'the perspectives backward'. 'Spenser, Milton, Pope and Thomson', he remarks, 'were as automatically conscious of the classical penumbra behind their own efforts as most of today's students are unconscious of it'.[89] The phrase 'classical penumbra' is suggestive too, since Heaney implies that the penumbra, the meeting-point of light and shade, is a vital quality in a landscape, not merely an incidental of lighting effects.

Famously, Carson attacked what he took to be the implications of 'Punishment':

> It is as if [Heaney] is saying, suffering like this is natural; these things have always happened; they happened then, they happen now, and that is sufficient ground for understanding and absolution. It is as if there never were and never will be any political consequences of such acts; they have been removed to the realm of sex, death and inevitability.

Carson decried what one might call the 'mythologizing' vein of Heaney's poetry, which Carson felt had 'degenerated into a messy historical and religious surmise – a kind of Golden Bough activity, in which the real difference between our society and that of Jutland in some vague past are glossed over for the sake of the parallels of ritual'.[90] At root, Carson is objecting to the extension into the realm of contemporary political conflict of a fundamental procedure of Heaney's writing, namely the allusive sounding for points of origin through the 'fieldworker's archive' ('The Backward Look', in *Wintering Out*, p. 20). The meditative search for points of origin is not only a basic feature of Heaney's work, it is also a common feature of a great deal of poetry in the European tradition: it is a feature that can only be traced back to Virgil with neon caveats. Heaney's avowed practice in 'Personal Helicon' – rhyming 'to see myself, to set the darkness echoing' – may be described as 'Wordsworthian', as may indeed the aim to trace the 'making of a poet's mind'.[91] In Heaney's first four collections, an imaginary is developed of landscape and environment altogether suggestive of deep continuities, as abiding and mutable as the elements and the weather. By the time *North* appeared – 'Belderg' is the first in the book's series of poems with an archaeological theme – Heaney had already composed a rich 'archive' (to adopt metaphors from 'The Backward Look') of 'gleanings and leavings' in the 'comb' of his *oeuvre* for the ideas and images of his subsequent poems to settle into. As Jon Stallworthy observed in an early scholarly article on Heaney, the figure of the poet as archaeologist had evolved steadily from the poet's first collection.[92] The archaeological-mythical poems that appeared in *Door Into the Dark* (1969) and continued in *Wintering Out* (1972) had been anticipated in *Death of a Naturalist*. The poem 'In Small Townlands' in that collection, a meditation on the art of the painter Colin Middleton, celebrates the artist's creative violence in his act of reconstituting the elements of landscape and terrain – the artist splitting apart, stripping and paring down the elements of the land and its light like a farmer, scientist and archaeologist. It is from this carefully prepared poetic context (or pre-text) that the historico-mythic themes of *North* are cultivated.

North presents itself self-consciously as a composition, everywhere drawing attention to the poet's act of composing a virtual landscape from references to physical materials and objects as well as figures from an archaeo-historical and mythological past. 'Belderg' re-imagines the archaeological site of the neolithic settlement in County Mayo ('a landscape fossilized') as a world-tree or Yggdrasil of balanced quernstones excavated from the bog, 'Querns piled like vertebrae, | The marrow crushed to grounds' (pp. 4–5). In the poem's reported conversation with a local guide, based on an encounter with the archaeologist Seamus Caulfield, Heaney offers the derivation of his own 'bogland name', Mossbawn, and observes 'how its foundation | Was mutable as sound' in its derivation from either English *bawn* ('fortified farmhouse') or Irish *bán* ('white') as well as the Ulster Scots *moss*, 'bog'. But *moss*, Heaney finds, has a Norse derivation too from the Scandinavian and Germanic *mose*, 'bog', and the Norse 'growth rings' in the language allow him to reconfigure the entire scene with its 'mutable' components in the image of Yggdrasil, the ancient world tree of Norse myth. This backward-tracing impulse of the imagination toward the archaic and the archetypal is not only strong in Heaney but distinctive. To say 'archaic' and 'archetypal' is precisely *not* to say 'accurately historical' in the sense of something corresponding to either factual event, chronology, or causal sequence. When Heaney identifies his great-uncle Hughie as the presence informing the figure of his grandfather in 'Digging' as well as '"the god of the waggon" in the fifth section of "Kinship"' (Hugh Scullion is the family ancestor whose face Heaney 'recognized' in Glob's photograph of the Tollund Man), Heaney is revealing a personal archetype of great importance: 'To me he was always the ur-ancestor on the Heaney side of the family.'[93] Heaney's imagination is archetypal, even 'aetiological', in its tendency to establish archetypes as points of origin.

Divination and filial piety

Heaney's prose has greatly helped to establish certain archetypes in his work, such as the pump in the yard at the beginning of *Preoccupations*, identified at the head of his memoir essay 'Mossbawn' (1978) as the quietly enduring *omphalos* of his childhood world, triumphantly impervious to the ephemeral passage of American bombers 'groan[ing] towards the aerodrome at Toomebridge'. 'There the pump stands, a slender, iron idol, snouted, helmeted, dressed down with a sweeping handle, painted a dark green and set on a concrete plinth, marking the centre of another world.'[94] The 'helmeted pump' is there too in the earlier 'Mossbawn' I: 'Sunlight' (*North*, p. ix). The pump of the essay – an auditory memory as well, the plunger described as 'slugging up and down, *omphalos, omphalos, omphalos*' –needn't absolutely be associated with 'the invisible, untoppled omphalos' of Heaney's contemporary poem 'The Toome Road' (in *Field Work*, p. 7), but readers who know Heaney's work in prose as well as verse will make the connection, and see too that the poem's distinction is precisely to break free from the concrete figure and assert the power of pure symbol (in the poem, the *omphalos* is no longer a pump, still 'vibrant' but 'invisible') over the patrolling soldiers or 'charioteers', who are as mocked by Heaney's Hellenizing diction as the memoir essay's 'helmeted' idol (the pump) is honoured by that diction. (The element of instability in the balance between high diction and mundane subject matter is of course recognizable as one of Virgil's most distinctive features.) Heaney's imagination, then, casts back to archetypes as points of origin: once the connection is made, his poetic craft typically strives to transcend the point of origin. Heaney has often explained his attraction, from earliest childhood, to what Wordsworth calls 'hiding places': 'All children want to crouch in their secret nests'.[95] Quoting Wordsworth's *Prelude* (1805) 11.335–42 at the head of his key essay 'Feeling into Words' (1974), Heaney identifies these places in the poet's memory and imagination as 'the hiding places' of his 'power'.[96] Antaeus is the heroic figure in Heaney's early poetry that represents the state of deep connection with this source.[97]

On the one hand, Heaney characteristically presents himself as a fabricator, drawing attention to the act of composition. On the other, he represents the process of poetic composition as an act of divination, evoking and invoking the numinous, or as he calls it in his later work, 'the marvellous'. Either way, Heaney foregrounds the figure of the artificer or the diviner, which is quite different from Virgil's much slighter self-presentation as poet (and different too from the medieval notion of Virgil as magus). In the *Georgics*, Virgil's greatest evocation of the marvellous occurs in the so-called Aristaeus epyllion, which describes the Egyptian miracle of the regeneration of bees from the rotting carcass of a ritually bludgeoned ox (4.281–314). Virgil's evocations of the awe-inspiringly numinous, however, are mainly a feature of the *Aeneid*, where the divine is frequently associated with place, for instance in the description of Pallanteum in Book 8, where at the site of the future Capitol 'even then the dread sanctity of the region awed the trembling rustics; even then they shuddered at the forest and the rock' (349–50, *iam tum religio pavidos terrebat agrestis* | *dira loci, iam tum silvam saxumque tremebant*). The thrill of horror in the presence of the holy involves the uncanny: something is dimly recognized, yet not quite identified. A sense of wonder in the presence of immanent mystery distinguishes Heaney's early work, not least his poems of childhood at Mossbawn. In 'The Barn', discussed earlier, the inanimate objects and surfaces, even the dark itself, are instinct with menacing force: Heaney is apprehending primal mysteries. Many have observed Heaney's affinity with Wordsworth in this respect, often citing the boat-stealing episode in *The Prelude* (1805, 1.372–451). Heaney's creative impulse strikes inward and backward, psychically as well as culturally, as in his seminal bog poem 'Bogland' (*Door into the Dark*, 1969), where the sublime is figured as bottomlessness, and the bog's intimately familiar frontier-habitat is identified as the source of mystery, as well as the path toward origins and self-knowledge, by the steady process of unearthing, seen as a kind of divination.[98]

Interiority, the probing of the inner self, is not where Virgil and Heaney converge. Rather they coincide in the filial impulse, as well as in the disposition to bind back to ancestral origins. ('Glimmerings are what the soul's composed of. [...] And a whole late-flooding thaw of ancestors.' 'Shelf Life 3. *Old Pewter*, *Station Island* [1984], p. 23.) In Heaney's early poetry, it is principally the figure of the father-son relationship that evokes a Virgilian theme – a theme from the *Aeneid*, but in Heaney set in a rural community that recalls the agricultural world of the *Georgics*. Filial piety is the basis of a tribal piety. 'I shouldered a kind of manhood, | stepping in to lift the coffins | of dead relations.' ('Funeral Rites', *North*, p. 6): this is the sense of community Heaney sometimes evokes with the term 'tribe' ('Punishment'; 'Casualty'; 'Tollund'). This distinctive aspect of Heaney, ballasted as well as burdened with his own sense of responsibility and guilt, 'dragged upon' yet 'buoyant' ('Shelf Life 2. *Old Smoothing Iron*, *Station Island*, p. 22) – a paradox described as a conflict in 'Oysters', the opening poem of *Field Work* – this strikes me as Heaney's most 'Virgilian' dimension. It is commonplace to observe that Heaney's poetry issues from deep inner fissures and dualities. The dichotomous nature of his work may be illustrated by the pair of poems to his children at the centre of the first section of *Station Island*. 'A Hazel Stick for Catherine Ann' fashions itself as a poem of familial and poetic investiture from the perspective of childhood marvels, while 'A Kite for Michael and Christopher', which adjures Heaney's sons to 'take the strain', does the same from the perspective of shouldering adult responsibilities.[99] It is through the perspectives of child and parent that Heaney draws us to Virgil, as well as through the perspective of Dantean pilgrim, haunted by the shades and ghosts of his ancestors and predecessors.

Virgil through Dante

The Dantean motif of encountering shades that reaches its first culmination in *Station Island* begins to gather force in the previous collection, *Field Work*, which concludes with 'Ugolino', Heaney's translation from *Inferno* 22–3. Near the beginning of *Field Work*, 'The Strand at Lough Beg', Heaney's elegy in memory of his second cousin Colum McCartney, assassinated by Loyalist paramilitaries in 1975, not only takes its epigraph from *Purgatorio* I.100–03 but echoes the whole closing passage of that canto in which Virgil gathers 'cold handfuls' of the morning dew (p. 10) to wipe the pall of Hell from Dante's grimy face before the purgatorial journey. At the close of 'Casualty', another poem in *Field Work* on a victim of contemporary sectarian violence, Heaney implores a visitation from his wayward subject, begging the 'dawn-sniffing revenant' to 'question me again' (p. 17). (Notice how Heaney reverses the Dantean roles of pilgrim-questioner and shade-respondent.) In a lighter mood of rueful self-mockery, Heaney in 'An Afterwards' (p. 40) pictures himself cast in the glacial ninth circle of Dante's Hell where his wife 'would plunge all poets' for their backbiting, and where, 'aided and abetted by' Virgil's imaginary wife, she delivers the poem's imagined conjugal verdict. Dante's Hell is becoming a familiar presence in Heaney's poetry. In 'Leavings' (p. 54), Heaney musingly asks himself which circle of hell would serve to punish Thomas Cromwell for his destruction of pre-Reformation English church art, imagining that Cromwell's penalty would take the form of 'scalding on cobbles, | each one a broken statue's head' such as that from the decapitated statue of the Virgin Mary in Ely Cathedral's Lady Chapel. Presenting himself as travelling 'down England' (passing Ely), Heaney describes the fields blackened by stubble-burning fires and imagines walking 'on a sparking field' in the small hours, 'to smell dew and ashes | and start Will Brangwen's ghost | from the hot soot'. Heaney's allusion to Lawrence's Will Brangwen, a figure who conjoins the field and the cathedral (see *The Rainbow*, Chapters 4 and 5), suggests that Heaney's ghosts are sometimes kindred spirits, if not necessarily alter egos. Whereas Thomas Cromwell is imagined as confined in hell for 'threshing clear' the cathedral chapel's 'sumptuous windows', Cromwell's Lawrentian counter-spirit Brangwen is 'started' and set 'abroad' by the poet's imagination as 'a breaking sheaf of light [...] in the hiss | and clash of stooking'.[100] In this audacious and little-discussed poem Heaney is effectively laying claim to the 'leavings' – the gleaned cultural inheritance – of pre-reformation England.

These references to Dante in *Field Work* are quite disparate, but taken together they adumbrate the ghostly interrogations and self-interrogations that will characterize Heaney's subsequent engagement with Dante, Virgil and other poets. The adjective 'ghostly' comes readily, since the word 'ghost' features prominently in Heaney's lexicon (even 'ghosting', twice), together with a host of kindred words such as *shade* and *shadow* (used as verbs as well as nouns), *haunt* and *haunted*, *revenant*, *visiting* and *visitation*, and such spectral figures as the 'apparitions' sent 'abroad' in 'The Digging Skeleton' (*North*, pp. 17–18); or Brigid and her sisters in 'A Migration', figured as 'familiars' and 'ghosts' (*Station Island*, p. 26); or the figures of Seamus and Marie Heaney themselves on hearing the news of the ceasefire in 'Tollund', finding themselves 'at home beyond the tribe' and described as 'ghosts who'd walked abroad [...] to make a new beginning' (*The Spirit Level*, p. 69).[101] When the first part of *Seeing Things* (1991) begins, 'Larkin's shade surprised me' ('The Journey Back'), the reader is probably less surprised by the sudden apparition of a *shade* than by the fact that it is *Larkin's* shade.[102] But even this should come as no surprise. The poets who speak to Heaney address themselves to his imagination as the leech-gatherer appears to Wordsworth in 'Resolution and Independence', as an 'admonishing agent [...] who appears in a haunted, dreamy light, like a messenger "from some far region sent".[103] Poets are not the only apparitions. In the second part of *Seeing Things*, the word 'shade' is used again almost casually, without a hint of drama: 'I cannot mention keshes or the ford | Without my father's shade appearing to me | On a path towards sunset' ('Squarings xxxii', p. 90). As we have seen, *haunt* is a favoured expression in Heaney's critical prose as well as verse. Commenting on 'the feeling of unease' experienced by the speaker in the title poem of *District and Circle* (2006), Heaney observes that the figure travelling the underground is 'haunted' not only by memories of his former selves but 'by all kinds of new awarenesses' of danger.[104] But 'ghosthood' in Heaney involves the reassuringly familiar as much as the unsettlingly strange, and is not necessarily to be feared. 'Your proper haunt' is the most in-dwelled of environments, most intimately known ('Casualty', in *Field Work*, p. 17). One thinks of the figure of Heaney's 'undrowned father', whose 'ghosthood' appears as 'immanent' (etymologically, 'in-dwelling') in the third poem in the title sequence of *Seeing Things* (p. 18).[105] As Heaney explained in interviews, the death in 1985 of Robert Fitzgerald, translator of the Homer and Virgil, and 'a father figure' to Heaney at Harvard, and the death of his own father the following year, prompted him to translate the 'Golden Bough' passage from *Aeneid* 6 as a means of elicitation:

> Then when Robert died, there was a memorial reading held for him. And I thought, 'Book Six.' [...] And I had been thinking of the finding of the golden bough and of

being given the branch as symbolic of being given the right to speak. Then my father died, and I had a number of poems about him, and next thing someone asked me to contribute a piece to an Irish issue of *Translation* magazine, and I thought, 'I'll go and get permission to go down to the underworld to see him.' [...] It's like finding a voice, the beginning and end at once. So that was a raid, and it led into a book where I met my father in a poem called 'Seeing Things.'[106]

Heaney's understanding of the Golden Bough episode as 'symbolic of being given the right to speak' is unusual and interesting. In another of his poems about his father, 'The Ash Plant' in *Seeing Things* (p. 19), the deceased Patrick Heaney's ashplant is figured not only as 'a silver bough' that will allow him to 'come | Walking again among us' and speak his judgement on the living, but also as a 'phantom limb'.[107] As Peter McDonald has argued, Heaney's native river Moyola is itself as haunted by the Lethe of Virgil's Elysium as the figure of his father is haunted by Virgil's Anchises. Heaney's scene is spectral and uncanny, but not unsettling.[108] Patrick Heaney emerges from the river looking 'strange without his hat', and comically 'scatter-eyed | And daunted' (p. 18), almost a caricature of some virtuous soul reborn to a new body. But the vision the poet recalls of meeting his father 'face to face' that afternoon, recalling Aeneas's prayer for 'one face-to-face meeting' with his father in 'The Golden Bough', the translation that prefaces *Seeing Things* (p. 1), is conjured proleptically, gesturing toward an untroubled hereafter. In *Human Chain*, Heaney rewrites in a celebratory key Virgil's famous description of Aeneas's three-fold failure to embrace his father's ghost (*ter conatus ...*, *Aeneid* 6.700–02). In the poem 'Album', sections iv and v, Heaney's three imperfect opportunities in his own lifetime to hug his father are finally redeemed by his son's 'one-off' success – just at the moment, we are told, when Heaney is grappling with the *ter conatus* passage in his own translation of *Aeneid VI* (p. 8). The moment is seen to be hallowed by an apparently auspicious visitation of the 'phantom' Latin stem *verus* that Heaney detects in his own just-planted English phrase 'my very arms' (placed to appear fortuitous, but actually quite arbitrary, not least since it does not translate anything Virgilian).[109] On occasion, Heaney seems over eager to be haunted.

In *Station Island*, Heaney's most extensive engagement with Dante as well as with Virgil-through-Dante, visitations are a great deal less reassuring. 'The Underground' introduces the figure of the poet *nel mezzo del cammin* and haunted by memories of his own honeymoon, but less like Hansel 'retracing the path back' than like Orpheus, 'damned if I look back' (p. 13). *Station Island* does not mark any turning away from memory or personal experience, but seeks a poetic parallel for the disciplines of Catholic ritual and pilgrimage for the purposes of self-confrontation, self-judgement, and self-liberation. Station Island in Lough Derg is the site of St Patrick's Purgatory, and *Station Island* is purgatorial also in the sense of Anchises' words to Aeneas in the underworld about the manner in which guilty souls are purified, *quisque suos patimur manis* (6.743), literally 'each endures his own ghosts' (Loeb translates, 'each of us undergoes his own purgatory'). As with Heaney's Chekhov, who 'shadows a convict guide through Sakhalin', it is 'convicts' chains' that 'haunt' the Heaney of the early 1980s, and the burden that similarly 'rings on' through *Station Island* is that of the artist's 'freedom', specifically 'his freedom | To try for the right tone – not tract, not thesis | And walk away from floggings' ('Chekhov on Sakhalin', pp. 18–19). The figure of the writer's head 'swimming free' (p. 18) may once more recall the fate of Orpheus, whose severed head continues to sound Eurydice's name as it floats down the icy Hebrus in *Georgics* 4.523–7. The poet's freedom or *otium* is a central concern in the *Eclogues* and *Georgics*, though not explicitly in the *Aeneid* (where the word *otium* does occur twice, but with different meaning; 4.271, 6.813). The concern with freedom represented in the *Aeneid* that is increasingly relevant to Heaney's *oeuvre* (beginning quite early, arguably in *Station Island*) is the freedom gained by the souls in Virgil's Orphic Elysium, who are purified not merely of their mortal transgressions but of their very memory and sense of identity as individuals, until such a time as they may 'conceive the desire' for a second birth (6.724–51).

The ways to Virgil through Heaney's Dante are not easy to trace. Heaney's pressure on the verb 'venerate' in 'Sandstone Keepsake' (*Station Island*, p. 20), repeated in the poem's pregnant final phrase, 'one of the venerators', bears directly on Dorothy Sayers's translation of *Inferno* 12.120, 'the heart | they venerate still on the Thames' ('lo cor che 'n su Tamisi ancor si cola'). The 'keepsake' of the poem's title is a piece of red sandstone the poet picked up when fishing on the beach on the Inishowen peninsula in Donegal, facing the shore of Northern Ireland across the estuary that separates the Republic of Ireland from Magilligan Point in County Derry, where the poet can make out the lights coming on at dusk in the prison on the far shore, established in 1972 on the site of an army camp. 'A stone from Phlegethon | bloodied on the bed of hell's hot river?', Heaney asks, imagining the stone as the heart of Henry of Almain, murdered kneeling at Mass by his first cousin Guy de Montfort, whose shade in Canto 12 is identified by reference to the famous relic of his cousin-victim. Now if we were confident that Heaney expected at least some readers to know that Dante's phrase 'si cola', which Sayers translates as a form of the verb 'colere', 'to venerate', is taken by most other translators and commentators as the reflexive form of the verb 'colare', 'to drip', the resulting ambiguity might well be worthy of the term 'Virgilian'. For whereas Sayers's reading merely says that Henry's heart is still venerated by the Thames, the more common reading of Dante's line says that the heart *still drips itself*, i.e., still bleeds. According to the fourteenth-century Dante commentator Benvenuto Da Imola, Henry's heart was placed in the hand of the prince's statue in Westminster Abbey.[110] The heart's miraculous bleeding announces that its sacrilegious violation calls out to be avenged. On this reading, Heaney's self-portrait as 'one of the venerators' is darkened by the implication that such crimes cry out for vengeance. *Venerators* are those who bear witness to that cry. Heaney imagines how he appears to the watchman scanning the distant beach from his tower in the detention camp. The poem describes how the silhouette of the poet 'stooping along' is 'swooped on, then dropped by trained binoculars', taken as a figure 'not about to set times wrong or right' and 'not worth bothering about'. Yet Heaney's Latinate word 'venerators' has an ominous ring, not least by having accrued allusive resonances. To the reader, the communal veneration of victims of sacrilegious violence seems nowhere near as harmless or ineffectual as the poet's silhouette appears to the watchman metonymized out by the figure of his binoculars. For all its humility, the piety of 'the venerators' has gained the dimension of the terrible, perhaps even of menace.[111] Is this yet another instance of Heaney's literary cunning, comparable to the well-known case at the close of 'Funeral Rites' in *North*? In that poem, the miraculous singing corpse of Gunnar in *Njáls Saga* is presented, despite being said to remain 'unavenged', as a figure of poetry's capacity to transcend the call of vengeance, whereas in the saga Gunnar's violent death actually sets off a fresh cycle of blood-feuding.[112] Is the ambiguity of allusion in 'Sandstone Keepsake', as Heather O'Donoghue says of 'Funeral Rites', 'intertextuality of the highest order'?[113] If so, one might even speak of Heaney's 'two voices' in 'Sandstone Keepsake', in the sense that Adam Parry used that phrase about Virgil.[114] But Heaney gives the reader no firm grounds for assurance, and Heaney's self-conscious identification of his own position in 'the free state of allusion' does not alert us to any specific undersong of allusive meaning in the poem. Indeed, Heaney's pun on the Irish Free State would be a point well taken by the reader: allusion is *always* a 'free state'. Besides, Heaney's self-presentation as 'one of the venerators' is already chilled and sufficiently darkened by the Dantesque scene itself, the distant lights coming on one by one in the compound as darkness falls, evening frost and salt water making the poet's hand 'smoke'. Dante's Phlegethon, we remember, is the river of boiling blood in which violence against others is punished. Figuratively, then, Heaney the venerator is wading in his own Phlegethon (and to continue the Dantean parallel, looking across to the bank to the 'circle' where the violent against themselves are punished). Heaney has already described the red stone's 'reliably dense and bricky' feel, and how he often clasps it, throwing it 'from hand to hand'. This stone weighs like a weapon – like David's stone against Goliath, like a brick against soldiers – as well as like a holy relic. Like the sandstone with its 'underwater | hint of contusion', veneration itself begins to look 'ruddier' now. In one detail Heaney's evening scene is closer in atmosphere to Virgil's Phlegethon than to Dante's, since Virgil's Sibyl points out that 'night is coming on' (*nox ruit*; *Aeneid* 6.539). But Heaney's scene is powerfully Dantesque; to say the poem's atmosphere is 'Virgilian' sounds feeble by comparison, perhaps only recalling the critical cliché about Virgil's *sfumato* effects (by analogy to painterly blurred lines). Blurry allusions make uncertain signposts to Virgil.

Frustratingly, perhaps, it is similarly difficult to penetrate to Virgil through Heaney's powerful engagement with Dante in the title sequence of *Station Island*. 'What I first loved in the *Commedia*', Heaney explains in 'Envies and Identifications', 'was the local intensity, the vehemence and fondness attaching to individual shades, the way personalities and values were emotionally soldered together, the strong strain of what has been called personal realism in the celebration of bonds of friendship and bonds of enmity'.[115] These are qualities in which Dante will easily make Virgil seem redundant.[116] In fact, it seems as though Heaney reached back to Virgil when he wanted to leave local intensities behind. Such I take to be the main argument in a powerful essay by Peter McDonald. On this reading, it was Virgil's relatively *impersonal* universality that Heaney came to have need of in the second half of his life – a universality with stronger affinities to the ghostly impersonality of 'that region where dwell the vast hosts of the dead' at the close of Joyce's story than to the *Inferno*'s vividly particularizing mode of representation. (The two-part poem 'Uncoupled' in *Human Chain*, pp. 10–11, seems apposite: it imagines each of Heaney's parents as a solitary figure perceived indistinctly in an otherworldly dreamlike setting.) Heaney himself intimated that for him, Virgil was the poet of *lacrimae rerum*; but it was when he aspired to the plane of universality implied in seeing merely *res*, 'things', and *mortalia*, the common facts or sorrows of human existence, that Heaney had most need of Virgil's company.[117]

Unfazed by light

McDonald's essay '"Weird Brightness" and the Riverbank: Heaney, Virgil, and the Need for Translation' (2019) argues that 'Virgil in *Human Chain* takes Heaney away finally from his own deepest sources and strengths in the Wordsworthian poetry of memory. The translated work here is no longer a mirror in which to contemplate the poetic self, but a way out from that self into an impersonal, unreflecting "brightness".[118] McDonald's conclusion rests on a sustained close reading of Heaney's visitations of the riverbank scene from the title poem of *Seeing Things* (1991) to Heaney's final collection *Human Chain* (2010) and his posthumous translation, *Aeneid VI* (2016). My own understanding of Heaney's response to Virgil is indebted to McDonald's analysis, which I will be concerned to examine by extension. To me the most revealing line in 'The Riverbank Field' is that in which Heaney, putting *Aeneid* 6.748–51 into '[his] own words', expands Virgil's adjective *immemores* (*Aeneid* 6.750, literally 'deprived of their memory', referring to the Lethean souls at the time of their release for rebirth into the world) into a declarative sentence, 'So that memories of *this underworld* are shed' (*Human Chain*, p. 47, my emphasis). As Heaney points out, he is not merely translating Virgil's passage but 'continuing' it ('as enjoined to so often, | "in my own words"', p. 46), and so Heaney naturalizes the *Aeneid* passage within the framework of his own poem. In this context – that is to say, the context of this-worldly Moyola as distinct from otherworldly Lethe – Heaney's phrase 'this underworld' reads as a reference to *this world*, this our mortal being, from which we too may hope to be released into a higher plane. While in Heaney's poem 'memories' will be shed, 'soul' (without an article) will eventually long 'to dwell in flesh and blood | Under the dome of the sky' (p. 47).[119] Whether that longing will ever be fulfilled is not spelled out. But the yearning for release, for crossing over into something higher, is the dominant chord of the whole second half of Heaney's oeuvre, roughly from the time of the death of his parents in the mid-1980s. Heaney finds many ways to describe that translation, for instance in the paradox of the famous parable-poem about the monks of Clonmacnoise, who helped unfasten a stranded otherworldly ship so that its crewman could climb back 'out of the marvellous as he had known it' ('Lightenings' viii, *Seeing Things*, p. 62). The world – *this* world – appears 'marvellous' from the crewman's otherworldly perspective. As McDonald's essay explains, it is a perspective that Virgil helped Heaney to imagine. (Not Dante, who remains for Heaney a poet of local habitations.)

Time and again, Heaney describes joyful release as a distinctly ghostly experience. I have already mentioned 'Tollund', the penultimate poem of *The Spirit Level* (1996), which describes a revisitation of the Danish bog just as news arrives about the IRA ceasefire in September 1994. Heaney finds himself and his wife standing there

> footloose, at home beyond the tribe,

More scouts than strangers, ghosts who'd walked abroad
Unfazed by light, to make a new beginning
And make a go of it, alive and sinning,
Ourselves again, free-willed again, not bad.

Seeing Things, p. 69

Heaney's description of liberated ghosts walking abroad 'unfazed by light' may be compared with his later phrase 'weird brightness' in 'Wraiths' I *'Sidhe'* (*Human Chain*, p. 66), in which Peter McDonald hears an echo to Yeats's 1912 poem 'The Cold Heaven', in which the speaker describes himself as 'riddled with light'.[120] In McDonald's reading, 'Yeats's "Riddled with light" finds the image for radical (and profoundly alarming) translation from the human to the 'ghost' state; and it is this image which Heaney's "weird brightness" appropriates – or, indeed, which it translates, crossing it and confounding it with Virgil.'[121] It should be noted that Heaney himself traced the luminousness of ghostly encounters as far back as 'The Tollund Man': 'It was as if the Tollund Man and I had come from far away to a predestined meeting: a meeting where there was something familiar between us yet something that was also estranging and luminous'.[122] If we consider Heaney's 'unfazed by light' in 'Tollund' as an earlier recollection of Yeats's idea – taking note that the sense of Heaney's 'unfazed by light' differs greatly from Yeats's 'riddled with light', and indeed from the echo of Yeats that McDonald hears in Heaney's 'Wraiths' – then we may see how the light of an otherworld, glimpsed from this side of the grave, is for Heaney an intimation of a yearned-for liberation of the spirit; an earnest of a weirdly luminous, uncanny yet benign translation from an oppressively habitual condition to a state of 'ghostly' release, on *this* (mortal) side of the final 'Cut.' ('Wraiths' I 'Sidhe', *Human Chain*, p. 66). Speaking of the newly published *Human Chain* at the Aldeburgh Festival in 2010, Heaney remarked that if the volume had had an epigraph, 'it would be an epigraph from Eliot', and he recited the lines:

> See, now they vanish
> The faces and places, with the self which, as it could, loved them,
> To become renewed, transfigured, in another pattern.

Little Gidding III, 14–16[123]

A few lines earlier, Eliot's passage reads, 'This is the use of memory: | For liberation' (7–8). Certainly this section of *Little Gidding* III (lines 1–16) illuminates Heaney's conviction throughout *Human Chain*, but the passage would equally serve as a fitting epigraph for Heaney's entire *oeuvre*. In fact, the passage from *Little Gidding* narrowly missed publication as an epigraph thirty-five years before *Human Chain*, in Heaney's most momentous book. On the uncorrected title recto of *North* Part I, deleted by Heaney in his own proof copy, the cancelled epigraph is precisely *Little Gidding* III.7–16.[124] For the rest of his life, Heaney continued to quote the passage in his critical prose and conversation. As Anthony J. Cuda has shown, 'Heaney revisits Eliot's stanza from *Little Gidding* time and again until it becomes a permanent feature in his own imaginative landscape, one that repeatedly helps him to determine memory's role in calibrating the relationship between the irreducible particulars of history and the abstractions of the visionary'.[125]

Auditory imagination

As a poet of memory Heaney is not only 'Wordsworthian', but 'Eliotic' as well.[126] In his lecture 'Learning from Eliot' (1988) Heaney explains how in the 1950s, when he first began to read poetry as a schoolboy in Derry, 'one did not need to know any literary thing in particular [...] in order to know that Eliot was the way, the truth and the light, and that until one had found him one had not entered the kingdom of poetry'.[127] Heaney describes Eliot as 'more a kind of literary superego than a generator of the poetic libido' in those early years, and explained how Eliot only came to serve him as a useful tutelary figure once he had read C. K. Stead's book *The New Poetic: Yeats to Eliot* (1964), 'with its revelation of Eliot as a poet who trusted the "dark embryo" of unconscious energy'.[128] In John Hayward's Penguin paperback of Eliot's *Selected Prose* (1953), 'the particular tint' of its purple cover 'appropriately reminiscent of the confessor's stole', Heaney made the most enduringly important of his discoveries in Eliot's critical work, namely Eliot's 'definition of the faculty which he called "the auditory imagination"':

> WHAT I call the 'auditory imagination' is the feeling for syllable and rhythm, penetrating far below the conscious levels of thought and feeling, invigorating every word; sinking to the most primitive and forgotten, returning to the origin and bringing something back, seeking the beginning and the end. It works through meanings, certainly, or not without meanings in the ordinary sense, and fuses the old and obliterated and the trite, the current, and the new and surprising, the most ancient and the most civilised mentality.[129]

Heaney quotes from Eliot's passage at the head of his 1976 lecture 'Englands of the Mind' on 'the cultural depth-charges latent' in the poetic languages of Hughes,

Hill and Larkin.[130] A decade later, at the beginning of his lecture on Sylvia Plath ('The Indefatigable Hoof-Taps'), Heaney again quotes Eliot's passage, this time to add, expanding on Eliot, that 'the auditory imagination [...] unites reader and poet and poem in an experience of enlargement, of getting beyond the confines of the first person singular, or widening the lens of receptivity until it reaches and is reached by the world beyond the self'.[131] In the course of this lecture about 'the poet's need to get beyond the ego', Heaney finds that whereas Yeats and Eliot stood the full course of this 'widening' dialectic of self-discovery and self-transcendence towards an ideal universality of utterance, Plath falls short of this ideal, for all the intensity and command of her genius, which Heaney admiringly acknowledges. The poetics Heaney propounds by quoting Eliot's passage about the auditory imagination is a poetics that harks back to psychic points of origin in order to send these abroad and ultimately to transcend them.[132] Eliot's idea of the auditory imagination as a faculty working through 'recessive layers of meaning' has been described as 'archaeological' in Charles Martindale's essay on Eliot as a node in the modern reception of Rome, specifically as mediated by Virgil and Ovid.[133] The Eliotic 'conception of poetry as a quasi-archaeological project', Martindale observes, 'is not uncommonly encountered among modern poets. An obvious example would be Seamus Heaney's *North* [...]'.[134] And so the channels to (and back from) the banks of the Moyola run via Mincio and Missouri, as well as via 'Thames's "straunge stronde"' (*Electric Light*, title poem, p. 81). Heaney's 'archaeologies' are naturally thought of in spatial or geographical terms, but I would like to turn to what we might call the auditory 'archaeology' of Heaney's late poem 'Electric Light' (2001). How can the *sound* of Heaney take us back to Virgil, via Eliot?

'Electric Light'

Eliot is Heaney's tutelary figure as the poem traces a journey from its opening scene in Heaney's maternal grandmother's house in Castledawson, travelling geographically by ferry across the Irish Sea and by train to London, and in a kind of prefigurative parallel, travelling via the radio to 'roam at will the stations of the world'. The itinerary describes a journey backwards and forwards in time. The poem's first section describes a distressful night in Heaney's wartime early childhood, when his parents left him to stay overnight with his grandmother. The middle section describes Heaney's first trip to London in the summer of 1962, aged twenty-three. The third and final section revisits Heaney's Derry childhood, linking origins and ends in the poem's closing figure of perdurance, the talismanic thumb-nail which Heaney imagines 'must still keep | Among the beads and vertebrae in the Derry ground'. The trip to London in the middle section is presented as a self-consciously literary pilgrimage: 'To Southwark too I came' echoes Augustine's *Confessions* through Eliot's 'To Carthage then I came' (*The Waste Land*, 307). The mock-Chaucerian quotation would almost seem to mock the neophyte's self-consciousness, if it weren't for Heaney's evident sympathy with his younger self. The sheer foreignness and awkwardness of phrasing in 'Thames's "straunge stronde"', with its congestion of sibilants and quotation marks, trochees and alliterations, is naturalized by its proximity to the open vowellings of 'Moyola-breath', and irradiated by the speaker's emergence 'from tube-mouth into sunlight'. The refractive ruins of quotation glitter by a shore that is at once Thames and Moyola.

The 'puckered pearl' of the 'ancient' smashed thumb-nail acts as the poem's point of focus and centripetal force. 'Rucked quartz, a littered Cumae', the thumb-nail is a relic out of time, both pre- and post-historic, emblem of flickering candle light as well as the 'waste' of electric light. The poem's figure of the Sybil is not only Virgil's Deiphobe but also the ancient Sybil from Petronius' *Satyricon* in Eliot's epigraph to *The Waste Land*, the twentieth century's most celebrated poem about cultural belatedness and fragmentation. Heaney's grandmother is a figure of helplessness, in this regard less like Virgil's commanding figure than like Petronius' tiny Sybil in Eliot's epitaph, a pathetic figure whose thwarted wish is to die. But it is the strangeness of Heaney's grandmother's speech, her 'sybilline English', that sets in train the poem's crossing to 'Thames's "straunge stronde"'. The link from the childhood episode to the later trip to London was suggested to the ageing poet by his memory of his grandmother's speech, her 'urgent, sibilant | Ails'. '"What ails you, child?"', she asks ('what's wrong?'), using a verb that to Heaney sounded slightly alien. Explaining the poem's genesis in *Stepping Stones*, Heaney says that recalling that unhappy night with his grandmother, 'up came "ails" in its otherness and oddity – full, to my adult ear, of an *echt*-Englishness, so that led to memories of my first trip to England' (p. 403). Her strange English (wittily, '*echt*') is 'sibylline' in that it is linked, like Virgil's guiding Sybil, with the notion of transit, in Heaney's case from one cultural state to another. The grandmother's speech, compared to 'scaresome cavern waters' and 'splashes between a ship and dock', is proleptic of the ferry embarkment that the poem proceeds to describe. Like 'Alphabets' in *The Haw Lantern*, 'Electric Light' traces the development of the poet's soul from its 'pre-reflective' seed-time to the farthest extremity of its development, and back again to its points of origin. The word 'soul' is used advisedly: Heaney terms his childhood self '*animula*', the word used by the emperor Hadrian in his famous poem *Animula vagula blandula*, which Heaney would have first encountered in Eliot's poem 'Animula'. In this poem Eliot links the pagan 'little life-spirit' of his title with 'the simple soul' ('l'anima semplicetta') in the explanation offered by Dante's Marco Lombardo about the soul's proper freedom and discipline (*Purgatorio* 16.85ff.). As this miniature transmigration of the phrase 'animula' from Hadrian to Heaney might suggest, the journey of the soul is linguistic as well as archaeological, 'a littered Cumae'. Among the earliest of the ancient Greek colonies in Italy, Cumae is itself a figure of cultural palimpsest. It was in nearby Naples, a daughter colony, that Virgil says he wrote the *Georgics* (4.563–4). His way to Rome went through the Campania, littered with traces of Greece.

The verbal music of Heaney's poem is characteristically alliterative, assonant and elaborately patterned in stress and phrasing, as one can hear in the first line, 'Candle-grease congealed, dark-streaked with wick-soot . . .'. Balanced contrasts abound: the spondee of 'rucked quartz', abrading its craggy consonants like impact in a quarry, is followed by the musical dispersal of 'a littered Cumae', the delicate tinkling of the adjective swallowed by the cavernous vowels of 'Cumae'. The phonetics of 'Fur-lined felt slippers' is crushed and collapsed into an answering element, 'unzipped', and this line from the poem's first section is exactly repeated in the third. 'Lapping a boatslip' at the close of the poem's first section is chiastically answered by 'Lisp and relapse' at the beginning of the second. 'Helplessness' is immediately doubled by 'no help'. This is a language that not only mimetically enacts or expresses the things it describes, but makes its deliberate music in order to 'set the darkness echoing'. In sounding out the poem's music the reader experiences a sense of participating in its composition, as though under the sway of Heaney's own interest as a poet-critic in 'the relationship between the almost physiological operations of the poet composing and the music of the finished poem'.[135]

It is the sybilline grandmother's speech that scores itself into the poet's memory: 'urgent, sibilant | Ails'. Heaney's pun on 'sibilant' alerts us to the contrast between his grandmother's permanent whisper and the 'bellow' of Deiphobe's voice (*remugire*, 6.99) booming in the cavern's hundred mouths (6.81). What the voices do have in common is their uncanny, alien quality. Once the Sybil is possessed by Apollo, Virgil tells us, her voice sounds unearthly, 'not human' (*nec mortale sonans*, 6.50). The grandmother's incapacity before her grandson's relentless weeping contrasts with the very different helplessness of Virgil's Sybil overmastered by the god, but the brilliance of electric light in the Derry bedroom does more than contrast with the darkness of the sybilline cave, it also suggests Apollo's attribute of light evenly broadcast. In Virgil, the Cumaean prophecy heralds a new age. In *Aeneid* 6 the ultimate happy end is far distant, since the promised salvation through 'a Grecian city', Pallanteum, will only be reached long after the ordeal of a second Troy (83–97). But in Eclogue 4 the Apollonian renewal announced by 'Cumaean song' is imminent: the word *iam* ('now') occurs, with emphasis, four times in seven lines (4–9). The 'new age' of Heaney's lifetime is heralded by the coming of electric light to rural Derry in the 1930s and 40s, and with it, the Apollonian 'magic' of the radio, by which the young Heaney 'roamed at will the stations of the world'. In Heaney's poem, 'electric light' has ambiguous significance. Electricity is liberating as the mysterious power that illuminates the radio's dial, but Heaney's reference to 'Big Ben and the news' in wartime broadcasts also draws our attention to the dangers of that wider modern world (among his earliest memories was the Derry sky illuminated by the German bombing raids on Belfast), as does the radio's relapse into silence and dark during the blackout. Moreover, the link the poem makes between the first experience of electricity and the child's first traumatic separation from his parents also portends the final separation at their deaths long afterwards, as well as the many separations in between. The child's distracted weeping under the bedclothes, shielded from the bulb's glare, is unwittingly proleptic. What the child wittingly fears, however, is his grandmother's metamorphic nail with 'its dirt-tracked flint and fissure', its primal force imagined to endure 'among beads and vertebrae in the Derry ground'. The 'otherness and oddity' of 'ails' in the grandmother's speech may be heard as a pre-echo of the poet's future pilgrimage to England, a presaging hint of a glamouring future idiom in which soccer pitches may be said to measure 'the groin of distance' and grain fields are compared to 'the Field of the Cloth of Gold'.[136] (The conspicuous poetic simile has been compared to London's 'postal districts packed like squares of wheat' in Larkin's 'The Whitsun Weddings').[137] Yet the preservation of the 'glit-glittery' thumb-nail among the debris of buried bones and rosaries testifies not only to the gravitational pull of ancestral voices and the Catholic community, but to uncanny consonances and continuities that endure between archaic gleam and modern glare.

The link implied between the Sybil's 'Cumaean song' (*Eclogues* 4.4) and Heaney's own poem is sealed by his description of his grandmother's thumb-nail as 'plectrum-hard'. As often in Heaney, endurance as manifested in preservation is seen as emblematic of poetry itself. And we remember that for Heaney himself, the Sybil's disclosure of the secret of the Golden Bough is 'symbolic of being given the right to speak.[138] The mangled thumb-nail in the Derry ground appears an ancestral token of poetic investiture, linked to the permission granted by a familial and communal 'they' in Heaney's incantatory repeated phrase, 'they let me and they watched me'. 'A touch of the little pip would work the magic', says Heaney: the light bulb's magic comes easily, just as the Sybil tells Aeneas that the golden bough will come away easily in his grasp, if it comes away at all (*Aeneid* 6.146–8, though as it is freed, Virgil's bough is described as resisting, *cunctanctem*, 6.211). The radio is communal, it is 'theirs', the grown-ups': 'A turn of *their* wireless knob and light came on | In the dial' (my emphasis). It is to this initiation by his family that Heaney traces the origin of his future course of roaming 'at will the stations of the world'.

Virgilian music

What Virgilian strains might we hear, then, through Heaney's verbal music? The elaborately patterned and expressive quality in lines of 'Electric Light' that may call to mind similar qualities in Virgil: the surprisingly delicate alliterative stress and assonance of Heaney's 'puckered pearl', say, after his deliberate mangling of sibilants and labials in 'smashed', 'mangled' and 'thumb'. Or the inverted symmetry of sounds in 'lapping a boatslip'. Or the strenuous mouth-work involved in sounding the poem's first line ('Candle-grease congealed, dark-streaked with wick-soot . . .'). The ease with which we appreciate these musical qualities of Heaney's language, not least thanks to our familiarity with his recorded voice, reminds us that this facility is something we non-classicists tend to lack in our approach to Virgil. Neither trained nor attuned, our ear for Latin verse is far from adept. We strain to listen, unsure of what to listen for. But if we return to the entrance of the Sybil's cave after listening to Heaney, our hearing might be sensitized and better fit to appreciate the play of sound in Virgil. Once we have heard the two contrasting vowel parts of 'Cumae' in a line of Heaney – first the narrow pour and aim of rounded lips (/u/), then the wide-open deepening of the diphthong (/ae/) – once we have heard (and felt) these exotic sounds in the frequencies of English, we might be more alert to the sound effects of Virgil's Latin:

> Excisum Euboicae latus ingens rupis in antrum,
> quo lati ducunt aditus centum, ostia centum,
> unde ruunt totidem voces, responsa Sibyllae.

6.42–4

> The huge side of the Euboean rock is hewn into a cavern, into which lead a
> hundred wide mouths, a hundred gateways, from which rush as many voices, the
> answers of the Sybil.

Excisum Euboicae: one hears the chisel at work in *excisum*. The capaciousness of
Euboicae as it unfurls its concatenation of vowel sounds (at least two of them
dipthongs) suggests the amplitude of the rock face.[139] Then there is word-play on
the repeated *latus*, used first as a noun in line 43 and then as an adjective in line
44. First it denotes the 'face' of the rock, then it describes each cavern mouth as
'wide'. While the 'a' sound in the first *latus* is short, the second is long, so repetition
brings variation. Lines 42–4 may be scanned something like this:

> **Ex**cisum | **Eu**boi | **cae** latus | **in**gens | **ru**pis in | **an**trum,
> **quo** la | ti du | **cunt** adi | **tus** cent'[um], | **os** tia | **cen**tum,
> **un**de ru | **unt** toti | **dem** vo | **ces**, res | **pon**sa Si | **byl**lae.

Centum, 'a hundred' (i.e., 'countless'), is repeated in line 44, and R. G. Austin observes
that 'Virgil likes the repetition with the metrical ictus [or stress] falling differently
at the second occurrence'. Remarking on the expressiveness of these three lines,
Austin says they 'are subtly suggestive of echoes' when we perceive the pairings of
antrum/centum, *ducunt/ruunt*, and *Euboicae/Sibyllae*.[140] This vowelly, sonorous
language is first heard in Book 6 in its second line, *et tandem Euboicis Cumarum
adlabitur oris*. The vowel-richness of the names Euboia, Cumae and Sibylla lends
itself to suggestive uses in connection with ancient cavernous sites, as indeed does
their Greekness: the names themselves have an archaeological dimension. As we
have seen, the 'archaeological dimension' of Heaney's language, like the Sibyl's
cavern, has countless resonant mouths. So too does Virgil's, and we may the more
keenly appreciate this quality in Virgil when we come to him via Heaney.

Late Eclogues

Electric Light is conspicuous for its awareness of classical literature, and besides
its title poem, three other poems explicitly respond to Virgil: 'Bann Valley
Eclogue', 'Glanmore Eclogue' and the translation 'Virgil: Eclogue IX'. Heaney's
poetic interest in the *Eclogues* at this time was doubtless nourished by his
academic interest in pastoral: his Royal Irish Academy lecture 'Eclogues *in
extremis*' (2003) was also prepared during this period. By his own account,
Heaney's enthusiastic rediscovery of the *Eclogues* was inspired by David Ferry's
translation when it appeared in 1999:

[**O'Driscoll**]   *Electric Light* found you in eclogue – as well as loose-weave – form.

[**Heaney**]   David Ferry did a new translation of Virgil's *Eclogues*, published with the parallel Latin text, and for a while I was captivated entirely. I still have enough Latin to be susceptible to the mesmerism of the hexameters. You have *melopoeia* aplenty there; but it also struck me that there was something implacable in the way Virgil hewed to the artificiality of the convention. Here was a young poet coming back with an almost vindictive artistry against the actual conditions of the times. There was something recognizable at work, a kind of Muldoonish resistance. Virgil's eclogues proved an effective way for a poet to answer whatever the world was hurling at him, so I had a go at writing a couple of my own.[141]

Heaney's mention here of Paul Muldoon highlights the huge difference between these two poets. If we went looking for a poem of 'Muldoonish resistance', we'd soon find Muldoon's 'The Year of the Sloes, for Ishi' (1973), written not only 'just after' Bloody Sunday, but even said by its author to be 'to some extent a poem about Bloody Sunday' – despite the fact that this 'is not evident from the poem' itself.[142] Heaney's approach to Virgilian pastoral could hardly be more different. In Heaney's eclogues, his distance to political events is less a response of pointed obliquity than a corollary of polite literary manners. His urbanity comes from a position of considerable cultural security and self-assurance ('. . . so I had a go at writing a couple of my own'). This is by no means to criticize Heaney, who needed no reminding that he himself was no longer 'a young poet coming back with an almost vindictive artistry against the actual conditions of the times'. Heaney never wrote eclogues 'in extremis'; nor did he write them during the Troubles. Heaney's captivation in 1999 by the *Eclogues* and by Virgil is coloured by his own anticipations at the turn of the millennium. In 1999, we remember, Heaney's celebratory tribute 'Secular and Millennial Miłosz' drew comparisons between Virgil and the Polish poet. Of the three explicitly Virgilian poems in *Electric Light*, Heaney's translation of Virgil's Eclogue 9 is the only one written in anything like a hard-bitten style – fittingly, since Virgil's original offers the bleakest outlook in the *Eclogues* on the fortunes of the dispossessed and on the eventual outcome of the civil wars. By contrast, Heaney's 'Glanmore Eclogue', a highly allusive version of Virgil's first Eclogue, commemorates an *achieved* otium, and represents creative security by the most self-consciously literary means available. A full-dress pastoral pledge of gratitude to Heaney's friend and benefactor Ann Saddlemyer, the poem's 'Augusta', 'Glanmore Eclogue' is

Augustan in the neoclassical sense. What it highlights in Virgil's *Eclogues* is the element of allusive masquerade. 'Bann Valley Eclogue', on the other hand, is animated by real urgency, communicating the poet's sense that great things are at stake as well as at hand. Composing in the autumn of 1999, as his niece's pregnancy drew to a close alongside the millennium, Heaney prays that this birth will bring 'a flooding away of all the old miasma' (p. 11) to refresh the prophecy of Eclogue 4, in which the birth of the miraculous infant heralds an age of renewal. Virgil's Fourth Eclogue has a special personal importance for Heaney, by comparison to which his appreciation of the other eclogues, however genuine, seems more academic. Indeed, the Fourth Eclogue may be taken as the key text through which Heaney reconfigures *Aeneid* 6 in *Human Chain*, in which the long-awaited and much longed-for translation of the spirit at the end of life is prefigured by ordinary human childbirth.

Once again we see Heaney responding to Virgil through the Christian tradition, or rather *with* that tradition. The Fourth Eclogue is the poem that gave Virgil his medieval status as a proto-Christian poet. It is this poem that Dante has Statius quote back to its author in *Purgatorio* 22.70–2. It was the Virgil of the Fourth Eclogue, the purgatorial Statius testifies, who first lit his way to God (64–9). Heaney's Virgil is in essence Dante's Virgil, the poet of Eclogue 4 and *Aeneid* 6. This Dantean Virgil is a mainstay of the personal secular culture that Heaney fashioned for himself as a counterpart to religious doctrine. (He called this personal literary culture 'Jungian' for its fidelity to archetypes, including religious archetypes.) It is this Dantean Virgil that in later life lights Heaney's way towards a vision of his own life in what he called 'the poetic imagination', which he described as 'a shadow region – not so much an afterlife as an after-image of life'.[143] The augury of regeneration in Virgil's Fourth Eclogue also enables Heaney to anticipate in death a release from the social self, a release of the soul into its own separateness, relieved in the knowledge that generational life is being renewed.

Baby talk

This is why 'Route 110', *Human Chain*'s twelve-poem sequence that reworks *Aeneid* 6 in domestic miniature, ends with the joyful announcement 'And now the age of births', in place of Virgil's closing lament for the death of Marcellus, Augustus' nephew, son-in-law and heir (6.860–86). Earlier in Heaney's poem, at its centre, 'It was the age of ghosts', or funerals and wakes, and we are invited to observe that the neighbourly customs of wakes and the celebrations of births are governed by similar pieties of hospitality (Poems VI and VII, pp. 53–4). In the poem's present, the 'thank-offering' Heaney brings to welcome his new infant granddaughter is a bunch of oat stalks with 'silvered heads', a customary gift remembered earlier in the poem from an occasion in his own youth, 'each head of oats | A silvered smattering, each individual grain | Wrapped in a second husk of glittering foil | They'd saved from chocolate bars, then pinched and cinched | "To give the wee altar a bit of shine."' (p. 52). This is Heaney's version of Virgil's Golden Bough, which licenses the poem's descent into the underworld of memory as Heaney revisits the Troubles in Poem IX, an Elysian sports day in Bellaghy in Poem X, and evenings with his father by the riverbank in Poem XI.[144] What Heaney's domestic golden bough also licenses, even more crucially, is a release from his own literary idiom into the pentecostal language of 'baby talk'. We should observe that in his 'Translator's Note', Heaney expressed distaste for the whole prophetic conclusion of *Aeneid* 6 (pp. viii–ix), which goes some way towards explaining his own radical rewriting of this section in 'Route 110'.[145] This is not merely an audacious way to conclude his deployment of what he called the 'mythic method', but an astonishing final act of renunciation and refusal.[146] In the place that corresponds to Virgil's parade of spectral heroes from future generations, and the lament for Marcellus that crowns that set-piece culmination of *Aeneid* 6 (756–892), Heaney declines anything grander than 'Talking baby talk', the poem's trouncingly humble final line. In the preface to his translation, Heaney observes that in 'Route 110' his 'focus this time [i.e., in contrast to his earlier poetic visitations of *Aeneid* 6] was not the meeting of the son with the father, but the vision of future Roman generations with which Book VI ends, specifically the moment on the bank of the River Lethe where we are shown the souls of those about to be reborn and return to life on earth [6.703–51]' (viii–ix). Rachel Falconer's reading of the final section of 'Route 110' is cast in fittingly paradoxical language: 'for Heaney, the return via Lethe constitutes a forgetful rupture, a cutting loose from the past, but also a memorious continuity'.[147] The critical question is how to weight the respective terms of these dichotomies (rupture/continuity, oblivion/memory). Falconer introduces a very apposite term in speaking of the 'many images of divestiture' in 'Route 110'.[148] For Heaney, Virgil comes to serve as a preparation for the final shedding of personal memory, of the social self, even of poetic language: the shedding of everything except that mystery, the soul. In *Human Chain*, that is what Heaney's earlier phrase 'the forewarned journey back' has come to mean: a journey 'into the heartland of the ordinary', yes, but in a radical sense not foreseen in the title poem of *Seeing Things* (1991: 7). Heaney came to have use for Virgil as he began to prepare himself for something ordinary and forewarned as well as still-to-be-experienced, namely the soul's journey back to its 'pre-reflective' state ('Alphabets', in *The Haw Lantern*, p. 3).

Kites

After the Virgilian correspondences of 'Route 110', which have received a great deal of attention from critics, there are no further Virgilian echoes in the rest of *Human Chain*. If it is true that Heaney's engagement with Virgil in his later work expresses a yearning for a state of liberation or release of the spirit in what Heaney called the 'after-image of life', his own alternative to the traditional notion of an afterlife; and if it is accepted that this longed-for release is imagined specifically as a liberation from the social self, then a degree of confirmation may be found in 'A Kite for Aibhín', a poem based on Giovanni Pascoli's poem 'L'Aquilone' (1897), though radically recast. Whereas Pascoli's poem is an elegy for a dead child, Heaney's poem is a parable of the soul's release in death, dedicated to a newborn grandchild.[149] In this final poem of *Human Chain*, which is now hard not to read in a valedictory light, familial piety is joined together with the motif of release in the image of the string snapping and the kite breaking free. Familial piety is involved not only in the title's dedication but also because it evokes Heaney's earlier poem to his sons, 'A Kite for Michael and Christopher'.[150] Following Pascoli's original poem, which Heaney had translated some years before writing the free version that appears in *Human Chain*, Heaney expands on the 'longing' of the 'gazing' kite-flier, paying out string as he watches the kite climb higher and higher 'Until string breaks and – separate, elate – | The kite takes off, itself alone, a windfall' (*Human Chain*, p. 85). As in Pascoli's poem, the freed kite is an emblem of the soul's translation at death. Heaney's distinctive touch is to emphasize the kite's new condition of being apart: he describes the kite as not only 'elate' but 'separate'. 'The kite takes off, *itself alone*', and the phrase I have italicized echoes the Irish phrase 'Sinn Féin Amháin', 'we ourselves alone'. Heaney had echoed that phrase before, in the final lines of 'Tollund' discussed above, in which Heaney describes himself and Marie as 'ghosts who'd walked abroad | Unfazed by light, to make a new beginning | [...] Ourselves again, free-willed again, not bad' (*The Spirit Level*, p. 69). Heaney commented on the closing lines of 'Tollund': 'What we were experiencing, you could say, was hope rather than optimism, and that's why I liked the complicating echo of the words "Sinn Féin" in the phrase "ourselves again"'.[151] We have seen that 'In Tollund', the ghostly liberation is represented as a release into the light. In 'A Kite for Aibhín', the kite released into separateness, 'itself alone', is described as 'a windfall'. Now this word 'windfall' also occurs in Heaney's own direct translation of Pascoli's 'L'Aquilone', the tenth stanza of which reads, 'S'inalza; e ruba il filo dalla mano, | come un fiore che fugga su lo stelo | esile, e vada a rifiorir lontano' (p. 43), or as Heaney translates, 'It rises, and the hand is like a spool | Unspooling thread, the kite a thin-stemmed flower | Borne far away to flower again as windfall' (p. 42). And the word 'windfall' recurs in the fifteenth stanza of Heaney's translation, where the speaker addresses the object of his elegy, the deceased child: 'You who were lucky to have seen the fallen | Only in the windfall of a kite' (p. 42). 'Windfall' is Heaney's own word: it does not correspond directly to a word or phrase in the Italian original. It is a complex, even a paradoxical word, combining the notion of descent in 'fall' with the contrasting notion of flight in 'wind'. Its core sense is of an unexpected boon, literally a ripe fruit that has been freed by a gust of wind. In his direct translation of Pascoli, composed before 'A Kite for Aibhín', Heaney's description of the kite-flower 'borne far away to flower again as windfall' plays on the Christian paradox of life renewed in death and transfiguration. In 'A Kite for Aibhín', however, the word 'windfall' is shorn of this context, so that in this later poem we are freer to explore the possible connotations of the word. And if Heaney's 'windfall' recalls to us Dylan Thomas's adjectival use of the word in the line from 'Fern Hill', 'Down the rivers of the windfall light', we may supplement the word's core meaning of a fortuitous blessing with an accompanying image of a sweep of light.[152] If so, 'that earth-to-air thing', as Heaney's own children put it – the trajectory 'from earth to air, dark to light' that Heaney taught his audiences to notice in the arc of his work, from *Seeing Things* on – stands all the more firmly emplotted by the first and last poems in his twelve collections. As his son Christopher has remarked, Heaney's published work is now 'bookended by digging and a kite'.[153] Whereas the spade-pen is a figure of investiture, the freed kite is a figure of divestiture. 'A Kite for Aibhín' does not refer to Virgil, but it concludes a final stage in Heaney's work in which Virgil was vitally involved.

There is finally no part of Heaney's writing in which traces of Virgil are absent: Virgil's reception crosses Heaney's too variously for that. The *Georgics* especially casts a penumbra that deepened with the growth and diversification of his work, without becoming anything other than a penumbra. On the other hand, Heaney's direct response to Virgil is fairly limited, or rather it is delimited, focusing mainly on the *Eclogues* and the *Aeneid* (overwhelmingly, on Book 6), strongly mediated by Dante, via Eliot. This quality of focus and delimitation in direct response to Virgil suggests a tendency to grasp a tradition unfussily and acceptingly, and indeed Heaney's ideas of Virgil's career and canonical importance seem happy to be conventional. When Heaney's poetry begins to pay sustained attention to Virgil after the death of his parents in the 1980s, his reasons are transparent and he explains them with ease. In these regards, Heaney's engagement with Virgil is relatively straightforward. Drawing out a conversation between Heaney and Virgil, however, requires a third participant, the reader. Like all three-body problems, this rules out straightforwardness. Moreover, the critical enterprise is always provisional, and may always be extended as well as revised. In the present case, more remains to be said about many individual poems, perhaps especially the Bog People poems. But the most significant regard in which Heaney may instruct us in approaching Virgil afresh reflects the simple fact that Heaney himself is now read as a classic. This is not merely to observe that Heaney has an uncommonly wide readership throughout the English-speaking world, and a popular readership too, outside the academy. Heaney is read as 'a classic' because a great number of these readers command his whole *oeuvre*, and when reading or discussing any individual poem they will habitually (and with relative ease of memory) link it with others drawn from various parts of Heaney's body of work. Heaney's work rewards readers who perceive its coherence, and common experience concurs that his work is uncommonly coherent. This became apparent from very early on, and remains so now when the work stands complete. In other words, the reading practices that Heaney rewards, and which in turn sustain his reception, are about as close as we get in modern literature to the traditional reading practices by which Virgil is still mediated. The reading protocols that sustain Heaney have considerable exemplary force for a current pursuit of Virgil.

Conversely, Heaney can also help us appreciate the ways in which reading Virgil at any time during the two millennia since his death must differ greatly from our own experience of reading a poet who until recently was a contemporary author. Heaney's readers today will draw with ease on an incomparably greater wealth of contextual detail than is possible for any reader of Virgil, no matter how learned, for the simple reason that in Virgil's case so much contextual detail is irretrievably lost. For instance, there is a marvellous 'Dialect Glossary for Seamus Heaney's Works' (1998), a work of greater scope than its modest title suggests, published late enough to cover three-quarters of the *oeuvre* yet also early enough to leave plenty of time (as things turned out) to be corrected by peers in the poet's own lifetime.[154] What wouldn't one give for similar materials from Virgil's day? The sheer wealth of attention to nuance and textual detail that innumerable critics lavished on Heaney's work even as it unfolded, and the degree to which this contemporary reception is reflected in available records, stand in stark contrast to the meagreness of what has survived of Virgil's strictly contemporary reception. This is not to suggest that we can imagine Virgil's contemporary reception merely by projecting into the past a modified version of our own impressions of Heaney's reception. On the contrary, my point is that comparisons between Heaney's and Virgil's receptions will highlight, but also help us to gauge, the differences between them.

Heaney's final engagement with Virgil was his translation of *Aeneid VI*, published posthumously in 2016. Though generally well received, it remains to be seen whether this translation will assume a status comparable to Heaney's celebrated translation of *Beowulf* (1999), which was included in Faber's 2013 box set together with the twelve collections of original verse. A proper assessment of Heaney's *Aeneid VI* would have required a chapter of its own. (Fortunately, that is precisely what Heaney's translation is about to receive in Rachel Falconer's forthcoming book, *Seamus Heaney, Virgil and the Good of Poetry* (Edinburgh University Press, 2022), which I regret will appear too late by a cat's whisker for me to have drawn on it.) Although Heaney had translated parts of Book 6 before, he only undertook the full translation after he had already drafted the Virgilian poems that appeared in *Human Chain*. As he explains, 'the impulse to go ahead with a rendering of the complete book arrived in 2007, as the result of a sequence of poems written to greet the birth of a first granddaughter'.[155] Heaney's translation came too late to have an impact on the course of his *oeuvre*, which *Human Chain* brought to a remarkably coherent close. The translation may of course modify readings of Heaney, including Heaney's responses to his own earlier work. Still, the fact that the translation was produced concurrently with Heaney's last collection makes it likely that it lacked the distance in time to reflect critically on Heaney's final poems. The translation seems altogether ancillary to the original work. Read as English poetry, the sections of the translation that correspond to the Virgilian passages Heaney transformed in *Human Chain* are weaker than the original poems, the inspiration less palpable. This is hardly surprising, not least since Heaney had already made Virgil serve his own intimate and final purposes as a poet. Heaney said his translation was 'neither a "version" nor a crib' but 'more like classics homework': this is mere self-deprecation, and characteristically charming. We can better trust his insistence that the task was undertaken in a spirit of piety, partly to honour the memory of his Latin teacher at St Columb's College and partly to give thanks for the birth of his granddaughter.[156] But these motives seem almost too selfless, too disinterested. His own poetic task completed, Heaney doesn't need Virgil for himself anymore. A notable line in the penultimate section of 'Route 110' describes Heaney's father on the riverbank field, standing like the 'shades and shadows' in Virgil's Elysium 'waiting, watching' to cross Lethe and be reborn, 'Needy and ever needier for translation' (*Human Chain*, p. 58).[157] With *Human Chain*, Heaney seems to have freed himself from the urgent need for translation – and paradoxically perhaps, or else just as one might suspect, that is precisely when he finally got round to translating *Aeneid* 6 from beginning to end. He only turned to the 'homework' after the great work was finished.

The conceit of reaching Tara via Holyhead or Mossbawn via Mantua is obviously a paradox. One of the ideas it encapsulates is that each Holyhead or port leads on to other ports in a proliferation of interim destinations. The return to a point of origin is counter-intuitive: the map looks more like a garden of forking paths. I have now traced one such literary trajectory, trusting that its partly arbitrary course would provide a series of shifting angles from which to usefully examine the relationship between Heaney and Virgil. But it is clear that the itinerary cannot be repeated, and would necessarily take a different course if one should set off once more. Such obliquity goes against the grain of systematic argument and demonstration. The best that can be said is that it is genuinely experimental. What I think my discussion has made clear is that Heaney's lifelong engagement with Virgil has a distinct and coherent purpose when his career is viewed complete and as a whole, but that he reached for Virgil solely in response to local needs in the composition of any given poem. Heaney only ever turned to his 'exemplary' poets when he had real and present need of them, and his needs were very much his own.

Conclusion: Imagination and the Common Reader – Virgil through V. Sackville-West's two English Georgics, *The Land* (1926) and *The Garden* (1946)

Although Theodore Ziolkowski's *Virgil and the Moderns* (1993) describes the second half of the twentieth century as 'a post-Virgilian age', this invaluable work of reception history documents the persistence of responses to Virgil nearly to the end of century. What the book just missed was the millennial upsurge of interest in Virgil that encouraged Ziolkowski's immediate successor Fiona Cox to hail a new Virgilian age, especially in women's writing (*Sybilline Sisters: Virgil's Presence in Contemporary Women's Poetry*, 2011: 1–2). Together with more specialized or localized studies such as Florence Impens's *Classical Presences in Irish Poetry after 1960* (2018), these reception histories have enabled me to adopt a drastically selective approach.[1] While they too include a great deal of close reading in tandem with their comprehensive survey work, these studies do not set themselves the peculiar and narrower task that I have undertaken, namely to develop a few close readings of modern literature into extended critical essays that aim to test a reception-directed means of close-reading Virgil. My work is at once supplementary to theirs, and different. I have tried to develop a way of turning detailed attention to modern texts into a means for critical engagement with the detail of Virgil's texts.

Whether this way of approaching Virgil points in a viable direction must be for the reader to decide. This concluding chapter will in fact focus on the figure of the reader, raising several questions about readers and reading. 'The reader' is an abstraction that masks a multiplicity of beings, and of course a multiplicity of reading practices. As a teacher of literature, I am naturally anxious to promote the act of reading itself. But that word 'itself' begs questions that ought to be considered, for reading is not one practice but several. My own ideal 'close reader' reflects many of the aspirations associated with mid-twentieth-century New Criticism, less as a set of propositions from the writings of its pioneers than as an ethos of literary education as it came to affect me as a teenager in the 1980s.

Broadly speaking, this is an academic kind of reading. On the other hand, I picture another ideal reader, 'the common reader', who may be a 'close reader' too, but whose character is more multifaceted, and equally an abstraction. Instinctively I should wish my conclusion to suggest a close kinship between these two ideal kinds of reader, with a view to suggesting that each might serve as an example to the other. But it would be a shame to bypass Virgil in reaching any final judgement, since he intriguingly addresses at least two kinds of reader in the *Georgics*. Can Virgil help us think about the purpose or value, if not of reading 'itself', then of some of its attributes or varieties?

This book has been concerned to test the proposition that reading through modern reception 'helps one read Virgil better', as Rebecca Nagel has suggested with regard to Vita Sackville-West's two formal georgics, *The Land* (1926) and *The Garden* (1946).[2] In conclusion, I would like to discuss some of the implications of reading Virgil's *Georgics* today through Sackville-West's twentieth-century georgics, specifically with regard to questions of audience and the act of reading. This is not the only way to approach Virgil through Sackville-West: Susanna Braund, for instance, has recently heralded ecofeminist readings.[3] I take my direction from Philip Thibodeau's book *Playing the Farmer* (2011), which argues that Virgil invites the Roman landowners for whom he wrote to imagine themselves as farmers, partly for purposes that were political and ideological, and partly with designs that were imaginative also in ways that were more specifically literary.[4]

Thibodeau's reading of the *Georgics* through its earliest reception turns on Seneca's famous remark that Virgil wrote not to instruct farmers but to delight readers (*Ep.* 86.15). Seneca's distinction remains crucial, because the way we think about didactic poetry depends on the way we think about its intended audience.[5] And since the social character of Virgil's audience is a puzzle Virgil keeps before us all through the poem, the guessing reader is necessarily engaged in the act of *playing* the reader. This is true of all formal georgics. When we read Thomson's *The Seasons* (1726–46) or Dyer's *The Fleece* (1757), we try to picture the implied reader or intended audience of these poems. Drawing on whatever knowledge we might recover about the early reception of any poem, we chiefly imagine as we read.[6] My final question in this book is, can 'playing the reader', specifically with regard to Sackville-West's georgics, set us on a course that may lead toward Virgil and (at the risk of sounding like an eighteenth-century georgic poet) 'improve' us as readers?

The Land and *The Garden* are notable for their lyric beauty and exceptional for their popularity. Both georgics are in pentameter verse (mainly blank but threaded with rhyme, and occasionally interspersed with lyrics in other meters) and arranged in four books to trace the seasonal cycle, which is itself the fundamental theme of both works. Each found a wide audience, was favourably reviewed and sold exceedingly well. By 1971, *The Land* had gone into twenty-two editions and sold around 100,000 copies.[7] At the beginning of the twenty-first century, both poems were still in print. Each poem won a prestigious literary prize. *The Land* won the Hawthornden in 1927, and *The Garden* received the Heinemann in 1946.

Not since the eighteenth century had a georgic poem succeeded in engaging 'the common reader', a phrase revived by Virginia Woolf in her two-volume work of the same title. Woolf was recalling Samuel Johnson's famous pronouncement on Gray's *Elegy*, 'I rejoice to concur with the common reader, for by the common sense of readers uncorrupted with literary prejudices, after all the refinements of subtility and the dogmatism of learning, must be finally decided all claim to poetical honours'.[8] Johnson's distinction between 'the common reader' and the academic reader touches on my concerns in this chapter. Sackville-West's works represent a vanishingly rare moment when there did exist a 'common reader' of contemporary georgic poems with whose judgement a considerable number of academics and reviewers could rejoice to concur. In 1944, the classicist W. F. Jackson Knight described *The Land* as 'probably the most Vergilian of all recent poems'.[9] In his 1969 study of Virgil's *Georgics*, L. P. Wilkinson applauded *The Land* as 'perhaps the best of English georgics'.[10]

The subsequent shift in classics towards an ultra-literary, metapoetic view of Virgil's *Georgics*, with the more specialized approach this perception demands, has probably made it harder to perceive strictly literary continuities between Virgil's highbrow project and the middlebrow tenor of English georgics such as Sackville-West's. Spoofed as 'The Oak Tree' in Woolf's *Orlando* (1928), the fictional poem is praised by Woolf's fictional critic Nicholas Greene for bearing 'no trace [...] of the modern spirit'.[11] Sackville-West's engagement with 'the modern spirit' and modernist poetry is certainly more complex than Woolf's satire allows. Still, her diffidence vis-à-vis the high modernism of Eliot and Pound seems positively un-Virgilian today, when classicists tend to think of Virgil as a kind of proto-modernist, every bit as avant-garde in the *Georgics* as in the *Eclogues*, and more like the poet of *The Waste Land* than the poet of *The Land*.[12] True, Sackville-West does accommodate Virgil's metapoetic dimension. At the close of *The Land*, for instance, in her imitation of Virgil's *sphragis* (4.559–66), she describes herself thinking how Virgil, 'from Mantua reft, | Shy as a peasant in the courts of Rome', took the waxen tables in his hand and 'out of anger cut calm tales of home' (p. 107). Here Sackville-West reconfigures Virgil in her own self-image. She was living in London (and in 1926, visiting Tehran, where she finished *The Land*), prevented by her sex from inheriting her birthplace, the Sackville estate of Knole, and bent on resurrecting her ancestral home in poetry – for she had not yet acquired Sissinghurst.[13] Her autobiographical passage also admits a metapoetic reading, given that Virgil used epic hexameter ('anger') to write on rural and Epicurean subjects. Nevertheless, instead of reflecting a Roman ultra-modernist, Sackville-West's poems mainly reflect a Virgil who is naturalized, domesticated, and given a lyrical dimension during the course of the seventeenth through nineteenth centuries, in the accommodating and variegated traditions of the English country house poem and the blank verse georgic.[14]

Sackville-West maintained she had not yet read the *Georgics* when she conceived *The Land* in 1921, but certainly she did read Virgil in the course of composition, between 1923 and 1926.[15] She immediately identifies Hesiod and Virgil as her main predecessors ('as once at Thebes, as once in Lombardy', p. 3) and groups the pair with Homer (p. 89), but overall she takes Virgil as her principal model. Sackville-West's affinity with the British georgic tradition is less explicit though arguably just as important. Anyone familiar with William Cowper's *The Task* (1785) and his predecessor Thomson – as well as with Cowper's immediate successors, William Wordsworth and Charlotte Smith – will read Sackville-West with a sense of recognition. Didactic-descriptive pentameter verse about inhabiting the productive landscape, or topographical poetry that describes the speaker's passage through that landscape, represents a rich and varied tradition in British literature. Sackville-West's template for both her georgics is Thomson's *Seasons*, not least on account of her comparable focus on the seasonal round, each four-part work progressing from winter to autumn.[16] Woolf's critic Greene finds that Orlando's poem 'compared favourably with Thomson's *Seasons*': a barbed compliment, but unlike the one that precedes it ('it reminded him, he said as he turned over the pages, of Addison's *Cato*'), a comparison that holds true.[17]

In December 1928, Woolf wrote to Sackville-West reporting the response of her ten-year-old nephew, Julian Bell:

> [...] its frightfully good, he thinks; one of the best modern poems; the sort of poetry he likes; so solid; and she knows it all; and she has a sense of words; and she's honest; and thank God she doesn't imitate Tom Eliot [...][18]

Like the fictional critic Greene's remark that 'The Oak Tree' bears no trace of the modern spirit, young Bell's contrastive reference to Eliot (at any rate as it passes through Woolf's pen; and she repeats it for comic effect) is presumably a way of saying that the poem is not allusive in Eliot's supposedly Mandarin vein. This too holds true of *The Land*. Though Sackville-West occasionally refers explicitly to English poets, she rarely alludes to them and never implicates them as her own predecessors. She was aware of unconscious indebtedness, and guarded against it.[19] By contrast, we have observed that she claims Virgil as a distant ancestor. When she begins *The Garden*, '. . . of gardens in the midst of war | I boldly tell. Once of the noble land | I dared to pull the organ-stops . . ', it is Virgil she recalls, specifically the four-line prelude to the *Aeneid* from late antiquity (*ille ego, qui quondam . . .*), now considered extra-canonical but which commonly prefaced the epic in Renaissance editions.[20] Spenser is an intermediary (*The Faerie Queene* begins, 'Lo I the man, whose Muse whylome did maske . . ') and an even closer one is Cowper, whose *The Task* begins humorously, 'I sing the Sofa. I, who lately sang | Truth, Hope and Charity. . .'.[21] Despite Sackville-West's nods to English poets as common acquaintances – *The Land*, for instance, includes an artful cameo about summer that names as well as evokes the seventeenth-century poets of pastoral lyric – she generally gives the impression that her own native literary materials are traditional to the point of being anonymous.[22] Aside from her programmatic allusions to Virgil, her principal framework of allusive reference is biblical (for instance, *The Garden*, p. 76, 'Jewels of youth . . ' reworks Acts 17:28). Her single reference to a contemporary poet is a solecism. In *The Garden* (pp. 63–4), she quotes the famous first four lines of Eliot's *The Waste Land* at the head of 'Spring' and proceeds to lambast Eliot's treatment of the season.[23] All this is not to say that Sackville-West's verse is not allusive – it is, occasionally and in an understated way – only that it alludes differently from many of her modernist contemporaries.

Nor would it be right to say that the *The Land* is utilitarian: 'this is no more a didactic poem' than Virgil's *Georgics*.[24] For her epigraph, Sackville-West chose precisely the lines from Virgil's programmatic passage at the centre of *Georgics* 3 (284–93) that define the poet's work rather than the farmer's: *nec sum animi dubius*, verbis *ea vincere magnum | quam sit et angustis hunc addere rebus honorem*, 'And well I know how hard it is to win *with words* a triumph herein, and thus to crown with glory a lowly theme' (289–90, my emphasis).[25] Sackville-West's point becomes even clearer when we consider that at proof stage she cancelled a second epigraph she had chosen, Hesiod's line 'There is no shame in working, but the shame is in not working' (*Works and Days* 311, David Grene's translation. The Greek epigraph was untranslated, as is the Latin epigraph from Virgil that survived into print).[26] Contemporary reviewers took Sackville-West seriously on agricultural topics, as any critic should, and appreciated her acumen in these matters, but they recognized that poetry came first. Sidney Barrington Gates, reviewing anonymously in *The Nation and Athenaeum* (6 November 1926), conceded that *The Land* 'could be read aloud in a country alehouse, and if it were not announced as poetry, its rough and racy wisdom would win a gruff assent' – only to insist, 'But it is a poem, and a very remarkable one'. Gates was himself a poet as well as an aeronautical engineer. He praised not only 'the comely gravity and sweetness' of Sackville-West's music, but applauded the fact that this music could sustain such an extensive work.[27]

The review implies a poem that could hold its own with two distinct audiences. Like Seneca remarking that Virgil wrote not to instruct farmers but to delight readers, the reviewer draws a line between the two constituencies, subordinating one to the other.[28] A faultline will always exist between form and farm, in Alessandro Barchiesi's witty phrase, or between words and things in the world; between the literary and the literal.[29] Nor is that the sole divide. Even as the current proliferation of translations draws new readers into the fold, another fissure widens, between those who read the *Georgics* in Latin and those who read Virgil mainly in translation. More fundamentally still, there is the gap between those who read poetry (or even imaginative literature of any kind) and those who do not. But gaps exist to be bridged imaginatively, as indeed one might gloss Sackville-West's Virgilian epigraph about winning poetic glory for a lowly theme. In the twenty-first century, studies of the *Eclogues* by Timothy Saunders and the *Georgics* by Rebecca Armstrong see no conflict between Virgil's mapping of the physical world and his metapoetic mapping of Graeco-Roman literary culture.[30] One way in which ecocritical readings of Virgil 'through Sackville-West' might bridge the separation between form and farm would be to compare and contrast her georgics with Virgil's project of inviting the reader to imaginatively 'play the farmer', unfolding especially the political implications of this idea. As I have already suggested, I shall investigate a second route suggested by Thibodeau. For when we read Virgil or Sackville-West, indeed when we read any georgic poem, we are engaged in playing the reader.

We may picture a georgic's poetic predecessors, together with its notional audience, as a kind of 'imagined community' in the mind of its reader, to borrow Benedict Anderson's phrase. When we read Virgil or Sackville-West we try to imagine their previous readers and step into their circle, in part trying to read over their shoulders, in part acting a role ourselves as readers of georgic. This is because, as Seneca's remark shows, the way we think about the purpose of didactic poetry depends on the way we think about its intended audience. Virgil addresses Maecenas, a rich patron, but also claims to be writing for the benefit of labouring farmers. Being rich in Virgil's day meant owning land, though this did not necessarily involve doing farm work, or even managing one's estates oneself. Virgil's implied reader is a landowner who manages his own estate. Virgil himself was a landowner as well as a reader/poet.[31] Neither a landowner nor a reader is necessarily a farmer, but both can play at being one. We have learned to be suspicious of such play-acting, especially across class and occupation. The phenomenon is with us still, centuries after Marie Antoinette played shepherdess, and we are probably right to be wary of reimagining the farmer (or indeed the author) in georgic poems as, say, a proto-environmentalist. We should also be wary of conjuring up a 1930s and 40s community of readers equally in tune with Sackville-West and Virgil, lest this should merely indulge nostalgic fantasies about the activity of reading itself as once a binding element in 'the social fabric'.

But play-acting may also be a respectable form of vicarious imaginative experience. When we 'play the reader' we are imagining an audience, a community of readers, at the same time as we necessarily reflect on the distance or difference between ourselves and those imagined other readers. Sackville-West's conservatism in politics as well as poetry may prove an obstacle to those who seek to recruit her for progressivist readings.[32] Anyone who has read Raymond Williams, or been taught by someone who has, will (rightly) ask themselves what historical specificities are obfuscated by Sackville-West's celebration of the timeless agricultural cycle.[33] This may serve to check an otherwise uncritical willingness to find mere corroboration of personal preferences in an imagined past. We may be forced to imagine parts of her audience as different from ourselves (whoever 'we' are), as well as differently situated historically. In the polarized climate that characterized the years after *The Land*, Sackville-West's champions included people whose Toryism we may consider philistine, or even a great deal worse. Her immediate reception took place largely in the wakes of the two world wars. The stance of each of Sackville-West's georgics can be described as embattled against the dominant social upheavals of its time, first and foremost the impact of wartime on the rural and domestic sphere. Each georgic reflects the domestic experience of its moment. While *The Land* begins in the confident expectation that the 'classic monotony' of agriculture will remain 'undisturbed' by offstage 'modes and wars' (p. 3), *The Garden* situates the singer 'in the midst of war', acknowledging from the outset that in wartime it befalls the 'small pleasures' of 'agriculture's little brother' to 'correct great tragedies' (p. 13). Each georgic develops Virgil's fundamental idea that agriculture is an alternative form of warfare, waged not against human adversaries but against a recalcitrant

natural world bent on speeding everything towards the worse (*in peius ruere,*
Georgics 1.200). As Braund observes, Sackville-West's 'language of violence,
struggle and toil vividly recalls that in *Georgics* 1, especially the crucial lines
(1.145–6): *labor omnia vicit | improbus et duris urgens in rebus egestas*' – lines that
are difficult to translate because the founding of toil's world dominion can be
read as either a blessing or a curse.[34] Sackville-West's first 'mild continuous epic
of the soil' sings of the practical 'means | That break the *unkindly* spirit of the
clay' (*The Land*, pp. 3–4, my emphasis). A reviewer observed, 'Perhaps *The Land*
leans a little to the gloomy side; but, then, the particular county of which the poet
is singing is Kent, clayey Kent.'[35]

In *The Garden*, cultivation is explicitly ranged against the surrounding 'state
of war' as 'a miniature endeavour | To hold the graces and the courtesies | Against
a horrid wilderness', mirroring an endless cycle of 'advance, relapse, advance,
relapse, advance':

> So does the gardener in little way
> Maintain the bastion of his opposition
> And by a symbol keep civility;
> So does the brave man strive
> To keep enjoyment in his breast alive
> When all is dark and even in the heart
> Of beauty feeds the pallid worm of death.
>
> *The Garden*, pp. 14–15

The farmer and the gardener each engage in an elemental 'battle between man
and earth' (*The Land*, p. 7) that is presented as a counterpart of the seasonal cycle.
Time itself is Sackville-West's great theme, a feature that distinguishes the whole
tradition of English pastoral and georgic, but hers is the biological time registered
by the repetition of the seasons, not primarily by allusions to historical or
political events – apart from the fundamental wartime situation of *The Garden*.
Similarly, Sackville-West's literary time, or her sense of literary history, can only
be said to be lightly marked by the poetic points of reference aroused by literary
allusion. If this is remarkable, it is partly because her georgics are engrained in
literary traditions of British and Virgilian georgic that on the whole are strongly
allusive, and partly because they are written at a time when allusive reference
was a currency by which to gain poetic prestige. Her first reviewer, the appreciative
J.C. Squire, did make detailed comparisons between *The Land* and Thomson's
Seasons, observing points of contrast between a passage from each poet on the
exploitation of the beehive.[36] But Squire quotes each poet at length in order to

illustrate the historical differences between them, not to argue that Sackville-West was inviting readers to compare her passage with Thomson's. It is likely that the greater part of Sackville-West's audience did not read for the literary recognitions of allusion, which typically uses some linguistic trigger to invite comparison for the sake of registering a contrast, but read instead for a sense of observing deep historical continuities, literary as well as occupational, in times of pronounced social disruption.

Readers familiar with Virgil as well as Philips, Thomson, Dyer and Cowper will nonetheless be tempted to scribble in the margins of Sackville-West's georgics, if only out of habit. In the third and fourth verse paragraphs of *The Land*, beginning 'Why should a poet pray thus?' and 'The country habit has me by the heart', it is hard not to recognize a rewriting of Virgil's *makarismos* passage and the *laudes ruris* or 'praises of the countryside' section of *Georgics* 2 (475ff.). Sackville-West's taciturn, calculating farmer is reminiscent of Virgil's *agricola avarus* (*Georgics* 1.47–8), and her verb-driven description of that farmer as he 'Compels, coerces, sets in trim, allots, | Renews the old campaign' (*The Land*, p. 22) will recall Virgil's vigorous military vocabulary when he describes the farmer who 'turns his plough and again breaks crosswise through the ridges which he raised when first he cut the plain, ever at his post to discipline the ground, and give his orders to the fields' (*proscisso quae suscitat aequore terga, | rursus in obliquum verso perrumpit aratro | exercetque frequens tellurem atque imperat arvis, Georgics* 1.97–9). Sackville-West's 'Else shall your toil be all in vain' (*The Land*, p. 45) echoes the theme of wasted labour in the *Georgics*, whether it be of oxen (1.325–6, 3.525) or of Orpheus, whose toil to save Eurydice is 'spilt' (*effusus*, 4.492). Her description of the emblematic craftsman who 'out of need made inadvertent art' (p. 81) recalls the Jupiter theodicy at *Georgics* 1.143–6. And in her beautiful tercet

> My life was rich; I took a swarm of bees
> And found a crumpled snake-skin on the road,
> All in one day, and was increased by these.
>
> *The Land*, p. 55

it is tempting to discern an oblique Callimachean-style cameo of the Aristaeus epyllion (*Georgics* 4.281–558), which embeds the story of Eurydice in Virgil's account of Aristaeus' discovery of a miraculous means to regenerate a beehive. (Fleeing Aristaeus' embrace, Eurydice was fatally bitten by a snake, then nearly rescued from Hades by her husband Orpheus.) But Sackville-West also presents classics-minded readers with the challenge of imagining a different kind of reader, who might well notice such parallels (and many less obvious ones) but who equally might not, and who in any case is not reading principally on their account.

What then is this imagined reader reading for? Sackville-West's own manuscript notes for *The Garden* include a telling self-instruction: 'No vague imagination any use; must have precision and knowledge, and yet not allow them to impair sense of beauty. The connoisseur's lack of aesthetic taste. Possible to become too highbrow.'[37] Sackville-West's paramount concern is to convey the 'sense of beauty', in *The Land* no less than in *The Garden*. She told her husband Harold Nicolson that she found her second georgic poem harder to write than her first, because the topic of gardening lacked 'the inherent dignity of agriculture', and because 'seed-boxes are not so romantic as tilth.'[38] *The Garden* begins by contrasting the 'pretty treble' of gardening's plucked string with the full-voiced 'organ' music of the earlier poem, which had described 'husbandry's important ritual' (p. 13). Sackville-West's sense of gardening's lesser stature is revealing, for in persisting with her second georgic she abided by the Virgilian epigraph of her first ('And well I know how hard it is to win with words a triumph herein, and thus to crown with glory a lowly theme', *Georgics* 3.289–90). Sackville-West's remark about 'the inherent dignity of agriculture' might seem at odds with Virgil's own sense that herding sheep and goats, the topic he announces in the lines she used for her epigraph, is inherently *angustum*, 'narrow' (lowly, or mean).[39] But Sackville-West knew that these contrasts and paradoxes of georgic are structural. For all its inherent dignity, agriculture is not well represented in the nakedness of Milton's Adam ('in native virtue clad'), but demands all the resources of poetic art, as Milton's description itself demonstrates of nudity. Any dogmatic belief in 'the inherent dignity of agriculture' will stand in the way of grasping the real problems and paradoxes involved in writing poetically about it. ('How can a man write poetically about serges and druggets?', Samuel Johnson demanded scornfully about Dyer's *Fleece*. The answer is, one can, but probably not if one doesn't see a problem in the first place, as Dyer certainly did.)[40] Sackville-West's choice of epigraph demonstrates her awareness that the difficulty of writing beautifully about supposedly undignified subjects is precisely the point of the georgic genre. In wartime especially, gardening lacks 'the inherent dignity of agriculture' because its primarily aesthetic character makes it seem frivolous. The fact that Sackville-West nevertheless insists on the value of gardening in wartime precisely by the elaborate act of dignifying it poetically, arguably draws her even closer to Virgil than her writing about agriculture during the twenties. Her audience read *The Garden* not in wartime but in the post-war era, but this makes little difference, not merely because wartime austerity stretched into the 1950s, but because in all likelihood they were anyway reading for 'the sense of beauty'.

Reading for beauty, or poetic 'beauties', seems 'very eighteenth century'. But clearly the habit survived throughout the greater part of the twentieth century.[41] In modern *Georgics* scholarship, the British classicist most sympathetic to this hedonistic form of appreciation was arguably L. P. Wilkinson (who, as we have seen, applauded *The Land*). In the opening passages of *The Garden*, Sackville-West points her reader toward the pleasures of local spots of beauty. She deprecates the slightness of 'agriculture's little brother' only to celebrate its capacity for delicate refinement and attention to intimate detail. Whereas *The Land* had celebrated the plough that 'Homer and Hesiod and Virgil knew' (p. 89), Sackville-West now describes the ploughshare and harrow as brutish instruments, preferring instead the 'smaller spade and hoe and lowly trowel | And ungloved fingers with their certain touch'. Gardening is eroticized, enclosed in the embrace of a parenthesis:

> (Delicate are the tools of gardener's craft,
> Like a fine woman next a ploughboy set,
> But none more delicate than gloveless hand,
> That roaming lover of the potting-shed,
> That lover soft and tentative, that lover
> Desired and seldom found, green-fingered lover
> Who scorned to take a woman to his bed.)
>
> p. 13

As a cliché of academic discourse, the notion of a textual 'erotics' often falls short of actual hedonism. But in Sackville-West's passage the aroused language of the potting-shed is of a piece with the hedonistic lyric principle that animates her poetry. Sackville-West is thoroughly Wordsworthian in her attention to the poetic 'necessity of giving immediate pleasure to a Human Being' and in turn, her regard for 'the grand elementary principle of pleasure'.[42] Sackville-West's poetry is 'lyrical' in this Wordsworthian sense, and *The Garden* is especially lyrical also in the different sense that the poem was 'strung' together like a 'necklace' from individual lyrics or 'beads of verse', as she explains in her opening verse paragraph (p. 13). The admission encourages the reader to enjoy the poem's verse paragraphs and stanzas for their local felicities, and this tendency is reinforced by Sackville-West's increasing use of rhyme, especially in *The Garden*. This is much as Virgil has been enjoyed for a great deal of his reception history.

Wilkinson harks back to Addison as well as Seneca in his insistence that the dominant and distinctive (though not exclusive) mode of the *Georgics* is descriptive rather than didactic, and caps his argument with Coleridge's definition of a poem as

> that species of composition which is opposed to works of science by proposing for its *immediate* object pleasure, not truth; and from all other species (having *this* object in common with it) it is discriminated by proposing to itself such delight from the *whole* as is compatible with a distinct gratification from each component part.[43]

Wilkinson proposes that the pleasures of the *Georgics* arise mainly from description, whether of things or of phenomena, or of an ethos of country life. Thibodeau's study of the immediate reception of the georgics largely supports this view. In Sackville-West's case, the question could easily be put directly to 'the common reader'.

The powerful attractions of georgic are its delight in variety and plenitude, as well as in human resourcefulness in the face of austerity and danger.[44] Variety is a principle not only of the physical world but a principle of poetic invention, and the poet's inventiveness mirrors that of the farmer – or, unexpectedly elevated to a heroic plane in Sackville-West's wartime georgic, the resourcefulness of the soldier, or even (in a flight of exoticism) of the bullfighter. Sackville-West reminisces at length about the wartime summers, 'a strange, a fierce, unusual time' when civilians found themselves living 'exalted to a different clime' and performing 'not as spectators' but inside 'the stainèd ring' (p. 91). The heroic and the abject are strikingly juxtaposed in her description of civilian resistance to the threat of German invasion. Picking up her own refrain 'Strange things we did' from a passage about Englishmen finding themselves 'in a profane | Lunatic twist where guardian science fought | With murderous science' (perhaps echoing Churchill's famous phrase about 'the lights of perverted science'), Sackville-West continues,

> Strange things indeed, that none had thought to do!
> Dug trenches in the orchard when the fruit
> Hung for September's picking; hung, and fell
> Into the gashes open at the root.
> We thrust our children in that clammy cell;
> Like beasts we went to earth, for their small sake;
> The vixen's litter, hidden in the brake,
> Slept softer than the infant sons of men.

And we created darkness. Sons of light
By God's intention, over sea and land
In one wide gesture of erasing hand
We swept that symbol from our natural night.
No window in the sleeping village street,
No window in the cottages discrete;
Hidden, and like a child afraid
Shrinking beneath the bed-clothes that persuade
Into a sense of safety, then
We cowered in our darkness, yet we made
Different light, and watched it from the shades.

The Garden, p. 95

The sheer unnaturalness of wartime is described with remarkable vividness, and by a great variety of means. The 'clammy cell' of the makeshift shelter dug in the orchard seems all the more sinister for sounding like a perversion of Keats's line in his ode 'To Autumn', 'For summer has o'erbrimmed their clammy cells'. Biblical allusion is skilfully deployed. 'The vixen's litter . . . slept softer than the infant sons of men' feminizes 'The foxes have holes . . . but the Son of Man hath not where to lay his head' (Matthew 8:20, Luke 9:58). Biblical language ('Sons of light') heightens the passage's register and intensifies its pathos. The 'erasing hand' of the population working collectively in the nightly blackout to make darkness fall across the land travesties the Creation of Genesis in a way that seems both heroic and apocalyptic. (We are probably not supposed to recall the dying of the light before the 'uncreating word' of Dulness at the end of Pope's *Dunciad*, but Sackville-West's reversal of Genesis is along similar lines, and similarly bold.) The population 'shrinking beneath the bed-clothes' is presented at once in the position of children and as a disciplined civilian army. This passage is a good example of a style that is at once resourceful and unstrained, poetic yet also conversational. For all its poetic and biblical echoes, it is not allusive in the modernist style that indicates points of rupture with a historic target text and the past culture it represents, but rather a style in which opportune adaptation rests on the continuity of common pieties. It is easy to understand the broad appeal of this style, and how it could be felt to be well suited to speak with plural pronouns and represent a genuinely collective experience.

But it is 'Winter', *The Garden*'s longest book, that most clearly showcases the poem's appeal to the reader's imaginative craving for poetic creativity. Like life in wartime drabness, winter brings a 'valuable and enforced retreat' that 'liberates the vision of the soul' (p. 21) from the darkness of the season. (As Pomeroy well

observes, the whole poem is cast as 'a talisman against darkness'.)[45] The existential
fears this book confronts are not seasonal, though that is how they are manifested,
but presented instead as 'an unmanageable intimation' which rouses forth 'that
rabble in the basement of our being [...] that seldom rush to light' but that,
summoned by wartime anxieties, harry 'the frightened rabbit of the soul' (p. 23).
Winter is a time for the imagination to dispel these fears, by extravagant dreaming
as well as by prudent planning: 'The gardener dreams his special own alloy | Of
possible and the impossible' (p. 26). This appeal to a kind of imagination and
vicarious experience that is universally familiar outside the poetic arts not only
won Sackville-West large audiences, but aligns her with the georgic tradition.

As Addison observes, georgic 'addresses itself wholly to the imagination'.[46] He
writes in *Spectator* 411 (21 June 1712), 'A man of polite imagination ... often feels
a greater satisfaction in the prospect of fields and meadows, than another does in
the possession. It gives him, indeed, a kind of property in every thing he sees, and
makes the most rude uncultivated parts of nature administer to his pleasures.'[47]
Thoreau writes similarly,

> In imagination I have bought all the farms in succession, for all were to be
> bought, and I knew their price. I walked over each farmer's premises, tasted his
> wild apples, discoursed on husbandry with him, took his farm at his price, [...]
> – cultivated it, and him too to some extent, I trust, and withdrew when I had
> enjoyed it long enough, leaving him to carry it on.
>
> *Walden*, ch. 2, 'Where I Lived, and What I Lived For'[48]

The winter reveries of Sackville-West's imaginary gardener are not only detailed
by exact knowledge of fruit varieties and the like (in his dream orchard, 'Cox's
Orange jewels' – that is, sparkles – together 'with the red | Of Worcester Permain')
but also by 'extravagant, excessive' flights of fancy, in which New England 'Scarlet
Oaks would flush our English fields | with passionate colour as the Autumn
came, | *Quercus coccinea*, that torch of flame | Blown sideways as by some Atlantic
squall | Between its native north America | And this our moderate island' (pp.
26–7).[49] Sackville-West, who knew many parts of the world, loves 'opening
sudden windows on other lands', as Gates observes in his review of *The Land*.[50]
Her aim is not primarily to inform her readers, but to delight them. Of her
extensively 'imagined woods' in *The Garden* (p. 27) she writes

> They are more lovely than known loveliness,
> They are the consummation of a vision
> Seen by rare travellers on Tibetan hills
> – Bitter escarpments cut by knives of wind,

Eaves of the world, the frightful lonely mountains, –
Or in Yunnan and Sikkim and Nepal
Or Andes ranges, over all this globe
Giant in travelled detail, dwarf on maps;
Forrest and Farrer, Fortune, Kingdon-Ward,
Men that adventured in the lost old valleys,
Difficult, dangerous, or up the heights ,
Tired and fevered, blistered, hungry, thin,
But drunk enough to set a house on fire
When the last moment of their worthless quest
Startled them with reward, a flash as sudden
As the king-fisher's blue on English stream.

p. 28[51]

In this set-piece, reminiscent of the poetic circumnavigations of the globe in the fourth book of Dyer's *The Fleece*, Sackville-West evokes the romance of scientific exploration not only to dignify and variegate her theme, but to conjure an ideal of beauty that can only be pictured in the imagination. Sackville-West offers her 'invented woods' and 'imagined forest', beckoning the reader, 'Think, and imagine: this might be your truth; | Follow my steps, oh gardener, down these woods' (pp. 28–9). (She admits that while she dreams, mixing lyrical 'impossibilities' with sober 'sense', the practical gardener sits apart 'in the lamplight'. Yet being herself a 'poor practised gardener', she knows as well as he 'the Yes and better still the No', p. 29.) Such set-pieces are knowingly escapist fantasies. 'Luxuriate in this my startling jungle', she proposes (p. 29). And these poetic luxuries are all the more enticing to the reader who vicariously enjoys them in the knowledge of their being earned by the poet's own experience of austerity (and in many cases, also by the reader's own, not least during the extraordinarily severe first winter after *The Garden*'s publication). Such forms of vicarious experience must surely be licit. Whatever else is literature for?

One way that Sackville-West may help one 'read Virgil better', as Nagel puts it, is by sensitizing one to the opulence of his imagination.

ac prius ignotum ferro quam scindimus aequor,
ventos et varium caeli praediscere morem
cura sit ac patrios cultusque habitusque locorum,
et quid quaeque ferat regio et quid quaeque recuset.
hic segetes, illic veniunt felicius uvae,
arborei fetus alibi, atque inussa virescunt
gramina. nonne vides, croceos ut Tmolus odores

India mittit ebur, molles sua tura Sabaei,
at Chalybes nudi ferrum, virosaque Pontus
castorea, Eliadum palmas Epiros equarum?
continuo has leges aeternaque foedera certis
imposuit natura locis, quo tempore primum
Deucalion vacuum lapides iactavit in orbem,
unde homines nati, durum genus. ergo age, . . .

Georgics 1.50–63

And ere our iron cleaves an unknown plain, be it first our care to learn the winds and the wavering moods of the sky, the wonted tillage and nature of the ground, what each clime yields and what each disowns. Here corn, there grapes spring more luxuriantly; elsewhere young trees shoot up, and grasses unbidden. See you not, how Tmolus sends us saffron fragrance, India her ivory, the soft Sabaeans their frankincense; but the naked Chalybes give us iron, Pontus the strong-smelling beaver's oil, and Epirus the Olympian victories of her mares? From the first, Nature laid these laws and eternal covenants on certain lands, even from the day when Deucalion threw stones into the empty world, whence sprang men, a stony race. Come then, . . .

This is one of the passages in Virgil which most powerfully stirred the imaginations of later writers. It inspired Addison's rhapsodic *Spectator* no. 69 on London's Royal Exchange (19 May 1711), in which Mr Spectator finds 'this Metropolis a kind of *Emporium* for the whole Earth'.[52] Pope's description of Belinda at her dressing table draws on Addison's essay as well as on its Virgilian model (*The Rape of the Lock* 1.129–36). The 'Foreign Lands' theme in Virgil, as Wilkinson calls it (for an example, see *Georgics* 2.114–42), is much elaborated in eighteenth-century georgics on British commercial expansion, most notably in Dyer's *The Fleece*.[53] Virgil's phrase for cleaving an unknown plain, *scindere ignotus aequor* (1.50), uses a word for plain, *aequor*, that Virgil also uses frequently of the sea.[54] As Mynors observes (*ad loc.*), the maritime parallel is 'not far below the surface'. Plough and ship equally are vessels of restlessly expansive cultivation.

The imperialist implications of Virgil's passage are clear, and discussed in Charlie Kerrigan's recent study *Virgil's Map: Geography, Empire, and the Georgics* (2020).[55] Kerrigan also draws attention to Virgil's stimulation of the geographical imaginary through his delight in ethnography, history, and myth.[56] When Virgil addresses the reader-farmer, *Nonne vides* ('Don't you see' . . . 1.56), he is using a formula he expects the reader to recognize as distinctive of Lucretius (see Mynors's and Thomas's commentaries *ad loc.*), but as Kerrigan observes, the imperative to use one's senses 'kindles the reader's geographic imagination'.[57] Virgil's use of evocative place names and references to the specialities of foreign lands is a development of Homeric epic: the catalogue of ships and warriors in *Iliad* 2 is also a gazetteer of the Greek world. Virgil's great inheritor in English is Milton, who achieves extraordinarily complex effects by using geographical references for evocative purposes (for a famous example, see *Paradise Lost* 4.268–86). Virgil's list of foreign produce at 1.56–9 not only balances the exquisiteness of saffron, ivory and frankincense against the boldness of iron, castoreum and champion mares, but also incites the reader's imagination to luxuriate across an expanse of exotic places. Tmolus is a mountain range in Lydia (modern Turkey). The Sabaeans are Arabs, famous for their trade in spices. The Chalybes are a people from the southern shore of the Black Sea, legendary for having invented iron-working. Epirus is a mountainous and coastal region in western Greece. The allure of armchair geography is overlaid with the enchantment of myth and legend. Tmolus was not renowned for producing saffron but rather for its wine (*Georgics* 2.98). Yet the mountain range feeds the river Pactolus, said to carry gold dust from its slopes, and it is but a step from crocus threads to gold. Myth aids the step if we remember the aetiological tale of Midas washing off his golden touch in the Pactolus (Ovid, *Metamorphoses* 11.142–5). 'Armchair geography' is a (harmlessly?) belittling phrase, but Keats teaches us not to disparage a reader's longing for enchantment. ('Oft have I travelled in the realms of gold . . .') At the same time, such flights of imagination rest on political realities that Kerrigan and others teach us not to relegate but to incorporate into our own imaginaries.

Sackville-West's georgics once invited a large reading audience to daydream and delight in richly evocative language. The appeal is hedonistic, and Virgil's is as well. His passage on the specialities of various remote regions of the world ostensibly illustrates (by analogy) the rather obvious precept 'learn what you can about your land', and digresses from his topic of early ploughing. But the whole notion of his 'digressing' from a didactic purpose gives the wrong idea.[58] From the very beginning of the *Georgics*, Virgil's reader is encouraged to enter imaginatively into the scene:

> Vere novo, gelidus canis cum montibus umor
> liquitur et Zephyro putris se glaeba resolvit,
> depresso incipiat iam tum mihi taurus aratro
> ingemere, et sulco attritus splendescere vomer.

Georgics 1.43–6

> In the dawning spring, when icy streams trickle from snowy mountains, and the crumbling clod breaks at the Zephyr's touch, even then would I have my bull groan over the deep-driven plough, and the share glisten when rubbed by the furrow.

Here is a cosmic drama in miniature. The plough cuts deep, requiring an effort that makes the bull groan, *ingemere*. It is the process of being worn down, *attritus*, that makes the ploughshare glisten, *splendescere*. Our attention is drawn to the animal pain involved in making the metal gleam. But equally salient is the aesthetically pleasing contrast that Virgil's emphasis on gruelling toil presents to the preceding lines (1.43–4), which depict the effortless power of the spring sun melting the snow and of the west wind crumbling the unresistant clods. This poignant contrast between effortlessness and toil can be said to present a small tableau of an indifferent universe, since the spring blithely accomplishes what the bull must be goaded to achieve with pain. The speaker-poet is himself implicated, since he 'would have the bull groan' (*mihi* is a dative). He wills the bull's work, assimilating it to the blind course of the seasonal cycle. And the reader is implicated, vicariously, at many removes. The reader is 'playing the farmer', and is also conscious of the fact that 'playing the farmer' means acting in the character of a reader. But 'being a reader' of the *Georgics* is not as straightforward as it sounds, precisely because the poet is speaking to us as though he and we were farmers ('Come then', *ergo age*, start ploughing, the poet urges us at 1.63). We know this game has been played by others before. What were these readers like? What did they steer by?

I echo these questions rather than pose them. Empirical investigation is not my purpose here, but rather to observe how such questions necessarily form part of our responses to the text. As I have already suggested, questions about readership and reception (e.g., 'Who read the *Georgics*? For instruction or delight?') are part of what we read the text with. When we read a passage by Sackville-West, we form our own response within a context we are simultaneously forming in our imagination, of an audience of readers whose 'horizons of expectation' we are continuously and provisionally reconstructing, aided by whatever we know about historical reception. (This is the province of reader-response theory and *Rezeptionsästhetik*.) We know that Sackville-West was an actual landowner and gardener, but that the life she represents is also partly a fiction. We can assume that most of her readers were not landowners or farmers of gardeners, but that many of them were knowledgeable about agricultural and horticultural matters, and that they too wished to enter imaginatively into the world she represents. The political implications of writing and reading her georgic poems, in light of Britain's domestic as well as imperial history, are too extensive to be pursued here. But teasing them out will inevitably involve imagining her readers and putting ourselves in their place. Something similar occurs when Kerrigan imagines Virgil's first readers encountering the end of *Georgics* 2:

> Dacians, who appear threateningly crossing the Danube at G.2.497, fought in mass combat in Rome in 29, the year in which it is assumed the *Georgics* was completed. One can perhaps imagine the first Roman readers of the *Georgics* reading of this Dacian threat and then going to view Dacian prisoners fighting in the city.[59]

Next one might imagine how those first readers (or as Kerrigan says, listeners, an audience in the root sense) can have taken Virgil's reference to the Dacian threat in its immediate context, a poetic passage that praises the life of obscure rural piety, oblivious to world affairs (2.493–9).[60] Happy the man, Virgil's next line continues, who is 'not swayed [...] by the state of Rome and the kingdoms | slated for destruction', *non [flexit] res Romanae perituraque regna* (2.498, trans. Chew).[61] The line can be construed in several ways, depending on the reader. (Do we perceive a contrast between (Eternal?) Rome and those ephemeral kingdoms that are doomed by its might, or is the state of Rome *peritura* too, ephemeral, like the condition of other realms? Chew's translation highlights the parallel between *res Romanae* and *regna*, rather than the contrast.)[62] To pursue a little further Kerrigan's act of imagination, what might it have been like to recall Virgil's line during a gladiatorial spectacle, as Augustus or Maecenas, two very different men, might conceivably have done?[63] Or to hear the line read by the poet himself in a country villa, as Augustus and Maecenas actually did?[64] Or to read it, say, in a military camp, perhaps not far from the Danube? How might Virgil's early readers, however situated, have responded to Virgil's praise of a life utterly divorced from the cares of Rome – a life of ideal indifference not only to the metropolis, but to the empire as well? How literally, how figuratively, should one take the line? Is it an exhortation or a fantasy? How do we – and how did others – understand its Epicurean subtext? Reconstructing contexts, which is the aim of scholarship, also engages the imagination.

To the question about the ways in which reading Sackville-West, and indeed the other authors treated in this book, might be supposed to 'improve' us as readers of Virgil, my own response has been practical, one might even say procedural, in the sense that my written readings are composed as demonstrations of a form of practice or procedure. I have 'read through reception' in the company of an imaginary audience peopled in part by exemplary readers, mainly poets and academics. But Sackville-West's genuinely popular readership reminds us that 'the common reader' is exemplary as well. Who then is the common reader? For Johnson, it was the mass of readers who were not dons, or clergymen, or educated members of the legal or medical or other professions, or literary professionals such as himself. When Johnson rejoiced to concur with the common reader, he was not self-identifying as a common reader, nor was he merely agreeing with what he took to be the popular consensus on Gray's *Elegy*. He was asserting that after the scholars and pundits and professionals have had their say, it is 'by the common sense' of those nameless non-professional readers that the verdict of posterity must finally be decided (and therefore in this instance it was lucky for him that he agreed with them). Woolf placed Johnson's statement at the head of *The Common Reader* as a sentence 'which might well be written up in all those rooms, too humble to be called libraries, yet full of books, where the pursuit of reading is carried on by private people'.[65] It is now Woolf's opening paragraph that might well be written up in rooms – in libraries, even – to define the 'qualities' of readers and dignify their aims, as she puts it, and even bestow the sanction of her approval, great woman that she was, 'upon a pursuit which devours a great deal of time, and is yet apt to leave behind it nothing very substantial'.

In the sense of mass readership, common reading is historically a rarity, and not to be taken for granted. Yet even in the rare epochs of widespread reading, such as Woolf's, reading is apt to leave behind it nothing very substantial. For all our empirical recovery of individual readers' experiences of the act of reading – and valuable work has been done in this area – we must acknowledge that the greater part of reading evaporates instantly. However much data we manage to recover, the common reader is essentially The Unknown Reader, that is to say the imagined reader whose company we seek, together with that of readers that we recognize more specifically – Woolf, for instance, or Johnson – who are not imaginary but nonetheless imagined. Reading is a practice or exercise that is never lastingly achieved but always a step away from oblivion, and always in need of support, above all from the imagined presence of earlier readers whose company we seek. Without the company of these spectral presences we cannot read; conversely, their absence means we are no longer reading.

Sackville-West was a voracious reader in an age of voracious readers, whose example makes me anxious that my own practice lags behind. We typically emulate what we most suppose ourselves to want. Being a scholar of English, I admire classicists (inevitably, perhaps, idealize them) for their rigour and versatility in endlessly reinterpreting a relatively small canon. Emulation is a force that drives all reading. We want to read something because it has meant something to someone else. It bears the traces of their attention, which we cannot perfectly share, but what mainly matters is their company, and we understand ourselves partly by the company we keep. It is the differences we surmise between our own experience and that of, say, Vita Sackville-West, that drive us to seek her company. If reading Sackville-West 'improves' us as readers of Virgil, it will be by engaging us in reading as a pursuit, as Woolf put it – a pursuit of company, which is precisely an act of the imagination.

Woolf realized that 'private people' might find needed encouragement in 'the sanction of the great man's approval'. (Always, that glint in her eye.) Woolf's figure of the common reader, like Johnson's, 'differs from the critic and the scholar. He is worse educated': he is less gifted; 'he reads for his own pleasure rather than to impart knowledge or correct the opinions of others'. The mainstay of this 'private person' is a resourceful imagination, and as Woolf proceeds to describe this reader's imagination with her signature exuberance, it seems clear that she is drawing a caricature of herself:

> Above all, he is guided by an instinct to create for himself, out of whatever odds and ends he can come by, some kind of whole – a portrait of a man, a sketch of an age, a theory of the art of writing. He never ceases, as he reads, to run up some rickety and ramshackle fabric which shall give him the temporary satisfaction of looking sufficiently like the real object to allow of affection, laughter, and argument.

'Affection, laughter, and argument': these too are words that might well be written up in all those rooms where the pursuit of reading is carried out, whether by 'private people' or by critics and scholars – and of course, the overlap between these figures is considerable. Woolf is clear eyed about the shortcomings of her cartoon autodidact: 'Hasty, inaccurate, and superficial, snatching now this poem, now that scrap of old furniture, without caring where he finds it or of what nature it may be so long as it serves his purpose and rounds his structure, his deficiencies as a critic are too obvious to be pointed out'. In her preface to *The Common Reader*, Woolf is playing with two caricatures, 'Dr Johnson' (a figure of authority and finality, and not identical with Samuel Johnson, hence Woolf's use of the conventional title) and the protean 'common reader'. Of course, she herself is neither figure; or rather, she knows herself as both, though for the purposes of decorous self-deprecation, as well as to deflect attention from the Cham in her own character, she pretends that her essays are produced by the 'hasty, inaccurate, and superficial' – imaginative – figure. The best implication, I think, is that there should be traffic between the two.

Both 'imagined communities', then, are exemplary; we need to emulate both. Few communities today seem to me to read quite as seriously and attentively as classicists and poet-critics. If we wish to remain readers in any full sense of the word, we will do well to play the reader in an imaginary company of exemplary practitioners, even as we aspire to the condition of common readers. This book has been an attempt to sound out readings of Virgil through the process of reading modern literature along the lines proposed by reception studies, in hopes of vindicating the effort by its fruit. If the book has given pleasure – or better, given encouragement to seek delight – it will have succeeded.

Notes

Introduction

1 'Purification': Miller, *Apollo, Augustus, and the Poets*, 28, 48–51.

2 Sheeler, *Little Sparta* , 69.

3 Miller, *Apollo, Augustus, and the Poets*, 206–10.

4 Maenalus is a mountain in Arcadia, the area in the Peloponnese associated with the pastoral deity Pan. Unless otherwise specified, translations are from the revised Loeb translation (Fairclough-Goold).

5 The *tibia* is part of the family of pipes associated with the pastoral genre (e.g. the *calamus* of *Eclogues* 6.69–71), which includes the generically emblematic pan-pipe or *fistula* (*Eclogues* 3.22).

6 Sheeler, *Little Sparta*, 16–17. Accounts of the dispute vary slightly: see https://www. littlesparta.org.uk/ian-hamilton-finlay-his-work/, accessed 7 April 2021.

7 Barchiesi, 'Learned Eyes', 285, on S. J. Heyworth's observation of an allusion to Callimachus' *Hymn to Apollo* line 24 in Propertius 2.31.6.

8 For a critique of reception that insists on its condition as an ongoing process, see Whitmarsh, 'True Histories'.

9 Virgil alludes to the equally programmatic passage in which Callimachus seems to reject epic, *Aetia* fr. 1.21–4.

10 Saunders, *Bucolic Ecology*, ch. 4, 'Topography', esp. 96–101.

11 Virgil, *Georgics*, ed. Thomas, *ad* 3.36. (Henceforth 'Thomas, *Georgics*'.) Miller discusses 3.36 (*Apollo, Augustus, and the Poets*, 5–6), cautioning that Augustus' championship of Apollo is not automatically relevant everywhere the god is mentioned in Augustan poems, but that relevance depends on context, i.e., contextualization.

12 For a discussion of 'Apolline poetics and Augustus', see Miller, *Apollo, Augustus, and the Poets*, ch. 6 (298–331).

13 Lee, *Virgil as Orpheus*, 127, and Nelson, *God and the Land*, 138–40. For the Callimachean intertext, Thomas, *Georgics*, *ad* 4.560–1. See also Hollis, 'Octavian in the Fourth Georgic', 305–8. For a critique of reductive juxtapositions of Callimachus and Virgil, see Hunter, *The Shadow of Callimachus* 2; also 126–7. On the *sphragis*, see Peirano, 'Illo ego qui quondam: on authorial (an)onymity'; on the end of the *Georgics*, esp. 269–72.

14 The composition of the *Georgics* and the erection of the temple on the Palatine are roughly coterminous. Virgil wrote the *Georgics c.* 36–29 BC. Miller, *Apollo, Augustus, and the Poets*, 3, 185.

15 Miller, *Apollo, Augustus, and the Poets*, 140–1. At 97, 139 and 185–6, Miller also observes that Aeneas' vow at Cumae to build a temple to Apollo and Diana (6.69–70) is similarly proleptic.

16 Miller, *Apollo, Augustus, and the Poets*, 2–6, 148.

17 Virgil is also inviting the reader to draw connections between Hercules and Aeneas and to make these connections anticipate Octavian, whose triple triumph of 29 BC, celebrating the victory at Actium, began on 13 August, the annual festival of Hercules at the Ara Maxima, the very occasion of Evander and Aeneas' first meeting; see G. K. Galinsky, *The Herakles Theme* 141. It is important to realize that figures such as Aeneas or Augustus are commonly enriched by associations with more than one hero or deity. For a marvellously rich reading of the 'wormhole' of 12–13 August in *Aeneid* 8 that links Aeneas and Hercules with the battle of Actium and Augustus' triple triumph, see Feeney, *Caesar's Calendar*, 161–3.

18 On Apollo's prophecy at 3.97–8, its Homeric derivation (*Iliad* 20.307–08) and Callimachaean intertext, see Miller, *Apollo, Augustus, and the Poets*, 109–11. On Virgil's tracing of a common ancestry of Evander's people and the Trojans, see Papaioannou, 'Founder, Civilizer and Leader', 695.

19 Eliot, 'Tradition and the Individual Talent', 15.

20 Lodge, *Small World*, 51–2.

21 Martindale, *Redeeming the Text*, 54. The book has had an extraordinarily rich reception; see the special issue of the *Classical Receptions Journal* 5.2 (2013), 'Redeeming the Text: Twenty years on', https://academic.oup.com/crj/issue/5/2, accessed 7 April 2021.

22 Martindale, *Redeeming the Text*, 49.

23 Sheeler, *Little Sparta*, 130–3. At *Georgics* 4.141 Finlay's text reads *pinus* (pine) as in Thomas's text, rather than the *tinus* (laurustinus) of Mynors and the Loeb edition; see Virgil, *Georgics*, ed. Mynors, *ad* 4.112–15. (Hereafter, 'Mynors, *Georgics*'.) Accordingly (or vice versa), Finlay has had pines planted among the encircling trees.

24 Sheeler, *Little Sparta*, 22–3.

25 The word *umbra* is pointedly recalled at the end of the *Georgics* and *Aeneid* too – and placed, incidentally, in the above-mentioned passage about the old Corycian's garden, *Georgics* 4.146. On Marvell's reading of Virgil, see Martindale, 'Green Politics', 175. On *umbra* in Virgil, see Theodorakopoulos, 'Closure and the Book of Virgil', 236–9. The translation of the Latin inscription on Finlay's urns is in Sheeler, *Little Sparta*, 78. Another of Finlay's garden meditations on *umbra* is the representation of an evening shadow by a line of bricks set in the ground behind a tree, with each brick stamped 'VIRGIL': Sheeler, *Little Sparta*, 106–7.

26 Henkel, 'Vergil Talks Technique', 58.

27 Henkel, 'Vergil Talks Technique', 61.

28 Thomas, *Virgil and the Augustan Reception*, 18.

29 Pellicer, 'Reception, Wit, and the Unity of Virgil's *Georgics*', 90–115.

30 On the experiential-experimental principle or method in seventeenth-century science generally, see Shapin and Schaffer, *Leviathan and the Air-Pump*.

31 Philips, *Cider*, ed. Dunster, 54. On the paradox familiar to the Renaissance humanists that 'an author is less likely to remember what he knows best', see G. W. Pigman, 'Versions of Imitation in the Renaissance', 13–15.

32 Vida, *De Arte Poetica* 3.257–8, as cited in Pigman, 'Versions of Imitation in the Renaissance', 14.

33 Sheeler, *Little Sparta*, 65–7.

34 Martindale, 'Paradise Metamorphosed: Ovid in Milton', 325.

35 Miller, *Apollo, Augustus, and the Poets*, 15, 28, 350.

36 Sheeler, *Little Sparta*, 75. In Virgil, the storm is associated with Tellus (Earth) and Juno, 4.166–7. The frieze that runs along the grotto wall reads, 'ONE CAVE A GRATEFUL SHELTER SHALL AFFORD TO THE FAIR PRINCESS AND THE TROJAN LORD' (Dryden's translation of *Aeneid* 4.124–5 [4.174–5]). Inside there are busts of Aeneas and Dido.

37 Sheeler, *Little Sparta*, 76–7.

38 Sheeler, *Little Sparta*, 74–5 and 101–3.

39 Sheeler, *Little Sparta*, 79.

40 'A "reference" is a "specific direction of the attention"; an "allusion", in the words of the *OED*, is "a covert, implied or indirect reference"'. Hinds, *Allusion and Intertext*, 22. In chapter 2, Hinds seeks an ideal method (which he compares to 'fuzzy logic' in computing) to steer a middle way between the intentionalism implied by the term 'reference' and the consensualism implied by 'intertextuality'; see esp. 47–51.

41 Hinds, *Allusion and Intertext*, 11; I modify slightly.

42 As Hinds puts it, 'The ideal of a reader who sees exactly the same cues within the *topos* as the author, and constructs them in the same order and in the same way, will always in the final analysis be unattainable' (*Allusion and Intertext*, 46).

43 Edmunds, *Intertextuality and the Reading of Roman Poetry*, xvii, quoting an email from Richard Thomas.

44 For a good discussion, see Hinds, *Allusion and Intertext*, 34–47.

45 Tarrant, 'Poetry and Power', 260. In fairness to Frost, it should be said that his poem is more ironically self-aware than selective quotation easily allows (... '"New order of the ages" did we say?' ...). Frost, *Collected Poems, Prose & Plays*, 436. For a positive reappraisal of the poem (as rhetorically even closer to Horace than to Virgil), see Ziolkowski, 'Robert Frost in Roman Mode'.

46 Buxton, *Robert Frost and Northern Irish Poetry*, 113–20.

47 Pope, *The Dunciad in Four Books*, ed. Rumbold, 101.

48 Muldoon, *Why Brownlee Left*, 10. Buxton, *Robert Frost and Northern Irish Poetry*, 116.

49 Donaghy and Muldoon, 'A Conversation with Paul Muldoon', 84, and Buxton, 115–16, also citing Muldoon, 'Getting Round: Notes towards an *Ars Poetica*', 117.

50 Ziolkowski, 'Robert Frost in Roman Mode', 2–3.

51 Thomas, *Virgil and the Augustan Reception*, 4.

52 'Augustan hermeneutics': Thomas, *Virgil and the Augustan Reception*, 6.

53 This holds true as well if one takes Shakespeare's 'chimney sweepers' to (also) mean dandelion clocks, and 'dust' their dispersing pollen. For another version of the gold/lead topos in Muldoon, see his elegy 'Incantata', which speaks of building from pain 'a monument to the human heart | that shines like a golden dome among roofs rain-glazed and leaden' (and repeats the description of the roofs in the subsequent stanza). Paul Muldoon, *The Annals of Chile*, 19.

54 For an excellent introduction to this subject, see Feeney, *Caesar's Calendar*, 131–7.

55 For an overview, see Perkell, 'The Golden Age and Its Contradictions in the Poetry of Vergil'.

56 Martindale, 'Introduction: The Classic of All Europe', 6. (Regarding the literal sense of 'golden', consider *Aeneid* 8.656, describing the Capitol's gilded colonnades represented – in gold? – on Aeneas' shield.) There is a brilliant reading of Aeneas' arrival at the site of the future Roman Forum in Feeney, *Caesar's Calendar*, 161–6.

57 'Bring to a close': Thomas, *Virgil and the Augustan Reception*, 4–5.

58 Brooks, '*Discolor Aura*. Reflections on the Golden Bough', 274–5, quoting Empson, *Seven Kinds of Ambiguity*, 195.

59 Virgil, *Aeneidos Liber Sextus*, ed. Austin, *ad* 6.204.

60 For an alternative construction of Heaney's oat stalks, as corresponding to the flowers strewn in memory of Marcellus at *Aeneid* 6.883–6, see Putnam, 'Virgil and Heaney: "Route 110"', 106, and Ware, 'The Ashplant and the Golden Bough', 236–7.

61 Falconer, 'Heaney and Virgil's Underworld Journey', 186–7.

62 Martindale quotes Gadamer via Frank Kermode: 'One understands differently when one understands at all'. *Redeeming the Text*, 54.

63 Harrison, *Generic Enrichment in Vergil and Horace*, ch. 1 (1–33).

Chapter 1

1 Alpers, *The Singer of the Eclogues*, 156, quoting Friedrich Klingner.

2 Jenkyns, 'Virgil and Arcadia', 26.

3 Martindale, *Redeeming the Text*; Martindale, 'Green Politics'; Skoie, 'Passing on the Panpipes'.

4 Martindale, 'Green Politics', 175.

5 I am indebted to the ideas and vocabulary of Fairer, *Organising Poetry*, 8–9 and *passim*.

6 The text of the first corrected Faber edition of *Arcadia* (1993, 'reprinted with corrections') was revised in the 2009 edition ('reprinted with revisions'). For readers' convenience I have adopted a double form of page reference (1993/2009), henceforth given parenthetically in my text.

7 To Virgil scholars, the combination of mathematics (or rather, numerological analysis) and the *Eclogues* is not unknown; for a brief discussion with bibliography, see Horsfall, *A Companion to the Study of Virgil*, 33–4.

8 The tutor Septimus Hodge's surname is suggestive in this respect. As Hardy explains in *Tess of the D'Urbervilles*, ch. 18, 'Hodge' is the stock name for the English rustic, a figure of simplicity. In mathematics, the name's connotations are quite different: the Hodge conjecture is a famous unsolved problem in algebraic geometry. The complementarity of Septimus Hodge's first and last names is a further case in point: while 'Septimus' connotes a) a numbered series, b) Latinity, and c) high culture, 'Hodge' connotes the native and the low.

9 Stoppard, *Rosencrantz and Guildenstern Are Dead*, 51.

10 Gleick, *Chaos*, 251, quoting Doyne Farmer, one of the pioneers of chaos mathematics at Santa Cruz: '"On a philosophical level, [chaos theory] struck me as an operational way to reconcile free will with determinism"'. Gleick's book is an avowed source of Stoppard's play. Other useful introductions to deterministic chaos include Stewart, *Does God Play Dice*; Hayles, *Chaos Bound*; and Gribbin, *Deep Simplicity*.

11 The example of cream going into coffee is a commonplace in popular accounts of chaos. The most relevant source is Gleick, *Chaos*, 24–5; also Hayles, *Chaos Bound*, 12, 150, and Stewart, *Does God Play Dice?*, 106.

12 Schmidt, 'Arcadia'. The essay that has done most to establish the view that pastoral is a post-classical invention is Jenkyns, 'Virgil and Arcadia'. For an account of what Arcadia meant for Virgil, see Kennedy, '*Arcades ambo*: Virgil, Gallus and Arcadia'.

13 Schmidt, 'Arcadia', 43.

14 Actually two articles by Panofsky, the first written in 1936 and the extensively revised version of 1955.

15 Rosenmeyer, *The Green Cabinet*, vii.

16 As Richard Hunter writes of structural variation in Theocritus, 'Constant difference within the apparently unchanging and familiar was indeed to remain a feature of the bucolic/pastoral tradition, and it already marks the world which Theocritus creates'. Introduction to Theocritus, *Idylls*, trans. Verity, xvii.

17 Stoppard, *Rosencrantz and Guildenstern Are Dead*, 63, quoted in Zeifman, 'The comedy of eros: Stoppard in love', 189.

18 Hamilton, 'The Argument of Spenser's *Shepheardes Calender*', 174.

19 Heaney, 'Eclogue IX', in *Electric Light*, 34.

20 Stoppard, *Rosencrantz and Guildenstern Are Dead*, 8.

21 Limon, 'Waltzing in *Arcadia*'.

22 Brater, 'Tom Stoppard's Brit/lit/crit', 209; Meisel, *How Plays Work*, 91.

23 Carrier identifies five themes in this passage, '1. the ancient world; 2. mortality; 3. awkwardness; 4. creating order from chaos; 5. intellectual activity', adding, 'They are common in the Poussin literature'. *Poussin's Paintings*, 63–4.

24 Rogers, 'Rhythm and Recoil in Pope's *Pastorals*', 4–6. See Panofsky, 'Et in Arcadia Ego' (1936), which also discusses Poussin's *Ballo della Vita humana* at 241–3, and develops most fully the link between pastoral and the theme of transience in Poussin.

25 For Poincaré's application of the principle to the universe, see Kragh, *Entropic Creation*, 183. But as Kragh immediately observes, Poincaré himself considered his own recurrence theorem and its 'prediction of a cyclic, recurrent universe to have no relevance for the real world'.

26 Atkins, *Galileo's Finger*, ch. 4.

27 For a history of scientific theories of the 'heat death' of the universe in the second half of the nineteenth century, see Kragh, *Entropic Creation*, ch. 3.

28 Gleick, *Chaos*, 308.

29 Atkins, *Galileo's Finger*, ch. 4, 'The Spring of Change'. See Hayles, *Chaos Bound*, 100.

30 Gleick, *Chaos*, 314: '. . . And as Lorenz discovered so long ago, dissipation is an agent of order.' This idea is most pronounced in the work of Ilya Prigogine and Isabelle Stengers, most influentially *Order Out of Chaos*. For an admirably critical discussion of Prigogine and Stengers' work, see Hayles, *Chaos Bound*, ch. 4.

31 Gleick, *Chaos*, 308.

32 Gleick, *Chaos*, 102–3.

33 There is probably deliberate irony in that several pioneers of chaos mathematics – to name only Henri Poincaré and Benoit Mandelbrot – have been French (compare Stoppard's joke about the nationality of calculus, 107/109).

34 Stewart, *Does God Play Dice?*, 73.

35 Fairer, *English Poetry of the Eighteenth Century*, 86.

36 The theoretical biologist and physicist Robert May, who advised Stoppard during the composition of *Arcadia*, comments that 'This passage from *Arcadia* is undoubtedly over the top, but it does capture what it felt like – for me and others – in the early 1970s to be part of the scientific revolution caused by chaos theory'. May, 'The Best Possible Time to Be Alive', 212.

37 Old Carr travesties Wordsworth's famous lines in the first act of Stoppard's *Travesties* (1993 edn, 10/2017 edn, 14).

38 May describes his own famous paper 'Simple mathematical models with very complicated dynamics' (*Nature* 261 [1976], 459–67) as 'evangelical' (the paper itself

uses this term in its introductory section), its style 'deliberately messianic'; 'The Best Possible Time to be Alive', 223.

39 Gleick, *Chaos*, 52.

40 Gleick, *Chaos*, 37.

41 Gleick, *Chaos*, 157.

42 Auerbach, *Mimesis*, 151.

43 Hinds, 'Pastoral and its futures: reading like (a) Mantuan'.

44 Du Quesnay, 'Vergil's Fourth *Eclogue*', 81.

45 Du Quesnay, 'Vergil's Fourth *Eclogue*', 81.

46 Gleick, *Chaos*, 163–5.

47 Quoted in Cassidy et al., *Understanding Physics*, 323.

48 Feeney, *Caesar's Calendar*, 132.

49 Gussow, *Conversations with Stoppard*, 89–90. Stoppard may be remembering an article entitled 'Chaos' by James P. Crutchfield, J. Doyne Farmer, Norman H. Packard and Robert S. Shaw, *Scientific American* 254/12 (Dec. 1986), 46–57.

50 Cf. T. S. Eliot's remarks on the difference between classicism and romanticism as 'the difference between the complete and the fragmentary, the adult and the immature, the orderly and the chaotic'. 'The Function of Criticism', *Criterion*, October 1923, cited in Martindale, 'Ruins of Rome: T. S. Eliot and the Presence of the Past', 112.

51 Pater, 'Postscript', in *Appreciations*, 247. I am indebted to Tim Saunders for drawing my attention to this passage.

52 Rosenmeyer, *The Green Cabinet*, vii.

53 Jenkyns, 'Pastoral', 159, 151.

54 *Norton Anthology of English Literature*, 9th edn, 4.502.

55 Stoppard's introduction of Cleopatra by choosing Enobarbus' famous speech for Septimus's variant on the 'Latin unseen' is apt in many respects, not least in light of Pascal's famous observation about Cleopatra's nose: 'had it been shorter, the whole aspect of the world would have been altered.' As quoted in Lively, 'Cleopatra's Nose, Naso and the Science of Chaos', 27.

56 Theocritus, *A Selection*, ed. Hunter, headnote to *Idyll* 11 (p. 221).

57 Muecke, 'Virgil and the Nature of Pastoral', 170, cited in Theocritus, *A Selection*, ed. Hunter, 11–12.

58 Johnson, *Lives of the Poets*, I.278 (§181). Johnson was discussing Milton's *Lycidas*, of all poems.

59 Alpers, *What is Pastoral?*, 351, of Montemayor's *Diana* (1559).

60 Virgil, *Eclogues*, ed. Coleman, 27.

61 Fantazzi, 'Virgilian Pastoral and Roman Love Poetry', 171.

62 Virgil, *Eclogues*, trans. Lee, 13.

63 Fantazzi, 'Virgilian Pastoral and Roman Love Poetry', 176.

64 Hunt, *The Figure in the Landscape*, 1.

65 Martindale, 'Green Politics', 179. On Virgil and elegy, see Kenney, 'Virgil and the Elegiac Sensibility', and Conte, 'An Interpretation of the Tenth *Eclogue*'.

66 Rosenmeyer, *The Green Cabinet*, 83.

67 Theocritus, *A Selection*, ed. Hunter, headnote to 11 (p. 220) and *ad* 11.80 (p. 242). For a rich reading of the many ironies of *Idyll* 11, see Goldhill, *The Poet's Voice*, 249–61.

68 We cannot, of course, assume that *Idyll* 30 was the final one in Virgil's own version of Theocritus' works.

69 On Virgil's combination of sources in Eclogue 8.37–41, see Kenney, 'Virgil and the Elegiac Sensibility', 53–7.

70 Conte, 'An Interpretation of the Tenth *Eclogue*', 225.

71 Harrison, *Generic Enrichment*, 62 – 3.

72 I owe the latter formulation to Fairer, *English Poetry of the Eighteenth Century*, 84.

73 Stoppard, *The Invention of Love*, 99; see also 13.

74 See Stewart, *Does God Play Dice?*, describing Lorenz as 'ahead of his time' (124): 'Lorenz had opened a door into a new world. | Nobody stepped through. | *Door? What door?*' (134).

75 Chloë's echo of Thomasina ('Valentine, do you think I'm the first person to have thought of this?', 97/99) has the additional irony of 'anticipating' that Chloë's idea itself ('it's all because of sex') has also been anticipated by Thomasina ('The Chater would overthrow the Newtonian system in a weekend', 112/114).

76 Snyder, *Pastoral Process*, 177–8.

77 Martindale, 'Thinking Through Reception', 12. Martindale has criticized Richard Jenkyns's pointedly synchronic reading of Eclogue 8.37–41, not for any undue subjectivity, but because Jenkyns fails to factor in the cultural underpinnings of his own literary taste; see *Redeeming the Text*, 4–6.

78 Jenkyns, 'Virgil and Arcadia', 30.

79 On framing as a poetic device, see Goldhill, *The Poet's Voice*, ch. 4.

80 I am adapting Hubbard, *The Pipes of Pan*, 45.

81 Snyder, *Pastoral Process*, 93.

82 As Guy Lee observes, this detail distinguishes Virgil from his source in Theocritus 11.25–9. Lee, 'Imitation and the Poetry of Virgil', 12.

83 Harrison, *Generic Enrichment*, 15–21.

84 *OLD* s.v. 'inanis' gives several instances that suggest that the adjective becomes associated with pastoral *tenuitas* after Virgil.

85 Hardie, *Virgil's Aeneid: Cosmos and Imperium*, 44, on the classical trope of *recusatio*, when a poet rhetorically declines one poetic undertaking in favour of another.

86 Stoppard had probably been long acquainted with *Headlong Hall*, but he could also have been reminded of Peacock's novel by the excerpt included in Hunt and Willis's anthology, *The Genius of the Place*, 376–9.

87 Vickers, 'Leisure and idleness in the Renaissance: The ambivalence of *otium*', Parts 1 and 2.

88 On period doubling, see Stewart, *Does God Play Dice?*, 147–9, a discussion that may have suggested Stoppard's use of piano music in the play, specifically Valentine's illustrative comparison, 60–1/62–4. It is tempting to think that several of Stoppard's ideas came to him as jokes in response to his own research. For instance, if he read Hayles's *Chaos Bound* in the course of his research, he will have noted her feminist response to Gleick's *Chaos*: 'I had a divided response to this absence of women [in Gleick's narrative]. On the one hand, Gleick can scarcely invent them where they do not exist'. Hayles, *Chaos Bound*, 171, discussing the gendered character of scientific narratives, 171–4. One imagines Stoppard thinking, 'But *I* can invent them'. And then of course he may have recalled Ada Lovelace.

89 Alpers, *What is Pastoral?*, 68–9.

90 Galinsky, Vergil's Second *Eclogue'*, 161.

91 Skoie, 'Passing on the Panpipes', 94.

92 Saunders, 'Making an Example out of Marsyas', 36.

93 Fitzgerald, 'Vergil in Music', 346.

Chapter 2

1 For Homer's phrasing in describing the act of representation in metalwork, see Heffernan, *Museum of Words*, 14–22.

2 On the influence on Virgil of Apollonius' great intermediary epic, the *Argonautica*, see Nelis, *Vergil's Aeneid and the Argonautica of Apollonius Rhodius*, 350ff. on the ekphrasis of Jason's cloak, *Argonautica* 1.1721–68, which corresponds to Homer's and Virgil's Shields.

3 Auden, *Collected Poems*, ed. Mendelson. All references to Auden's poems are to this edition.

4 Horsfall, 'Virgil and the Poetry of Explanations'.

5 Feeney, *Caesar's Calendar*; on Homer, see p. 70; on Virgil, esp. pp. 161–6.

6 Though Auden's strictures specifically relate to Virgil's description of the shield of Aeneas in *Aeneid* 8, they might equally apply to Virgil's prolepsis of spectral Roman heroes as revealed to Aeneas in the Underworld in *Aeneid* 6.756–853.

7 In his final chapter (71), Gibbon quotes the Florentine humanist Poggio (1380–1459): '"The forum of the Roman people, where they assembled to enact their laws and elect their magistrates, is now enclosed for the cultivation of pot-herbs, or thrown open for the reception of swine and buffaloes."'

8 Bespaloff, 'On the *Iliad*', 80. See Schein, 'Reading Homer in Dark Times', 17–18.

9 I am grateful to Kathleen Coleman for this suggestion. On the cup in Idyll 1, including this vignette of the boy in the vineyard, as a '"bucolicisation" of Homer's Shield of Achilles', see, *Theocritus, A Selection*, ed. Hunter, *ad* 1.27–61 (pp. 76–7).

10 Fairclough/Goold's translation of *labor* as 'sorrow' (or 'sorrows') is shared by many translators, including Day Lewis, Mandelbaum, Fitzgerald and Lombardo (with hendiadys, Ahl gives 'trouble and sorrow'). C. S. Lewis not only retains the singular, but with the austere and dignified 'adversity' also manages to convey the generalizing and capacious qualities of *labor*, as well as its dual objective/subjective dimension. Fagles gives 'ordeals'; Dryden 'disasters'; Patric Dickinson, 'miseries'; Ruden paraphrases, 'what we suffered in that war'.

11 Virgil, *Aeneidos Liber Primus*, ed. Austin, *ad* 461f. Other critics have observed that Aeneas' reading of the scenes tell us at least as much about his own perspective and mental state as about what the scenes 'actually' depict: the scenes can be construed differently, Aeneas may be misreading, or at least Virgil enables alternative historical perspectives. See Fowler, 'Narrate and Describe: The Problem of Ekphrasis', 32–3, and Barchiesi, 'Virgilian Narrative: Ecphrasis', 420.

12 As Hecht observes, the penultimate lines of each of the rhyme-royal stanzas are exceptional tetrameters ('metrical deviations' from the rest), enabling the final line in each of these stanzas to reassert the trimester pattern with striking gravity. *The Hidden Law*, 427–8.

13 Conte, 'The Virgilian Paradox', 28–9. On Schiller, see 24–6.

14 Conte, 'The Virgilian Paradox', 28.

15 Conte, 'The Virgilian Paradox', 28.

16 Conte, 'The Virgilian Paradox', 29.

17 Homer, *Iliad*, trans. Lattimore; the Chicago Homer, https://homer.library. northwestern.edu/, accessed 17 Feb. 2021.

18 Barchiesi, *Homeric Effects in Vergil's Narrative*, 91.

19 Kirsch, '"Our Grief is Not Greek"', 32–3.

20 Quoted in Kirsch, '"Our Grief is Not Greek"', 50.

21 Taplin, 'The Shield of Achilles within the *Iliad*', 15.

22 Hardie, *Virgil's Aeneid: Cosmos and Imperium*, 341.

23 Fuller, *W. H. Auden: A Commentary*, 449.

24 Auden, 'The Greeks and Us', 18. Quoted in Kirsch, '"Our Grief is Not Greek"', 50.

25 To impose Roman *pax* one must 'battle down the proud', as Fitzgerald translates *debellare superbos*, 6.853: it is a peace enforced on subjected people, *subjectis*.

26 Summers, '"Or One Could Weep Because Another Wept"', 220.

27 In a 1966 essay on the fall of Rome published posthumously in 1995, reprinted in the chapter 'Auden on the Fall of Rome' in Bowersock, *From Gibbon to Auden*, 213; quoted by Bowersock, 199.

28 Westlake, 'W. H. Auden's "The Shield of Achilles": An Interpretation', 54–5. Cf. Summers, '"Or One Could Weep Because Another Wept"', 221; Hecht, *The Hidden Law*, 429; and Kirsch, '"Our Grief is Not Greek"', 55.

29 Rewriting Homer, Virgil inverts the position of the Homeric ocean scene from its circumferent position on Achilles' shield – though Homer's ekphrasis begins and ends with the ocean, 'which serves as boundary both to the account and to the world of the object' (Thomas, 'Virgil's Ekphrastic Centerpieces', 175).

30 On *sulcare* as well as Virgil's *vastum aequor*, see Ovid, *Epistulae ex Ponto, Book I*, ed. Gaertner, *ad* 1.4.35 (p. 293). On *Aeneid* 2.780, García Ruiz observes, 'The phrase *maris aequor* echoes the formulas used by Ennius and Lucretius: *ponti/maris/campi aequor*. At the same time, *aequor arandum* is an expression of Virgil's own making, a beautiful image that harks back to the poet's voice in the *Georgics*.' 'AEQVOR', 696.

31 Hecht, *The Hidden Law*, 428.

32 Heffernan, *Museum of Words*, 19–20.

33 Heffernan, *Museum of Words*, 32–3. For an excellent discussion of Virgil's collapsing of narrative levels and *mise-en-abyme* effects in the 'Shield', see Barchiesi, 'Virgilian Narrative: Ecphrasis', 419.

34 For a searching analysis of 'the blurring of the comparison and the thing compared' in *Aeneid* 6, see Jenkyns, *Virgil's Experience*, 454–7. Note, though, that Virgil's shield may be 'indescribable' (*non enarrabilis*) only in the sense of 'not fully describable'.

35 E.g., 8.628, 630, *fecerat*, 'he had made', 637, *addiderat*, 'he had set (as well)'. See West, '*Cernere erat*'.

36 West, '*Cernere erat*', 304.

37 As Cicero puts it, 'in things that are new to us, ignorance of their causes produces wonder; correspondingly, if our ignorance concerns familiar things we do not experience wonder' (*Causarum enim ignoratio in re nova mirationem facit; eadem ignoratio si in rebus usitatis est, non miramur; De Divinatione* II.22 (49), cited in *OLD* s.v. *miratio*. Recall Prospero's rejoinder (to Miranda's 'O wonder! . . . O brave new world, | That has such people in't'), ' 'Tis new to thee'; *The Tempest*, 5.1.181–4.

38 Harrison, 'Survival and Supremacy of Rome. The Unity of the Shield of Aeneas'.

39 Jangfeldt, 'Form in Poetry', 197. For brief remarks regarding Yeats's 'Easter 1916' on trimeters as the English equivalent of the classical epic hexameter, see Vendler, *Our Secret Discipline*, 193.

40 Jangfeldt, 'Form in Poetry', 198.

41 West, '*Cernere erat*', 297.

42 '*Res ipsae*'; Becker, *The Shield of Achilles*, 125, 152. On 'disobedient' ekphrasis which 'breaks free from the discipline of the imagined object', see Laird, 'Sounding Out Ecphrasis: Art and Text in Catullus 64', 19. Laird, however, argues that Homer's Shield of Achilles 'in the end inclines toward obedience – we could just about visualize how it would be' (20).

43 Becker, *The Shield of Achilles*, 125.

44 Gransden, *Virgil's Iliad*, 89, quoted in Boyd, '*Non Enarrabile Textum*', 74.

45 See Hardie, 'Virgil, a Paradoxical Poet?'.

46 Hecht, *The Hidden Law*, 429–30. See Weil, 'The *Iliad*, of the Poem of Force', 3–7.

47 Kirsch, '"Our Grief is Not Greek"', 54.

48 For instance, Summers, '"Or One Could Weep"', 230.

49 I use the singular ('is') since I read 'mass and majesty' as a hendiadys, two words working to convey a single idea.

50 Lewis, *A Preface to Paradise Lost*, 38.

51 Virgil, *Aeneidos IV*, ed. R. G. Austin, *ad* 4.449.

52 *Classical Literature and its Reception*, ed. DeMaria, Jr., and Brown, 224. The editors' remark that 'In "Musée des Beaux Arts", Auden prefers the painting in which the fall of Icarus is barely noticed to the stirring tale in Ovid', seems to me to miss the point that Bruegel and Auden invert Ovid's disposition of foreground and background.

53 Just so, now Auden's reading of Bruegel reading Ovid 'is there' in *Metamorphoses* 217–20: and perhaps not only belatedly either. See Peter Green's comment in his Penguin translation of Ovid's *Erotic Poems*, 364.

54 I owe this sentence to Tim Saunders.

55 Less charitably, Simone Weil dismisses the *Aeneid* as 'an imitation which, however brilliant, is disfigured by frigidity, bombast, and bad taste'. 'The *Iliad*, of the Poem of Force', 33–44.

56 Kirsch, '"Our Grief is Not Greek"', 50–2.

57 Quint, 'The Virgilian Coordinates of *Paradise Lost*', 197.

58 Putnam, 'The *Aeneid* and *Paradise Lost*: Ends and Conclusions', 406–7.

Chapter 3

1 In a note in his sonnet sequence *The River Duddon* (1820), Wordsworth writes, 'The power of waters over the minds of Poets has been acknowledged from the earliest ages; – through the "Flumina amem sylvasque inglorius" of Virgil, down to the sublime apostrophe to the great rivers of the earth, by Armstrong [*The Art of Preserving Health* 2.352–76]'. Wu, *Wordsworth's Poets*, 241.

2 *NB*: At 2.483 the Loeb text misprints *pratis* for Virgil's *partis* (the accusative plural of *pars*, 'part, region').

3 Hardie, *Virgil's Aeneid: Cosmos and Imperium*, 43–4. My understanding of *Georgics* 2.475–94 is much indebted to Hardie's section 2.I, pp. 33–51. On prayer in the *Georgics*, see also Perkell, *The Poet's Truth*, 148–52.

4 Wordsworth, *Letters, 1811–20*, ed. de Selincourt, 790, cited in the excerpt from John Jones's *The Egotistical Sublime* (1954) in *William Wordsworth: A Critical Anthology*, ed. McMaster, 391.

5 Freer, 'Virgil's *Georgics* and the Epicurean Sirens of Poetry', 80, citing Kyriakidis, '*Georgics* 4.559–566: The Vergilian Sphragis', 284–5.

6   Putnam, *Virgil's Poem of the Earth*, 146.

7   Putnam, *Virgil's Poem of the Earth*, 147.

8   My reading runs counter to Barrell, 'The uses of Dorothy'.

9   Though the context may be taken as 'a prayer for mutual compatibility' (Putnam, *Virgil's Poem of the Earth*, 148), and the alternatives may very plausibly stand for the two kinds of poetry Virgil is concerned to fuse, scientific and pastoral.

10 *Eighteenth-Century Poetry*, ed. Fairer and Gerrard, 402–3. Fairer, *Organising Poetry*, 108–13.

11 *Eighteenth-Century Poetry*, ed. Fairer and Gerrard, 402.

12 On the Bacchic contexts of *Georgics* 2.486–9, see Freer, 'Virgil's *Georgics* and the Epicurean Sirens of Poetry', 84–8.

13 Auerbach, *Mimesis*, 151.

14 Interestingly, when Macaulay surveyed the view from a hilltop town in Umbria in 1838 and recorded his impressions in his diary, he not only compared it favourably with the prospects at Matlock in the Peak District and the Wye Valley, but reflected how 'happily' Virgil had captured the Italian landscape at *Georgics* 2.156–7. See Kerrigan, *Virgil's Map*, 68.

15 Wordsworth and Coleridge, *Lyrical Ballads*, ed. Mason, Headnote, 206.

16 A line that 'could qualify as the vaguest line in English poetry'. Fairer, *Organising Poetry*, 266.

17 Barrell, 'The uses of Dorothy', 149.

18 In the *Georgics*, the adjective *dulcis* combines elements from Theocritus as well as Lucretius. 'Sweet' (*hadu*) is Theocritus' first word, a programmatic epithet and a keynote of his reception, and at 2.475 Virgil prefers the Theocritean flavour of *dulcis* to Lucretius' more erotic epithet *suavis* in the corresponding passage in *DRN* 1.924, though Lucretius refers to the Muses' sweet honey, *DRN* 1.947. Compare *Georgics* 3.291. Virgil also uses *dulcis* with Epicurean associations in the *sphragis* at 4.563. On 'sweetness' in Theocritus, see Edquist, 'Aspects of Theocritean *otium*', esp. 102–04. *Dulcis* at *Georgics* 4.563, describing 'Parthenope' (Naples), 'recalls the Epicurean goal of pleasure': Freer, 'Virgil's *Georgics* and the Epicurean Sirens of Poetry', 80–1. See Freer, 82, on Lucretius' *suavis* at 1.924 ('the language of passion'), and 84 on Lucretius' *dulcis* at 1.947.

19 Fairer, '*Gaps and Tracings*'.

20 Putnam, *Virgil's Poem of the Earth*, 150.

21 At the conclusion of *The Prelude* 10 (1019–27, 1805 text; compare 11.441–9, 1850 text), Wordsworth evokes Theocritus' pastoral Sicily as a type of his own home landscape in Cumbria, though Wordsworth here is also specifically concerned to recall the story of Comatas in Theocritus 7.78–82, buried alive by a tyrant but fed by bees bringing honey from the Muses.

22 Thomas, *Georgics, ad* 4.219–21.

23 *Pace* Mason, *Lyrical Ballads, ad* 96–103, who takes Wordsworth's Virgilian sources to be 'all definite about the presence of a deity' so they 'make Wordsworth's "sense of something" even more strikingly tentative' (212).

24 Mason, *Lyrical Ballads*, Headnote, 205.

25 Armstrong, '"Tintern Abbey': From Augustan to Romantic', 262.

26 I am prompted by Hammond, *Dryden and the Traces of Rome*, 26–8.

27 Mason, *Lyrical Ballads*, Headnote, 206.

28 I have composed this text from the several versions in Dove Cottage MS 5 printed in the Cornell *Early Poems and Fragments, 1785–1797*, ed. Landon and Curtis, 618–19. The punctuation is mine. For a different arrangement of the text, see Bruce Graver, 'Wordsworth's Georgic Beginnings', 142–3.

29 Graver, 'Wordsworth's Georgic Beginnings', 143.

30 Wordsworth, *Translations of Chaucer and Virgil*, ed. Graver, 188. Wordsworth could also be remembering other examples of figurative uses of the verb 'to hang' that he discusses in the Preface to the *Poems* of 1815, including the goats seen to hang from a bushy crag in Eclogue 1.76 (*dumosa pendere . . . de rupe*).

31 For commentary on Wordsworth's translation of *Aeneid* 1.164–5 in a discussion that takes Wordsworth's approach to translating the *Aeneid* as proto-modern in privileging the fragmentary over completion, see Falconer, 'Wordsworth Un-Englished', 182.

32 Mynors' commentary *ad Georgics* 2.486 quotes T. E. Page's gloss on *amem*, 'i.e., not merely feel an affection for [the country gods'] but express it in verse', supported by Quintillian 10.3.24. For metapoetic readings of the double *makarismos*, see Gale, *Virgil on the Nature of Things*, 10–11, and Volk, *The Poetics of Latin Didactic*, 143–4.

33 Hardie, *Virgil's Aeneid: Cosmos and Imperium*, 36–7.

34 Fairer, *Organising Poetry*, 97 ('textual interplay'), 98 ('riparian revisiting').

35 Fairer, *Organising Poetry*, 97.

36 Fairer, *Organising Poetry*, 116.

37 In the present context, Wordsworth's rhyme of *waters* with *chatters* may remind us not only that he came from a northern province, but that Virgil did too.

38 'It is not in the *Eclogues* [. . .] but in the *Georgics* that Vergil's most mature examination of *otium* is to be found.' Davis, 'Vergil's *Georgics* and the Pastoral Ideal', 22; cited by Sambrook in *English Pastoral Poetry*, 140.

39 Scodel and Thomas, 'Virgil and the Euphrates', 339.

40 As has been seen, my argument is indebted to Fairer's *Organising Poetry*, not least ch. 2, 'Organic Constitutions: Identity' (33–57).

41 Wilkinson, *The Georgics of Virgil*, 104.

42 For an extensive discussion, see Perkell, *The Poet's Truth*, 130–7.

43 *Oxford Classical Dictionary*, ed. Hornblower and Spawforth, s.v. Tarentum.

44 Wilkinson, *The Georgics of Virgil*, 23. See O'Rourke, 'The Representation and Misrepresentation of Virgilian Poetry in Propertius 2.34', 473–5.

45 I owe the main formulations in this paragraph to David Fairer, by email.

46 Wordsworth, *The Excursion*, ed. Bushell et al.

Chapter 4

1 Heaney, 'Mossbawn via Mantua', 19–21.

2 Joyce, *A Portrait of the Artist as a Young Man*, 250 (Stephen's diary, 3 April, toward the end of the final chapter).

3 Heaney, 'The Impact of Translation', 40–1. The idea of a 'parabolic' progress has also been made familiar through Andrei Voznesensky's 'Parabolic Ballad', mentioned in James Fenton's lecture on Heaney in *The Strength of Poetry*, 98–9.

4 Heaney, 'Secular and Millennial Miłosz', in *Finders Keepers*, 411, with the caveat, 'There is no point in labouring this Virgilian parallel', 412.

5 Donnelly, '"The Digging Skeleton *After Baudelaire*"', 251. In October 2008 Heaney told Gerald Dawe in an interview, 'I am very fond of Virgil in that he was obviously a bit like the scholarship boy who's made good'. For this and a further fleshing out of parallels, see Parker, '"His Nibs"', 335.

6 Heaney, *Finders Keepers*, 411.

7 Heaney's review of Peter Fallon's translation of the *Georgics* adopts similar phrasing, concluding that 'Taken in parts or as a whole, [the *Georgics*] says, "Glory be to the world"'. Heaney, 'Glory be to the world', *Irish Times*, Sat. 23 October 2004, electronic version https://www.irishtimes.com/news/glory-be-to-the-world-1.1163328, accessed 23 November 2018.

8 'Blacksmith Shop' (1991), translated by C. Miłosz and R. Hass, in Miłosz, *New and Collected Poems 1931–2001*, 503.

9 For a trenchant analysis of Heaney's tribute to Miłosz, see Jarniewicz, 'The Way Via Warsaw', 106–8. As Jarniewicz observes, 'To see in Miłosz's literary career the history of the whole millennium is more than a rhetorical gesture; it is an indirect exposition of Heaney's own understanding of the role of the poet and the functions of poetry in the modern age' (106).

10 Heaney, *Finders Keepers*, 410.

11 Kay, 'Dialogues across the Continent', and Parker, 'Past Master'. According to Parker, p. 831, Heaney's engagement with Miłosz began in earnest with his reading Miłosz's 1980 Nobel lecture in the 5 March 1981 issue of the *New York Review of Books*. This may explain why no poems by Miłosz are included in *The Rattle Bag*, the popular anthology Heaney edited with Ted Hughes (1982), which does include poems by Miroslav Holub, Zbigniew Herbert, Vasco Popa (a favourite of Hughes), and several other poets from Eastern Europe.

12 *Finders Keepers*, 411.

13 B. O'Donogue, 'The Aisling'.

14 Corcoran, 'Antaeus on the Move', 31.

15 Warm thanks to Fiachra Mac Góráin for suggesting this allusion.

16 *OED*, s.v. 'bell', v.4.

17 For an extended reading, see Reckford, 'Recognizing Venus I'.

18 In her analysis of Heaney's annotations in his schoolboy copy of J. W. Mackail's prose translation of the *Aeneid*, Edith Hall observes that 'there are only two passages marked in Book XII, but they are of utmost importance to our understanding of Heaney's response to the *Aeneid*. They are the two speeches which determine the 'Act of Union' by which Italy shall be made into a single political body and governed in the future'. The two passages are lines 183–94 and 823–41. Of lines 823–41, Hall says, 'Before I first opened the volume [Heaney's copy of the 1953 reprint of the Mackail translation] . . . I predicted that if Heaney had marked just one passage from the *Aeneid* it would be this', and goes on to explain its relevance in Ireland, referring to the Act of Union of 1801. Beyond this apparent allusion to Heaney's 'Act of Union', however, Hall does not mention the poem explicitly. Hall, 'Paving and Pencilling', 236–8.

19 Griffin, 'Virgil', 144. Pitt's quotation in his speech of 31 January 1799, making slight changes to Virgil, is given in Hoppen, *Governing Hibernia*, epigraph page (between Abbreviations and Introduction). Pitt's famous quotation of Virgil was repeated 'yet again' by Macaulay in a parliamentary debate on 9 June 1840; Hoppen, *Governing Hibernia*, 110. In the parliamentary debate following Gladstone's proposal of the first Home Rule Bill in 1886, the Virgilian quotation was again much repeated; see Morley, *The Life of William Ewart Gladstone*, vol 3, ch. 6, 'The Introduction of the Bill (1886)'.

20 On military language in the *Georgics*, see Batstone, 'Virgilian didaxis', 206.

21 Heaney, 'Eclogues *in extremis*', 250.

22 Heaney, 'Eclogues *in extremis*', 247.

23 Heaney, 'Eclogues *in extremis*', 252–3. Notice Heaney's artful use of the word 'tegument', echoing Virgil's striking use of the noun *tegimen* ('cover') in the first line of the *Eclogues*.

24 Heaney, 'Eclogues *in extremis*', 253–6.

25 Heaney, 'Eclogues *in extremis*', 253–4.

26 For a sensitive exploration of tensions in and between Heaney's 'Eclogues *in extremis*' lecture and his translation of Eclogue 9 in *Electric Light*, see Heiny, '"Puny in My Predicaments"'.

27 Alpers, *What is Pastoral?*, 290 (in chapter 7, 'Modern Pastoral Lyricism').

28 'In the Country of Convention' (*TLS*, 1975), in Heaney, *Preoccupations*, 180.

29 A comparable though lighter poem is 'A Brigid's Girdle' in *The Spirit Level*, p. 5.

30 Brandes and Heaney, 'Seamus Heaney: An Interview', 21.

31 In an uncollected twelve-line poem presented to Michael Longley on his seventieth birthday (*Love-Poet, Carpenter: Michael Longley at Seventy*, ed. R. Robertson (London, 2009), Heaney says he and Longley are 'More pastoral/lyrical than epical'. The poem is reprinted in McDonald, '"Weird Brightness"', 175 (n. 30). Falconer remarks that even in *District and Circle* (2006), where 'the entire arc of Virgil's underworld journey gets taken up in Heaney's poetry [. . .,] one hesitates to describe Heaney's transfusions of the *Aeneid* as "epic", since there seems always to be a lyric or georgic pressure exerted on Virgil's imperial narrative'. 'Heaney and Virgil's Underworld Journey', 182.

32 Vendler's description of the lyric imperative strikes me as apposite: '[. . .] the only thing to which the genre of the lyric obliges its poet is to represent his own situation and his responses to it in adequate imaginative language'. Vendler, *Seamus Heaney*, 175.

33 Corcoran, *Poetry and Responsibility*, 90 and 201 (n. 33). Heaney's use of the term is cited from Heaney's 'Foreword' in *Lifelines: An Anthology of Poems Chosen by Famous People*, ed. Niall MacMonagle (Harmondsworth: Penguin, 1993). But he used it on other occasions too, as in his 1988 lecture 'Learning from Eliot', in *Finders Keepers*, 38.

34 Corcoran, *Poetry and Responsibility*, 82. For Peter McDonald, 'Wordsworth's importance for Heaney is so widely acknowledged as to be a critical truism'. '"Weird Brightness"', 163.

35 A rare allusion to *Paradise Lost* occurs in Heaney's translation of 'The Death of Orpheus' from Ovid's *Metamorphoses* 11 in *The Midnight Verdict*, a Gallery Press volume in which Heaney's translations of Ovid's Orpheus and Eurydice flank his translation of Brian Merriman's poem. Heaney's description of Orpheus happily reunited with Eurydice in the underworld reads: 'For Orpheus now walks free, is free to fall | Out of step, into step, follow, go in front | And look behind him to his heart's content' (p. 42).

36 On the theme of the 'exemplary' in Heaney, see Corcoran, 'Seamus Heaney and the Art of the Exemplary', 117–27.

37 Heaney, 'Envies and Identifications', 254. At 250 Heaney describes Eliot's Dante as having 'a stern and didactic profile'.

38 'Erotic': Heaney, 'Envies and Identifications', 246.

39 Heaney, 'Envies and Identifications', 251.

40 Heaney, 'Envies and Identifications', 253.

41 Parker, *Seamus Heaney*, 267, quoting Heaney, 'Envies and Identifications', 240.

42 O'Donoghue argues that Mandelstam's essay also serves Heaney as a means 'to escape from Dante's Catholic-Christian grip'. 'Dante's Versatility and Seamus Heaney's Modernism', 253.

43 Heaney, 'Envies and Identifications', 242.

44 Heaney, 'Learning from Eliot' (1998), in *Finders Keepers*, 31–2.

45 Heaney, 'Feeling into Words', in *Preoccupations*, 41.

46 For an interesting though flawed reading of Heaney's 'Exposure' (in *North*) as a sustained allusion to the *Aeneid*, see Williams, 'Seamus Heaney's *Exposure* and Vergil's *Aeneid*'. I do not find Williams's argument persuasive, and *caveat lector*: p. 249 attributes a speech to Aeneas (10.668–79) that is actually spoken by Turnus.

47 Burrow, 'You've listened long enough', 13–14.

48 Heaney himself occasionally described his own early work as pastoral: in a 1988 interview conducted by George O'Brien at Howard Community College, Maryland, for instance, Heaney describes *Death of a Naturalist* as 'pastoral of a sort, I suppose'; https://www.youtube.com/watch?v=GpdzarVGOfs.

49 O'Donoghue, 'Heaney's Classics and the Bucolic', 107.

50 O'Donoghue, 'Heaney's Classics and the Bucolic', 108.

51 O'Donoghue, 'Heaney's Classics and the Bucolic', 108. Interestingly, in a poem dedicated to Heaney ('Summer Lightning', *TLS* 25 July 1980), Donald Davie commends the poet's 'early Georgics'. Davie, *Collected Poems*, 432.

52 Rowena Fowler's essay on 'Heaney and Hesiod' makes the same omission.

53 O'Donoghue, 'Heaney, Yeats, and the Language of Pastoral', 151.

54 In his essay on the development of the Antaeus figure in Heaney's work, Corcoran considers the significance of the fact that in *Opened Ground* (1998), Heaney moved this poem from its original position at the head of the first part of *North* (1975), where it was dated '1966', to a separate and intermedial position between the poems from *Death of a Naturalist* (1966) and those from *Door into the Dark* (1969); see Corcoran, 'Antaeus on the Move'.

55 Davis, 'From Mossbawn to Meliboeus', 102–3.

56 When 'A Postscript' was first published in *The Irish Times* (10 October 1992), the lines ran, 'The surface of a slate-grey lake is hit | By the bolt lightning of a flock of swans'. On his copy of the newspaper, Heaney made substantial revisions that would survive into book form. See photo in Deirdre Falvey, 'Seamus Heaney, our dad, the poet', *Irish Times* Sat. 30 June 2018, https://www.irishtimes.com/culture/books/seamus-heaney-our-dad-the-poet-by-catherine-chris-and-mick-heaney-1.3546885, accessed 22 November 2019.

57 Davis, 'From Mossbawn to Meliboeus', 102–3.

58 On figures of ascent through the hierarchy of genres, see S. J. Harrison, *Generic Enrichment*, chapter 5.

59 O'Donoghue, 'Heaney's Classics and the Bucolic', 116.

60 Heaney himself was clearly delighted to perceive unintentional humour in the Miltonic idiom of eighteenth-century 'attempts at a native georgic'. He genially describes a passage from John Philips's *Cyder* as 'more diction than drink'. 'In the Country of Convention', in *Preoccupations*, 178.

61 This kind of presumption has an obverse counterpart. Writing in 2004, Heaney recalls his meeting with Patrick Kavanagh in 1967: 'I went over and sat with him for a very short while, with the result that I nearly lost whatever credit I had just gained. I asked him what he thought of the poetry of Thomas Hardy. He immediately saw where the question was coming from and that I had to be given a lesson for my presumption. He ignored the question – which implied that as country poets who had moved from the local rural world to a literary urban milieu Hardy and he must have much in common – and answered emphatically: "Pope's a good poet. Alexander Pope."'. 'In the light of the imagination', *Irish Times* 21 October 2004, p. 14. https://www.irishtimes.com/culture/in-the-light-of-the-imagination-1.1162882?mode=print&ot=example.AjaxPageLayout.ot, accessed 8 November 2019.

62 Heaney, 'Above the Brim: On Robert Frost', 293.

63 'For Heaney, [. . .] the lovely way [in which] Vergil's bucolic poetry effortlessly reflected contemporary Roman political reality in poetry of surpassing beauty was all the Vergilian he needed to be.' Tatum, 'Mrs Vergil's Horrid Wars', 12.

64 Thanks to Charles Martindale for reminding me about the old man of Tarentum in this connection.

65 O'Donoghue has drawn attention to Heaney's 'absolute concentration on lyric poetry in his criticism': *Seamus Heaney and the Language of Poetry* (1994), 144; cited in Wheatley, 'Professing Poetry', 127–8. See also O'Donoghue, 'Heaney's *ars poetica*: *The Government of the Tongue*', 185–6.

66 Heaney, 'Feeling into Words' (1974), in *Preoccupations* (1980), 41.

67 For an argument that allusion serves a lyrical purpose in the *Aeneid*, and that the animating principle of Virgil's epic is profoundly lyric, see Putnam, 'The Lyric Genius of the *Aeneid*'.

68 Heaney, '"Apt Admonishment": Wordsworth as an Example', 28. In Mason's Longman edition of *Lyrical Ballads*, the passage is lines 95–104 in the 1802 text of the Preface.

69 Thomas discusses 'The Pitchfork' in 'The *Georgics* of Resistance', 140–1.

70 There is a similar description in Heaney's early poem 'The Barn' (*Death of a Naturalist*, 1966: 5): 'The musty dark hoarded an armoury | Of farmyard implements, harness, plough-socks.'

71 Batstone, 'Virgilian Didaxis', 206.

72 Mynors, *Georgics, ad* 1.165.

73 Compare Philoctetes' description of handling his bow in Heaney's version of Sophocles' *Philoctetes*, *The Cure at Troy*, 54–5: 'I loved the feel of it, | Its grip and give, and the grain | That was seasoned with my sweat.'

74 'The Pitchfork' illustrates Heaney's late style, an aesthetic he himself identified and analysed before other critics. Heaney describes it succinctly in the fourth paragraph of 'The Placeless Heaven: Another Look at Kavanagh' (1985), in *The Government of the Tongue*, 4. 'An Artist', a poem about Cézanne in *Station Island* (p. 116), is an

anticipation: 'His forehead like a hurled *boule* | travelling unpainted space | behind the apple and behind the mountain'.

75 Heaney, 'Glory be to the world'. *Irish Times*, Sat. 23 October 2004.

76 *OED*, s.v. 'riddle', n.2, P.1 ('obsolete'). Mac Góráin, 'The Mixed Blessing of Bacchus in Virgil's *Georgics*', *Dictynna* 11 (2014), §10; https://doi.org/10.4000/dictynna.1069, accessed 15 April 2021.

77 To take another instance, the first line of Fallon's translation sets my teeth on edge: 'What tickles the corn to laugh out loud.' In the translation's first edition (Oldcastle: Gallery Press, 2004), Fallon's corn did not laugh 'out loud' but 'in rows'. Either way, the tone strikes me as misjudged.

78 Haughton, 'Power and Hiding Places: Wordsworth and Seamus Heaney', 61.

79 Heaney himself quoted Yeats's phrase in relation to pastoral, describing 'Theocritus, Virgil, Horace, Mantuan, Marot' as 'those informing, influencing voices that were "modified in the guts of the living"' ('In the Country of Convention', in *Preoccupations*, 175.)

80 Dante, *Divine Comedy*, trans. and comm. Singleton, 2.2 (*Purgatorio: Commentary*), 3.

81 Pöschl, 'The Poetic Achievement of Virgil', 296.

82 Ricks, 'Growing Up: Review of *Death of a Naturalist*', 23.

83 Heaney, *Preoccupations*, 65. In 'Sonnets from Hellas' 6, 'Desfina', Heaney describes 'hairpin bends looped like boustrophedon' (*Electric Light*, p. 43).

84 Burris, *The Poetry of Resistance*. See also Hart, *Seamus Heaney, Poet of Contrary Progressions*. A distinctly American use of the term 'pastoral' derives in part from Leo Marx's seminal book *The Machine in the Garden* (1964). Whatever else it does, the usage generalizes the term in ways at once reductive and over comprehensive, hardening 'pastoral' to a stereotype while also covering, *inter alia*, what might otherwise have been associated with georgic. In Helen Vendler's assessment of Heaney's first three collections, for instance, 'pastoral' is associated with 'nostalgic idyll', static scenes, and anonymity – a 'pastoral' on which 'a wider social world' will inevitably intrude. The poet's personality is attributed not to the autobiographical 'I' but to the artificer sensed behind the poem, the 'sharp and idiosyncratic observer silently arranging' even the 'tableaux and friezes' of 'his anonymities'. See Vendler, *Seamus Heaney*, ch.1, esp. 28 and 36–7. My quotations are from p. 37.

85 Carson, 'Escaped from the Massacre?', 268.

86 Most notably, Longley, '"Inner Emigré" or "Artful Voyeur"?'. Generally appreciative, Seamus Deane concedes 'that the Viking myths do not correspond to Irish experience without some fairly forceful straining', though he affirms that 'the potency of the analogy of the two was at first thrilling', Deane, 'Seamus Heaney: The Timorous and the Bold', 69.

87 Quoted in Longley, '"Inner Emigré" or "Artful Voyeur"?', 65. Longley cites John Haffenden, 'Meeting Seamus Heaney: An Interview', in *Viewpoints: Poets in Conversation* (London: Faber, 1981), 64.

88 In his 1977 essay 'The Sense of Place', Heaney traces the Irish preoccupation with place and local origin with the literary tradition of *dinnseanchas*, 'poetry and tales which relate the original meanings of place names and constitute a form of mythological etymology' (*Preoccupations*, 131).

89 Heaney, *Preoccupations*, 175.

90 Carson, 'Escaped from the Massacre?', 269, 268.

91 B. O'Donoghue, Introduction to *The Cambridge Companion to Seamus Heaney*, 3.

92 Stallworthy, 'The Poet as Archaeologist'.

93 O'Driscoll, *Stepping Stones*, p. 25.

94 'Mossbawn' (1978), *Preoccupations*, 17.

95 'Mossbawn' (1978), *Preoccupations*, 17.

96 'Feeling into Words' (1974), *Preoccupations*, 41. Haughton, 'Power and Hiding Places', 63.

97 'Antaeus' (1966) and 'Hercules and Antaeus' in *North*.

98 Speaking of 'Westering', the final poem in *Wintering Out* (1972), Heaney discusses the ethnicizing trends in contemporary poetry that 'disposed [him] towards origin and the inward path'. O'Driscoll, *Stepping Stones*, 142.

99 There is a gendered polarity here, of course (besides, presumably, some reflection of the respective ages of Heaney's children at the time each poem originated), and Heaney thinks in terms of 'masculine' and 'feminine' modes of poetic language in his 1974 lecture on Hopkins, 'The Fire i' the Flint', in *Preoccupations* (1980), 79–97, at p. 88. For an excellent discussion of this topic, see Haffenden, 'Seamus Heaney and the Feminine Sensibility', treating the relevant passage from Heaney's lecture at p. 95.

100 Heaney may also be inviting us to remember a stanza of Kavanagh's 'On Looking into E. V. Rieu's Homer': 'In stubble fields the ghosts of corn are | The important spirits the imagination heeds. | Nothing dies; there are no empty | Spaces in the cleanest-reaped fields.' Kavanagh, *Collected Poems*, ed. Quinn, 185.

101 Heaney tells O'Driscoll, 'For years I've been writing poems where I meet ghosts and shades; they are among the ones I like and value most'. *Stepping Stones*, 472.

102 Reviewing *Electric Light*, Robert Potts not only expressed exasperation with Heaney's 'enlisting of ghosts to say his lines', but snorted at the notion of Larkin quoting *Dante*: '[…] yes, that would certainly be a surprise.' 'The View from Olympia', in *The Guardian*, 7 April 2001, https://www.theguardian.com/books/2001/apr/07/poetry.tseliotprizeforpoetry2001, accessed 5 November 2019.

103 Heaney, '"Apt Admonishment": Wordsworth as an Example', 25.

104 O'Driscoll, *Stepping Stones*, 410.

105 '… as though the future were somehow contained and bodied into that "undrowned" man in the past': McDonald, '"Weird Brightness"', 165, a page notable for its exacting reading of this poem.

106 Robert Hass and Seamus Heaney, 'Sounding Lines: The Art of Translating Poetry'. Interview published February 1999, University of California, Berkeley: Townsend Center for the Humanities. https://townsendcenter.berkeley.edu/sites/default/files/publications/OP20_Sounding_Lines.pdf at p. 16, accessed 5 November 2019. Quoted in Riley, '"The Forewarned Journey Back"', 209.

107 Ware, 'The Ashplant and the Golden Bough', 243.

108 Indeed some have found it insufficiently unsettling. In McDonald's reading of the poem, 'the ending's note of wistfulness slips readily into a weak sentimentality'. For McDonald, '"Seeing Things" III is not fully successful in exploring its own ironies of setting, genre, and Virgilian perspective, for it allows these to become imperfectly reconciled forces'. '"Weird Brightness"', 165.

109 Falconer, 'Heaney and Virgil's Underworld Journey', 202.

110 Dante, *Divine Comedy*, ed. Singleton, I.2 (*Inferno: Commentary*), 200–201.

111 Neil Corcoran reads 'Sandstone Keepsake' quite differently. Since he reads through the prism of the allusion to *Hamlet* which he perceives in Heaney's 'not about to set times wrong or right', he accentuates the poem's elements of quietist self-criticism. 'Heaney's Shakespeare', 68–70.

112 H. O'Donoghue, 'Heaney, *Beowulf*, and the Medieval Literature of the North', 197–200.

113 H. O'Donoghue, 'Heaney, *Beowulf*, and the Medieval Literature of the North', 200.

114 Parry, 'The Two Voices of Virgil's *Aeneid*'.

115 Heaney, 'Envies and Identifications', 256.

116 'In *Station Island* (1984), it is Dante, not Virgil, who provides Heaney with an otherwordly guide through the purgatorial passage enacted in that volume.' Falconer, 'Heaney and Virgil's Underworld Journey', 181.

117 'Heaney's Virgil is a poet of tragedy and melancholy; quintessentially he gives voice to the *lacrimae rerum*.' Falconer, 'Heaney and Virgil's Underworld Journey', 180, citing Heaney's 'Secular and Millennial Miłosz' in *Finders Keepers*, 411–13. (Falconer continues, however: 'And yet Heaney also sees in Virgil a farmer-poet who delights in the earth's renewal, and a visionary who dreamed of the soul's metamorphosis and regeneration.')

118 McDonald, '"Weird Brightness"', 179.

119 As Falconer observes in a brilliant reading of this passage, in Heaney's translation in 'The Riverbank Field', 'the souls don't seem [as, presumably, in Virgil] to return in an entirely blank mental state; they have lost "memories of this underworld", but perhaps they retain memory of former lives before they died', so that 'for Heaney, the return via Lethe constitutes a forgetful rupture, a cutting loose from the past, but also a memorious continuity'. 'Heaney and Virgil's Underworld Journey', 196–7.

120 Heaney greatly admired Yeats's 'The Cold Heaven': see his Oxford lecture 'Joy or Night' in *The Redress of Poetry*, reprinted in *Finders Keepers*. McDonald also links

Heaney's 'weird brightness' with *Aeneid* 6.640–1, *largior hic campos aether et lumine vestit | purpureo, solemque suum, sua sidera norunt*, and Heaney's translation of these lines, 'Here a more spacious air sheds brightness | Over the land; they enjoy their own sun here | And their own stars'. McDonald, '"Weird Brightness"', 177–8. Virgil, *Aeneid VI*, trans. Heaney, 35 (ll. 869–771).

121 McDonald, '"Weird Brightness"', 178.

122 Heaney, '"Apt Admonishment": Wordsworth as Example', 28. Recalling the eel-fishing 'dawn journey' with Louis O'Neill and Pat O'Hagan commemorated in 'Casualty' (*Field Work*, pp. 14–17), Heaney tells O'Driscoll, 'The shine of morning light on the lough had an otherworldly quality, it reminded me of the dawn scene in *Hamlet*, when the ghost fades on the crowing of the cock – so in "Casualty" Louis then turns into a "dawn-sniffing revenant"' (*Stepping Stones*, 93).

123 Poetry Foundation podcast dated 16 November 2010, featuring a recording made at the Poetry Proms that year; https://www.poetryfoundation.org/podcasts/75876/seamus-heaney (at 19:39), accessed 25 October 2019. See Murphy, 'Heaney Translating Heaney, 361–2.

124 Cuda, 'The Use of Memory', 158.

125 Cuda, 'The Use of Memory', 159.

126 Indeed some of Eliot's ideas about poetic memory might be called 'Wordsworthian': see the passage from *The Use of Poetry and the Use of Criticism* (1933) excerpted under the heading 'Poetry Imagery' ('Only a part of an author's imagery comes from his reading. . . .'), on the recto page facing the passage about 'Auditory Imagination' in the Penguin *Selected Prose*, ed. Hayward, 95. By the term 'Eliotic' I mean to suggest, too, a Modernist poetics of fragmentation and synchronicity.

127 *Finders Keepers*, 27.

128 *Finders Keepers*, 36–7.

129 *Finders Keepers*, 33–4. T. S. Eliot, *The Use of Poetry and the Use of Criticism* (London: Faber, 1933), ch. 6, 'Matthew Arnold', at 118–19. In Eliot, *Selected Prose*, ed. Hayward, 94.

130 *Preoccupations*, 150–69, 150.

131 Heaney, 'The Indefatigable Hoof-taps: Sylvia Plath', in *The Government of the Tongue*, 148–9, in which Heaney's quotation of Eliot is slightly adapted.

132 Heaney, 'The Indefatigable Hoof-taps: Sylvia Plath', in *The Government of the Tongue*, 148–70 ('get beyond the ego': 148). 'I do not suggest that the self is not the proper arena of poetry. But I believe that the greatest work occurs when a certain self-forgetfulness is attained, or at least a fullness of self-possession denied to Sylvia Plath' (168). However, Heaney finally declares Plath to be consonant with the long quotation he offers as a definitive formulation of the ideal dialectic of poetic creativity, from Wordsworth's 1802 Preface to *Lyrical Ballads* (in Mason's Longman edition, lines 148–74), at 169.

133 Martindale, 'The Ruins of Rome', 116.

134 Martindale, 'The Ruins of Rome', 115.

135 'The Makings of a Music' (1978), in Heaney, *Preoccupations*, 61.

136 In Heaney's reading of 'Electric Light' in the RTÉ recording of his poems
(15-CD box set, RTÉ/Lannan 2009), Heaney skips the first two lines of the poem's
ninth stanza, so the sentence of the eighth stanza concludes, '. . . In the railway-
facing yards of fleeting England, | Fields of grain like the Field of the Cloth of Gold.'
The omission was obviously deliberate. Perhaps Heaney felt the lines were too
outlandish.

137 Larkin, *Complete Poems*, ed. Burnett, 58.

138 Hass and Heaney, 'Sounding Lines: The Art of Translating Poetry', 16.

139 Austin *ad Aeneid* 6.42 says 'the arrangement [of words in the line] is intricate, but
the rhythm suggests that *ingens* ['huge'] should be taken with *antrum* ['cave'], not
with *latus* ['rock face'].

140 Austin *ad Aeneid* 6.44.

141 O'Driscoll, *Stepping Stones*, 389. Ferry's translations continued to inspire Heaney. In
Stepping Stones (at 423) Heaney says he came across Horace's *Odes* 1.34, the
template for his 9/11 poem 'Anything Can Happen' (*District and Circle*, p.13), in
Ferry's translation of the complete *Odes* (published 1998).

142 Gauthier, 'An Interview with Paul Muldoon', 54–5.

143 O'Driscoll, *Stepping Stones*, 472; cited by Falconer, 'Heaney and Virgil's Underworld
Journey', 186.

144 As I observe in my Introduction, Heaney's oat stalks can also be read as
corresponding to the flowers strewn in memory of Marcellus at *Aeneid* 6.883–6. See
Putnam, 'Virgil and Heaney: "Route 110"', 106, and Ware, 'The Ashplant and the
Golden Bough', 236–7.

145 The fragment of Heaney's draft for an afterword to *Aeneid VI* reads: 'For the
contemporary reader, it is the best of books and the worst of books. Best because of
its mythopoeic visions, the twilit fetch of its language, the pathos of the many
encounters it allows the living Aeneas with his familiar dead. Worst because of its
imperial certitude, its celebration of Rome's manifest destiny and the catalogue of
Roman heroes . . .' 'Note on the Text', in *Aeneid Book VI*, trans. Heaney, 51.

146 Explaining his procedure in 'Route 110', Heaney explained that 'it was a matter [. . .]
of a relatively simple "mythic method" being employed over the twelve sections'.
'Translator's Note' in *Aeneid Book VI*, trans. Heaney, viii.

147 Falconer, 'Heaney and Virgil's Underworld Journey', 197.

148 Falconer, 'Heaney and Virgil's Underworld Journey', 196.

149 On the genesis of 'A Kite for Aibhín' and a text of Heaney's uncollected translation
of 'L'Aquilone', see Morisco, 'Two Poets and a Kite: Seamus Heaney and Giovanni
Pascoli', *Linguae* 12/1 (2013), 35–45 doi: 10.7358/ling-2013-001-mori, http://www.

ledonline.it\\linguae, accessed 26 November 2019. Parenthetical page numbers are
to this article. For a reading of 'A Kite for Aibhín', see Falconer, 'Heaney and Virgil's
Underground Journey', 203–4.

150 Murphy, 'Heaney Translating Heaney', 363.

151 O'Driscoll, *Stepping Stones*, 351.

152 *OED* 'windfall', compounds, C.1, 'Also applied (poetically) to a flood of unexpected
light', citing the line from Thomas's 'Fern Hill'.

153 Deidre Falvey, 'Seamus Heaney, our dad the poet, by Catherine, Chris and Mick
Heaney', *Irish Times* Saturday 30 June 2018, at https://www.irishtimes.com/culture/
books/seamus-heaney-our-dad-the-poet-by-catherine-chris-and-mick-
heaney-1.3546885, accessed 25 November 2019.

154 Wall, 'A Dialect Glossary for Seamus Heaney's Works'.

155 'Translator's Note', in *Aeneid VI*, trans. Heaney, vii.

156 'Translator's Note', Heaney, *Aeneid VI*, trans. Heaney, vii, ix.

157 McDonald, '"Weird Brightness"', 175–6.

Conclusion

1   Other important critical works include Fowler, '"Purple Shining Lilies": Imagining
the *Aeneid* in Contemporary Poetry'.

2   Nagel, 'Farming Poetry', 1. I am indebted to Alison Martin, who kindly sent me her
paper on Sackville-West's *The Garden*, presented at the conference 'Reworking
Georgic' at the School of English, University of Leeds, 10 September 2019.

3   Braund, 'Women and Earth' 199–200.

4   'My position may be summarized by saying that the persons for whom Vergil was
writing were *almost* farmers – and that the interest lies in the *almost*'. Thibodeau,
Playing the Farmer, 19. Thibodeau acknowledges Wilkinson, 53, who describes
Virgil's typical reader as 'an absentee landlord'.

5   Three important critical discussions that focus on tone, readership, rhetorical
address and authorial self-representation are Perkell, *The Poet's Truth*; Dalzell, *The
Criticism of Didactic Poetry*, chs 1 and 4; and Volk, *The Poetics of Latin Didactic*, chs 1
and 4.

6   Possibly the most momentous episode in the history of the reception of British
georgic, though not contemporary with the 'received' author himself, is John Clare's
account of his first teenage encounter with Thomson's *Seasons*, contextualized in
John Goodridge and Kelsey Thornton, 'John Clare: The Trespasser', in *John Clare in
Context*, ed. Hugh Haughton et al. (Cambridge: Cambridge University Press, 1994),
87–129, revised in Goodridge and Thornton, *John Clare, Trespasser*.

7   Glendinning, *Vita*, 166; Blyth, 'A Sort of English Georgics', 21.

8 Johnson, *Lives of the Poets*, ed. Lonsdale 4.184.

9 Knight, *Roman Vergil*, Preface, viii. See Ziolkowski, *Virgil and the Moderns*, 129–30.

10 Wilkinson, *The Georgics of Virgil*, 311.

11 Woolf, *Orlando*, ed. Whitworth, 163.

12 For an 'ultra-modernist' translation of the *Georgics*, see that by Kristina Chew (2002), mentioned by Braund, 'Women and Earth', 240, promising treatment in her *A Cultural History of Translations of Virgil: From the Twelfth Century to the Present*, forthcoming from Cambridge University Press.

13 Bazargan, 'The Uses of the Land', 31.

14 See Fowler, 'Country House Poems', and Chalker, *The English Georgic*.

15 Braund ('Women and Earth', 194, 241) observes that Sackville-West's 1919 novel *Heritage* bears an untranslated epigraph from *Georgics* 4.559–61, 565–6, so the *Georgics* can hardly have been quite unknown to her.

16 Blyth, 'A Sort of English Georgics', 22. The kinship with Thomson was pointed out by J. C. Squire in his two reviews, 'Books of the Day: British Georgics', *Observer*, 10 October 1926, and 'Poetry', *London Mercury*, January 1927, 318–21, at 318–19.

17 Woolf, *Orlando*, 163.

18 Quoted in Blyth, 'A Sort of English Georgics', 19. *Letters of Virginia Woolf*, ed. Nicolson and Trautmann, 3.569 (no. 1976, 29 December 1928).

19 Sackville-West wrote to her husband, 14 April 1945, 'As to remembering whether a line is by me or by someone else, you know very well that I never could. The first shock of this realisation came when I very laboriously hammered out a line, choosing every word most carefully, and arrived at: "Men are but children of a larger growth." Since then I have been cautious.' Harold Nicolson, *Diaries and Letters*, ed. N. Nicolson, 2.447–8. Quoted in Pomeroy, 'Within Living Memory', 273, 289. N. Nicolson and Pomeroy misattribute the line to Dryden's *Alexander's Feast*; in fact it is from *All for Love*, Act 4 (Dollabella).

20 On the *ego ille* incipit, see Mac Góráin, 'Untitled/*Arma virumque*'.

21 Sackville-West appears to have known Cowper remarkably well. Replying from Tehran on 11 March 1927 to a letter from Woolf dated 21 February 1927, in which Woolf gives her (mostly favourable) impressions of reading *The Task* for the first time, Sackville-West writes 'Yes, I have read Cowper' and then quotes him very aptly. '"The stable yields a stercoraceous heap . . ." [*The Task* 3.463] | It bears an unpleasant resemblance to *The Land*, doesn't it? But it has its good moments. | "While fancy, like the finger of a clock, | Runs the great circuit, and is still at home." [*The Task* 4.118–19]'. These are, or were, well-known lines, and Sackville-West was probably quoting from memory. (The 1785 text of *The Task* read 'stercorarious', changed in the third edition (1787) to 'stercoraceous' (*OED* s.v. 'stercorarious' and 'stercoraceous'). Sackville-West clearly knows Cowper well enough to quote him, first with the superiority of preemptive self-deprecation, and then with an attractive couplet that sounds like

something she herself could have written. It should also be remembered that *The Garden* shares its title with Book 3 of *The Task*. Woolf: *The Letters of Virginia Woolf* 3.333 (no. 1718, 18–23 February 1928). Sackville-West: *Selected Writings*, ed. Caws, 92.

22 In *The Land*, 'Summer', 76–8 , a sequence of italicized trimester and tetrameter stanzas that name Lovelace, Waller and Herrick, as well as Sackville-West's favourite, Marvell. Shakespearean echoes and vocabulary are rife in both georgics; see Pomeroy, 'Within Living Memory', 273 and 289. 'Scrannel' (*The Land*, p. 61) derives from Milton's *Lycidas*, but is not used allusively. 'With steps obedient and slow' (*The Garden*, p. 90) must be counted an allusion to the end of *Paradise Lost*. *The Garden's* 'Winter' includes a reference to Keats as a *lusus naturae* of native genius, p. 54. 'Spring' remarks that Wordsworth, for all that he admired celandine, 'was no gardener, his eyes were raised' (p. 70). One may well catch an echo of Blake's 'The Sick Rose' in 'even in the heart | Of beauty feeds the pallid worm of death' (p. 15, quoted below), but whether this is a meaningful allusion is another matter.

23 *The Garden* p. 63 also alludes to *The Waste Land* 19–30, a passage Sackville-West criticizes in her lecture 'Some Tendencies of Modern English Poetry' (1928), *Selected Writings*, ed. Caws, 176–7.

24 'This [the *Georgics*] is no more a didactic poem than Ovid's *Ars Amatoria*': Wilkinson, *The Georgics of Virgil*, 3.

25 On the titlepage bearing the title 'Husbandry' (cancelling an even earlier title, 'Work') in the typescript/manuscript of *The Land*, 1926, Huntington Library HM 41088, Sackville-West copies out the Latin epigraph together with Fairclough's Loeb translation (unrevised, naturally), which I quote.

26 Grene's translation in Nelson, *God and the Land*, 17. See Pomeroy, 'Within Living Memory', 274.

27 *The Nation and Athenaeum* (6 November 1926), 188. The reviewer is identified by Virginia Woolf in a letter to Sackville-West, tentatively dated 12 October 1926; *Letters of Virginia Woolf*, 3.298 (no. 1679). See Thomas and Küchemann, 'Sidney Barrington Gates. 1893–1973'.

28 Seneca made this incidental remark polemically, in the specific context of criticizing Virgil on an agricultural point, namely whether beans and millet should be sown in spring or summer. Though Seneca's distinction goes straight to Virgil's basic priorities, it should not be entirely divorced from its original context. See Spurr, 'Agriculture and *the Georgics*', at 164–6.

29 'By using the interesting concept of "economic fantasy", Thibodeau rightly avoids separating (as many have done) form and farm, culture and agriculture in his new discussion of Vergil's agrarian poem'. Alessandro Barchiesi's dustjacket blurb for Thibodeau, *Playing the Farmer*.

30 Saunders, *Bucolic Ecology*. Rebecca Armstrong, *Vergil's Green Thoughts*; see her Introduction, esp. 41–9.

31 Thibodeau, *Playing the Farmer*, 245–7.

32 See Raitt, *Vita and Virginia*, ch. 2.

33 Raitt (*Vita and Virginia*, 11–13) cites Williams, *The Country and the City*, 248 and 254. See Williams's ch. 21, a contextualizing ideological critique of Georgian literature with rural settings.

34 Braund, 'Women and Earth', 195. See Perkell, 'The Golden Age and Its Contradictions in the Poetry of Vergil', 22. For a thorough discussion, see Gale, *Virgil on the Nature of Things*, ch. 5, 'Labor Improbus'.

35 C. [Clarence] Henry Warren [1895–1966], 'Gems and Coloured Glass', *Spectator Literary Supplement*, 30 October 1926, p. 758. A writer and broadcaster on agricultural topics, the reviewer was brought up in Kent; see Warren, 'C. Henry Warren: A Contented Countryman?'.

36 Squire, 'Books of the Day, English Georgics', *Observer* 10 October 1926, p. 6, comparing Thomson's passage on a plundered beehive ('Autumn', 1172–86) with a passage from Sackville-West's treatment of bees in her 'Spring' (*The Land*, pp. 42–3, from 'But if you shake them from their wicker hutch' through 'May reap his wealth from their calamity'). Squire admired Sackville-West's section on beekeeping especially (his 1927 review in the *London Mercury* quotes the verse paragraph beginning 'I have known honey from the Syrian hills', *The Land*, pp. 39–40), valuing particularly the poet's digressive flights of the imagination.

37 Quoted in Pomeroy, 'Within Living Memory', at 283. Thanks to Alison Martin for kindly supplying the reference, Huntington Library, MS HM 43232.

38 Letter to Harold Nicolson dated Sissinghurst, 8 December 1942. Nicolson, *Diaries and Letters*, 2.265. She must also have feared that *The Land* had exhausted the topics it shares with *The Garden*.

39 At this transitional point in *Georgics* 3, Virgil engages in paradox as well as ambiguity. He has just reined himself in lest he get carried away with *amor* or love of his theme, 3.285, yet as Richard Thomas observes, that theme is *amor* itself: specifically, how love possesses the grander animals, horses and cattle. With pointed contrast, Virgil announces his next topic of tending sheep and goats as *angustum*, though this also plays a part in 'the poem's development of Callimachean programmatic ideas'. Thomas ed. *Georgics ad* 3.290.

40 Boswell, *Boswell's Life of Johnson*, ed. Hill, rev. Powell, 2.453.

41 Kerrigan, *Virgil's Map*, seeks precisely to redress the imbalance of 'an aesthetic trend in the poem's scholarly reception', 2.

42 Wordsworth, 1802 version of the Preface to *Lyrical Ballads*, ll. 506–7, 520–1, in Mason, ed., *Lyrical Ballads*, 2nd edn (pp. 73–4). On Wordsworth's radical insistence on the principle of poetic pleasure, Mason cites Trilling, 'The Fate of Pleasure', 58.

43 Wilkinson, *The Georgics of Virgil*, 4–15, Addison quoted at 4 and Coleridge at 15 (from *Biographia Literaria*, ch. 14, end of seventh paragraph).

44 On variety, see Wilkinson, *The Georgics of Virgil*, ch. 4 *passim* but esp. 71–5,
   and 142–3. See too Fitzgerald, *Variety*; on English 'variety', Latin *varietas*, and
   Greek *poikilia*, ch. 1, esp. 12–21, and on the idea of variety in *Georgics* 1,
   pp. 43–6.

45 Pomeroy, 'Within Living Memory', 282.

46 Addison, 'Essay on the *Georgics*', 146.

47 *The Spectator*, ed. Bond, 3.538.

48 Thoreau, *Walden*, ed. Fender, 75.

49 On Sackville-West's use of botanical names, see Nagel, 'Naming Plants in *The
   Garden*'.

50 Gates, review in *The Nation and Athenaeum*, 6 November 1926, 188.

51 George Forrest (1873–1932), Reginald Farrer (1880–1920), Robert Fortune (1812–
   80), Frank Kingdon-Ward (1885–1958): celebrated British botanists/plant collectors
   and explorers.

52 *The Spectator*, ed. Bond, 1.293.

53 On the 'Foreign Lands' theme, see Wilkinson, *The Georgics of Virgil*, 67, 77, 87. On
   imperialism in British georgic, Kaul, *Poems of Nation, Anthems of Empire*; Griffin,
   Patriotism and Poetry, and Kerrigan, *Virgil's Map*.

54 García Ruiz, '*AEQVOR*', esp. 694–5.

55 See Kerrigan, *Virgil's Map*, 23ff.

56 Thomas speaks of Virgil's 'ethnographical interest'; *Georgics* ed. Thomas *ad* 1.56–9,
   see also *ad* 2.136–76. For an excellent introduction to Virgil's geographical
   imaginary, see Kerrigan, *Virgil's Map*, ch. 1.

57 Kerrigan, *Virgil's Map*, 23–5; quotation refers to *Georgics* 2.114–21.

58 'As a piece of logical argument, the passage fails to hold together – yet the
   inconsequence is quite beside the point.' Thibodeau, *Playing the Farmer*, 135. Thomas
   comments in the headnote to 1.43–70 that the passage, while didactic in character,
   'establish[es] from the outset the aesthetics behind even the more "mundane"
   sections of the poem'.

59 Kerrigan, *Virgil's Map*, 29.

60 Kerrigan, *Virgil's Map*, 1. Thibodeau reads *Georgics* 2.497 through its Horatian
   reception in *Satires* 2.6.53, where Horace's speaker on his farm is happy to declare
   he's heard no news about the Dacians (*Playing the Farmer*, 213).

61 Virgil, *Georgics*, trans. Kristina Chew (Indianapolis: Hackett, 2002), 74.

62 See Mynors as well as Thomas *ad* 2.498, and Putnam, *Virgil's Poem of the Earth*,
   152–3.

63 Augustus, of course, attended gladiatorial spectacles. Maecenas must have done so
   occasionally too. But do we imagine Maecenas seeking out the games? In his first
   Satire, Horace humorously casts himself in the role of retired gladiator and
   Maecenas as the old gladiator's patron. The humour depends on a perceived

incongruousness in the comparison between literary and gladiatorial arenas, but of course the games themselves are equally familiar to poet and implied reader.

64 Thibodeau, *Playing the Farmer*, 204–5. See ch. 6 *passim*, 'The Reception of the *Georgics* in Early Imperial Rome'.

65 Woolf, *The Common Reader*, vol. 1, 1.

Bibliography

Addison, Joseph. 'Essay on the *Georgics*'. In *The Works of John Dryden*. Gen. ed. H. T. Swedenberg, Jr. (Berkeley: University of California Press, 1956–), vol. 5, *Poems: The Works of Virgil in English, 1697*, ed. William Frost and Vinton A. Dearing (1987). 145–53.

Addison, Joseph. *Spectator* nos 69 and 411. In *The Spectator*, edited by Donald F. Bond. 5 vols. Oxford: Clarendon Press, 1965.

Alpers, Paul. *The Singer of the Eclogues*. Berkeley: University of California Press, 1979.

Alpers, Paul. *What is Pastoral?* Chicago: University of Chicago Press, 1996.

Armstrong, Isobel. '"Tintern Abbey": From Augustan to Romantic'. In *Augustan Worlds: Essays in Honour of A. R. Humphreys*, edited by J. C. Hilson, M. M. B. Jones and J. R. Watson, 261–79. Leicester: Leicester University Press, 1978.

Armstrong, Rebecca. *Vergil's Green Thoughts: Plants, Humans, and the Divine*. Oxford: Oxford University Press, 2019.

Atkins, Peter. *Galileo's Finger: Ten Great Ideas of Science*. Oxford: Oxford University Press, 2003.

Auden, W. H. *Collected Poems*, ed. Edward Mendelson. Rev. edn. London: Faber, 2007.

Auden, W. H., 'The Greeks and Us'. In Auden, *Forewords and Afterwords*, edited by Edward Mendelson, 3–32. London: Faber, 1973.

Auerbach, Erich. *Mimesis*, trans. W. R. Trask. Princeton: Princeton University Press, 1953, reprinted.

Barchiesi, Alessandro. *Homeric Effects in Vergil's Narrative* (*La traccia del modello*, 1984), trans. Ilaria Marchesi and Matt Fox. Princeton: Princeton University Press, 2015.

Barchiesi, Alessandro. 'Learned Eyes: Poets, Viewers, Image Makers'. In *The Cambridge Companion to the Age of Augustus*, edited by Karl Galinsky, 281–305. Cambridge: Cambridge University Press, 2005.

Barchiesi, Alessandro. 'Virgilian Narrative: Ecphrasis'. In *The Cambridge Companion to Virgil*, 2nd edn, edited by C. Martindale and F. Mac Góráin, 413–24. Cambridge: Cambridge University Press, 2019.

Barrell, John. 'The uses of Dorothy: "The Language of the Sense" in '"Tintern Abbey"'. In Barrell, *Poetry, Language and Politics*, 137–67. Manchester: University of Manchester Press, 1988.

Batstone, William. 'Virgilian didaxis: value and meaning in the *Georgics*'. In *The Cambridge Companion to Virgil*, 2nd edn, edited by C. Martindale and F. Mac Góráin, 193–215. Cambridge: Cambridge University Press, 2019.

Bazargan, Susan. 'The Uses of the Land: Vita Sackville-West's Pastoral Writings and Virginia Woolf's *Orlando*'. *Woolf Studies Annual* 5 (1999): 25–55.

Becker, Andrew Sprague. *The Shield of Achilles and the Poetics of Ekphrasis*. Lanham, MD: Rowan & Littlefield, 1995.

Bespaloff, Rachel. 'On the *Iliad*' (1943, trans. 1947). In Simone Weil/Rachel Bespaloff, *War and the Iliad,* trans. Mary McCarthy. intro. Christopher Benfey, 39–100. New York: New York Review of Books, 2005.

Blyth, Ian. 'A Sort of English Georgics: Vita Sackville-West's *The Land*'. *Forum for Modern Language Studies* 45 (2009): 19–31.

Boswell, James. *Boswell's Life of Johnson,* ed. G. B. Hill, rev. L. F. Powell. 6 vols. Oxford: Clarendon Press, 1934.

Bowersock, G. W. *From Gibbon to Auden: Essays on the Classical Tradition*. Oxford: Oxford University Press, 2009.

Boyd, Barbara Weiden. '*Non Enarrabile Textum*: Ekphrastic Trespass and Narrative Ambiguity in the *Aeneid*'. *Vergilius* 41 (1995): 71–90.

Brandes, Rand, and Seamus Heaney. 'Seamus Heaney: An Interview'. *Salmagundi* 80 (1988), 4–21.

Brater, Enoch. 'Tom Stoppard's Brit/lit/crit'. In *The Cambridge Companion to Tom Stoppard*, edited by Katherine E. Kelly, 203–12. Cambridge: Cambridge University Press, [2001] 2002.

Braund, Susanna. 'Women and Earth: Female Responses to the *Georgics* in the Twentieth and Twenty-First Centuries'. In *Reflections and New Perspectives on Virgil's Georgics*, edited by B. Xinyue and N. Freer, 185–200. London: Bloomsbury, 2019.

Brooks, R. A. '*Discolor Aura*. Reflections on the Golden Bough', *AJP* 74 (1952): 260–80.

Burris, Sidney. *The Poetry of Resistance: Seamus Heaney and the Pastoral Tradition*. Athens, OH: Ohio University Press, 1990.

Burrow, Colin. 'You've listened long enough: Review of Heaney, trans., *Aeneid: Book VI*', *London Review of Books* 38/8 (April 2016): 13–14.

Buxton, Rachel. *Robert Frost and Northern Irish Poetry*. Oxford: Clarendon Press, 2004.

Carrier, David. *Poussin's Paintings: A Study in Art-Historical Methodology*. University Park, PA: Pennsylvania State University Press, 1993.

Carson, Ciaran. 'Escaped from the Massacre?' (*The Honest Ulsterman* 50 (1975): 183–6.) In *A Twentieth-Century Reader: Texts and Debates*, edited by S. Gupta and D. Johnson, 267–71. London: Routledge, 2005.

Cassidy, David, et al. *Understanding Physics*. New York: Springer, 2002.

Chalker, John. *The English Georgic: A Study in the Development of a Form*. London: Routledge and Kegan Paul, 1969.

Classical Receptions Journal 5.2 (2013), special issue, edited by Lorna Hardwick, 'Redeeming the Text: Twenty years on'.

Conte, Gian Biagio. 'An Interpretation of the Tenth *Eclogue*' (1980; trans. 1986). In *Vergil's Eclogues* (Oxford Readings in Classical Studies), edited by Katharina Volk, 216–44. Oxford: Oxford University Press, 2008.

Conte, Gian Biagio. 'The Virgilian Paradox: An Epic of Drama and Pathos' (1998, trans. 1999). In G. B. Conte, *The Poetry of Pathos: Studies in Virgilian Epic*, edited by S. J. Harrison. Oxford: Oxford University Press, 2009.

Corcoran, Neil. 'Antaeus on the Move'. In *Seamus Heaney and the Classics: Bann Valley Muses*, edited by S. Harrison, F. Macintosh and H. Eastman, 26–37. New York: Oxford University Press, 2019.

Corcoran, Neil. 'Heaney's Shakespeare'. *Essays in Criticism* 70 (2020): 64–86.

Corcoran, Neil. 'Seamus Heaney and the Art of the Exemplary'. *YES* 17 (1987): 117–27.

Corcoran, Neil. *Poetry and Responsibility*. Liverpool: Liverpool University Press, 2014.

Cox, Fiona. *Sybilline Sisters: Virgil's Presence in Contemporary Women's Writing*. Oxford: Oxford University Press, 2011.

Crutchfield, James P., J. Doyne Farmer, Norman H. Packard and Robert S. Shaw. 'Chaos'. *Scientific American* 254/12 (Dec. 1986): 46–57.

Cuda, Anthony J. 'The Use of Memory: Seamus Heaney, T. S. Eliot, and the Unpublished Epigraph to *North*'. *Journal of Modern Literature* 28 (2005): 152–75.

Dalzell, Alexander. *The Criticism of Didactic Poetry: Essays on Lucretius, Virgil, and Ovid*. Toronto: University of Toronto Press, 1996.

Dante. *Divine Comedy*, trans. and comm. Charles S. Singleton. Corr. edn. Princeton: Princeton University Press, 1977.

Davie, Donald. *Collected Poems*, ed. Neil Powell. Manchester: Carcanet, 2002.

Davis, P. J. 'Vergil's *Georgics* and the Pastoral Ideal'. In *Virgil's Ascraean Song: Ramus Essays on the Georgics*, edited by A. J. Boyle, 22–33. Berwick, Victoria: Aureal, 1979.

Davis, Wes. 'From Mossbawn to Meliboeus: Seamus Heaney's Ambivalent Pastoralism'. *Southwest Review* 92 (2007): 100–15.

Deane, Seamus. 'Seamus Heaney: The Timorous and the Bold' (excerpt from *Celtic Revivals* (London, 1985): 174–86). In *Seamus Heaney* (New Casebooks Series), edited by Michael Allen, 64–77. Basingstoke: Macmillan, 1997.

DeMaria, R., Jr., and R. D. Brown, eds. *Classical Literature and its Reception*. Malden, MA: Blackwell, 2007.

Donaghy, Michael, and Paul Muldoon. 'A Conversation with Paul Muldoon'. *Chicago Review* 35 (1985): 76–85.

Donnelly, Brian. '"The Digging Skeleton *After Baudelaire*". Seamus Heaney'. *Irish University Review* 39/2 (2009): 246–54.

Du Quesnay, Ian M. LeM. 'Vergil's Fourth *Eclogue*'. In *Papers of the Liverpool Latin Seminar, 1976*, edited by Francis Cairns, 25–99. Liverpool: Cairns, 1977.

Edmunds, Lowell. *Intertextuality and the Reading of Roman Poetry*. Baltimore: Johns Hopkins University Press, 2001.

Edquist, Harriet. 'Aspects of Theocritean *otium*'. *Ramus* 4 (1974): 101–14.

Eliot, T. S. 'Tradition and the Individual Talent'. 1929. In *Selected Essays*, 3rd edn. London: Faber, 1951 (reprint).

Empson, William. *Seven Kinds of Ambiguity*. 2nd edn. New York: New Directions, 1947.

Fairer, David. *'Gaps and Tracings: Gothic Lines in the 1790s'*. The Landor Lecture: 1. Centre for Romantic Studies, English Department, University of Wales, Aberystwyth, 2006. Pamphlet (ISBN 978-0-9554345-0-1).

Fairer, David. *English Poetry of the Eighteenth Century 1700–1789*. London: Longman, 2003.

Fairer, David. *Organising Poetry: The Coleridge Circle, 1790–1798*. Oxford: Oxford University Press, 2009.

Fairer, David, and Christine Gerrard, eds. *Eighteenth-Century Poetry: An Annotated Anthology*. 2nd edn. Oxford: Blackwell, 2004.

Falconer, Rachel. 'Heaney and Virgil's Underworld Journey'. In *Seamus Heaney and the Classics: Bann Valley Muses*, edited by S. Harrison, F. Macintosh and H. Eastman, 180–204. Oxford: Oxford University Press, 2019.

Falconer, Rachel. 'Wordsworth Un-Englished'. In *Fashioning England and the English: Literature, Nation, Gender*, edited by Rahel Orgis and Matthias Heim, 171–200. London: Palgrave Macmillan, 2018.

Falvey, Deirdre. 'Seamus Heaney, our dad, the poet'. *Irish Times,* Sat. 30 June 2018. https://www.irishtimes.com/culture/books/seamus-heaney-our-dad-the-poet-by-catherine-chris-and-mick-heaney-1.3546885, accessed 22 November 2019.

Fantazzi, Charles. 'Virgilian Pastoral and Roman Love Poetry'. *AJP* 87 (1966): 171–91.

Feeney, Denis. *Caesar's Calendar: Ancient Time and the Beginnings of History*. Berkeley: University of California Press, 2007.

Fenton, James. *The Strength of Poetry*. Oxford: Oxford University Press, 2001.

Fitzgerald, William. 'Vergil in Music'. In *A Companion to Vergil's Aeneid and its Tradition*, edited by Joseph Farrell and Michael C. J. Putnam, 341–52. Malden, MA: Wiley-Blackwell, 2010.

Fitzgerald, William. *Variety: The Life of a Roman Concept*. Chicago: University of Chicago Press, 2016.

Fowler, Alastair. 'Country House Poems: The Politics of a Genre'. *The Seventeenth Century* 1 (1986): 1–14.

Fowler, Don. 'Narrate and Describe: The Problem of Ekphrasis'. *Journal of Roman Studies* 81 (1991): 25–35.

Fowler, Rowena. '"Purple Shining Lilies": Imagining the *Aeneid* in Contemporary Poetry'. In *Living Classics: Greece and Rome in Contemporary Poetry in English*, edited by S. J. Harrison, 238–54. Oxford: Oxford University Press, 2009.

Fowler, Rowena. 'Heaney and Hesiod'. In *Seamus Heaney and the Classics: Bann Valley Muses*, edited by S. Harrison, F. Macintosh and H. Eastman, 38–49. Oxford: Oxford University Press, 2019.

Freer, Nicholas. 'Virgil's *Georgics* and the Epicurean Sirens of Poetry'. In *Reflections and New Perspectives on Virgil's Georgics*, edited by Bobby Xinyue and Nicholas Freer, 79–90. London: Bloomsbury, 2019.

Frost, Robert. *Collected Poems, Prose & Plays,* ed. Richard Poirier and Mark Richardson. NY: Library of America, 1995.

Fuller, John. *W. H. Auden: A Commentary*. Princeton: Princeton University Press, 1998.

Gale, Monica R. *Virgil on the Nature of Things: The Georgics, Lucretius and the Didactic Tradition*. Cambridge: Cambridge University Press, 2000.

Galinsky, G. K. 'Vergil's Second *Eclogue*: Its Theme and Relation to the *Eclogue* Book'. *Classica et Medievalia* 26 (1965): 161–91.

Galinsky, G. Karl. *The Herakles Theme: The Adaptations of the Hero in Literature from Homer to the Twentieth Century*. Oxford: Blackwell, 1972.

García Ruiz, M. Pilar. 'AEQVOR: The Sea of Prophecies in Virgil's *Aeneid*'. *Classical Quarterly* 64 (2014): 694–706.

Gates, Sidney Barrington. Review. *The Nation and Athenaeum* (6 November 1926): 188.

Gauthier, Dominique. 'An Interview with Paul Muldoon by Dominique Gauthier, 18 September 1995'. *Études irlandaises* 22:1 (1997): 53–70.

Gleick, James. *Chaos: Making a New Science* (1987). 2nd edn. London: Vintage, 1998.

Glendinning, Victoria. *Vita: The Life of Vita Sackville-West*. London: Tauris Parke, 2018.

Goldhill, Simon. *The Poet's Voice: Essays on Poetics and Greek Literature*. Cambridge: Cambridge University Press, 1991.

Goodridge, John, and Kelsey Thornton. *John Clare, Trespasser*. Nottingham: Five Leaves, 2016.

Gransden, K. W. *Virgil's Iliad: An Essay on Epic Narrative*. Cambridge: Cambridge University Press, 1984.

Graver, Bruce. 'Wordsworth's Georgic Beginnings'. *Texas Studies in Literature and Language* 33 (1991): 137–59.

Gribbin, John. *Deep Simplicity: Chaos, Complexity and the Emergence of Life*. London: Penguin, 2005.

Griffin, Dustin. *Patriotism and Poetry in Eighteenth-Century Britain*. Cambridge: Cambridge University Press, 2002.

Griffin, Jasper. 'Virgil'. In *The Legacy of Rome: A New Appraisal*, edited by Richard Jenkyns, 125–50. Oxford: Oxford University Press, 1992.

Gussow, Mel. *Conversations with Stoppard*. New York: Grove Press, 1995.

Haffenden, John. 'Seamus Heaney and the Feminine Sensibility'. *YES* 17 (1987): 89–116.

Hall, Edith. 'Paving and Pencilling: Heaney's Inscriptions in J. W. Mackail's Translation of the *Aeneid*'. In *Seamus Heaney and the Classics: Bann Valley Muses*, edited by S. Harrison, F. Macintosh and H. Eastman, 223–43. New York: Oxford University Press, 2019.

Hamilton, A. C., 'The Argument of Spenser's *Shepheardes Calender*' ELH 23 (1956), 171–82.

Hammond, Paul. *Dryden and the Traces of Rome*. Oxford: Clarendon Press, 1999.

Hardie, Philip R. *Virgil's Aeneid: Cosmos and Imperium*. Oxford: Clarendon Press, 1986.

Hardie, Philip. 'Virgil, a Paradoxical Poet?'. In *Paradox and the Marvellous in Augustan Literature and Culture*, edited by P. Hardie, 95–112. Oxford: Oxford University Press, 2010.

Harrison, S. J. *Generic Enrichment in Vergil and Horace*. Oxford: Oxford University Press, 2007.

Harrison, Stephen J. 'Survival and Supremacy of Rome. The Unity of the Shield of Aeneas'. *Journal of Roman Studies* 87 (1997): 70–6.

Hart, Henry. *Seamus Heaney, Poet of Contrary Progressions*. Syracuse, NY: Syracuse University Press, 1992.

Hass, Robert, and Seamus Heaney. 'Sounding Lines: The Art of Translating Poetry'. Interview published February 1999, University of California, Berkeley: Townsend Center for the Humanities. https://townsendcenter.berkeley.edu/sites/default/files/publications/OP20_Sounding_Lines.pdf at p. 16, accessed 5 November 2019.

Haughton, Hugh. 'Power and Hiding Places: Wordsworth and Seamus Heaney'. In *The Monstrous Debt: Modalities of Romantic Influence in Twentieth-Century Literature*, edited by Damian Walford Davies and Richard Marggraf Turley, 61–100. Detroit: Wayne State University Press, 2006.

Hayles, N. Katherine. *Chaos Bound: Orderly Disorder in Contemporary Literature and Science*. Ithaca: Cornell University Press, 1990.

Heaney, Seamus. 'Above the Brim: On Robert Frost'. *Salmagundi* 88/89 (1990–1991): 275–94.

Heaney, Seamus. '"Apt Admonishment": Wordsworth as an Example'. *Hudson Review* 61 (2006): 19–33.

Heaney, Seamus. 'Eclogues *in extremis*: On the Staying Power of Pastoral'. (2003) In *Vergil's Eclogues* (Oxford Readings in Classical Studies), edited by Katharina Volk, 245–60. Oxford: Oxford University Press, 2008.

Heaney, Seamus. 'Envies and Identifications: Dante and the Modern Poet'. In *The Poets' Dante*, edited by Peter S. Hawkins and Rachel Jacoff, 239–58. New York: Farrar, Straus and Giroux, 2001 (paperback edn 2002).

Heaney, Seamus. 'Glory be to the world'. Review of Peter Fallon, trans., *Georgics* (Gallery Press, 2004). *Irish Times*, Sat. 23 October 2004, electronic version https://www.irishtimes.com/news/glory-be-to-the-world-1.1163328, accessed 23 November 2018.

Heaney, Seamus. 'In the light of the imagination'. *Irish Times* 21 October 2004, p. 14. https://www.irishtimes.com/culture/in-the-light-of-the-imagination-1.1162882?mode=print&ot=example.AjaxPageLayout.ot, accessed 8 November 2019.

Heaney, Seamus. 'Mossbawn via Mantua'. In *Ireland in/and Europe: Cross-Currents and Exchanges. Irish Studies in Europe 4*, edited by Werner Huber and Julia Novak, 19–26. Trier: Wissenchaftlicher Verlag Trier, 2012.

Heaney, Seamus. *Death of a Naturalist* (1966). London: Faber, 1991.

Heaney, Seamus. *District and Circle*. London: Faber, 2006.

Heaney, Seamus. *Door into the Dark* (1969). London: Faber, 1972.

Heaney, Seamus. *Electric Light*. London: Faber, 2001.

Heaney, Seamus. *Field Work* (1979). London: Faber, 2001.

Heaney, Seamus. *Finders Keepers: Selected Prose 1971–2001*. London: Faber, 2002 (paperback edn 2003).

Heaney, Seamus. *Human Chain*. London: Faber, 2010.

Heaney, Seamus. *North* (1975). London: Faber, 2001.

Heaney, Seamus. *Philoctetes, The Cure at Troy*. London: Faber, 1990 (republished 2018).

Heaney, Seamus. *Preoccupations: Selected Prose 1968–1978*. London: Faber, 1980.

Heaney, Seamus. *Seeing Things* (1991). London: Faber, 2001.

Heaney, Seamus. *Station Island*. London: Faber, 1984.

Heaney, Seamus. *The Government of the Tongue: The 1986 T. S. Eliot Memorial Lectures and Other Critical Writings*. London: Faber, 1988.

Heaney, Seamus. *The Haw Lantern*. London: Faber, 1987.

Heaney, Seamus. *The Midnight Verdict*. 2000. Oldcastle: Gallery Press, 2014 (reprint).

Heaney, Seamus. *The Spirit Level*. London: Faber, 1996.

Heaney, Seamus. *Wintering Out*. London: Faber, 1972.

Hecht, Anthony. *The Hidden Law: The Poetry of W. H. Auden*. Cambridge, MA: Harvard University Press, 1993.

Heffernan, James A. W. *Museum of Words: The Poetics of Ekphrasis from Homer to Ashbery*. Chicago: University of Chicago Press, 1993.

Heiny, Stephen. '"Puny in My Predicaments": Seamus Heaney's Readings of Virgil's Ninth Eclogue'. *Vergilius* 64 (2018): 53–70.

Henkel, John. 'Vergil Talks Technique: Metapoetic Arboriculture in *Georgics* 2'. *Vergilius* 60 (2014): 33–66.

Hinds, Stephen. 'Pastoral and its futures: reading like (a) Mantuan'. *Dictynna* 14 (2017), https://doi.org/10.4000/dictynna.1443, accessed 28 Jan. 2021.

Hinds, Stephen. *Allusion and Intertext: Dynamics of Appropriation in Roman Poetry*. Cambridge: Cambridge University Press, 1998.

Hollis, A. S. 'Octavian in the Fourth Georgic'. *Classical Quarterly* 46 (1996): 305–8.

Hoppen, H. Theodore. *Governing Hibernia: British Politicians and Ireland, 1800–1921*. Oxford: Oxford University Press, 2016.

Horsfall, Nicholas. 'Virgil and the Poetry of Explanations'. *Greece & Rome* 38 (1991): 203–11.

Horsfall, Nicholas. *A Companion to the Study of Virgil*. Leiden: Brill, 2011.

Hubbard, Thomas K. *The Pipes of Pan: Intertextuality and Filiation in the Pastoral Tradition from Theocritus to Milton*. Ann Arbor, MI: University of Michigan Press, 1998.

Hunt, John Dixon and Peter Willis, eds. *The Genius of the Place* (1975). Cambridge, MA: MIT Press, 1988.

Hunt, John Dixon. *The Figure in the Landscape: Poetry, Painting, and Gardening during the Eighteenth Century*. Baltimore: The Johns Hopkins University Press, 1976.

Hunter, Richard. *The Shadow of Callimachus: Studies in the Reception of Hellenistic Poetry at Rome*. Cambridge: Cambridge University Press, 2006.

Impens, Florence. *Classical Presences in Irish Poetry after 1960: The Answering Voice*. London: Bloomsbury, 2018.

Jangfeldt, Bengt. 'Form in Poetry: Joseph Brodsky and Derek Walcott in a conversation with Bengt Jangfeldt'. *Kenyon Review* 23 (2001): 185–200.

Jarniewicz, Jerzy. 'The Way Via Warsaw: Seamus Heaney and the Poet-War Polish Poets'. In *Seamus Heaney: Poet, Critic, Translator*, edited by Ashby Bland Crowder and Jason David Hall, 103–20. Basingstoke: Palgrave, 2007.

Jenkyns, Richard. 'Pastoral'. In *The Legacy of Rome: A New Appraisal*, edited by R. Jenkyns, 151–75. Oxford: Oxford University Press, 1992.

Jenkyns, Richard. 'Virgil and Arcadia'. *Journal of Roman Studies* 79 (1989): 26–39.

Jenkyns, Richard. *Virgil's Experience. Nature and History: Times, Names, and Places*. Oxford: Clarendon Press, 1998.

Johnson, Samuel. *The Lives of the Most Eminent English Poets; With Critical Observations on their Works*, edited by Roger Lonsdale. 4 vols. Oxford: Oxford University Press, 2006.

Joyce, James. *A Portrait of the Artist as a Young Man*. 1916. New York: Viking, 1964 (reprint).

Kaul, Suvir. *Poems of Nation, Anthems of Empire: English Verse in the Long Eighteenth Century*. Charlottesville, VA: University Press of Virginia, 2000.

Kavanagh, Patrick. *Collected Poems*, ed. Antoinette Quinn. London: Penguin, 2005.

Kay, Magdalena. 'Dialogues across the Continent: The Influence of Czesław Miłosz on Seamus Heaney'. *Comparative Literature* 63 (2011): 161–81.

Kennedy, Duncan F. '*Arcades ambo*: Virgil, Gallus and Arcadia'. *Hermathena* 143 (1987): 47–59.

Kenney, E. J. 'Virgil and the Elegiac Sensibility'. *Illinois Classical Studies* 8 (1983): 44–59.

Kerrigan, Charlie. *Virgil's Map: Geography, Empire, and the Georgics*. London: Bloomsbury, 2020.

Kirsch, Arthur. '"Our Grief is Not Greek": Auden's Poems on War'. *Yale Review* 96 (2008): 32–55.

Knight, W. F. Jackson. *Roman Vergil* (1944). 2nd edn. London: Faber, 1945.

Kragh, Helge S. *Entropic Creation: Religious Contexts of Thermodynamics and Cosmology*. London: Ashgate, 2008.

Kyriakidis, Stratis. '*Georgics* 4.559–566: The Vergilian Sphragis'. *Kleos* 7 (2002): 275–86.

Laird, Andrew. 'Sounding Out Ecphrasis: Art and Text in Catullus 64'. *Journal of Roman Studies* 83 (1993): 18–30.

Larkin, Philip. *The Complete Poems*, ed. Archie Burnett. Rev. edn. London: Faber, 2018.

Lee, Guy. 'Imitation and the Poetry of Virgil', *Greece & Rome* 28 (1981): 10–22.

Lee, M. Owen. *Virgil as Orpheus: A Study of the Georgics*. Albany: SUNY Press, 1996.

Lewis, C. S. *A Preface to Paradise Lost*. 1942. London: Oxford University Press, 1960 (reprint).

Limon, Jerzy. 'Waltzing in *Arcadia*: A Theatrical Dance in Five Dimensions'. *New Theatre Quarterly* 24 (2008): 222–8.

Lively, Genevieve. 'Cleopatra's Nose, Naso and the Science of Chaos'. *Greece & Rome* 49 (2002): 27–43.

Lodge, David. *Small World: An Academic Romance* (1984). London: Penguin, 1985.

Longley, Edna. '"Inner Emigré" or "Artful Voyeur"? Seamus Heaney's *North*'. In *The Art of Seamus Heaney*, 4th edn, edited by Tony Curtis, 65–95. Brigend: Seren, 2001.

Mac Góráin, Fiachra. 'The Mixed Blessing of Bacchus in Virgil's *Georgics*'. *Dictynna* 11 (2014). https://doi.org/10.4000/dictynna.1069.

Mac Góráin, Fiachra. 'Untitled/*Arma virumque*'. *Classical Philology* 113 (2018): 423–48.

Martin, Alison. '"Struggle. Weeds. Death and Loss. Success and Reward": The Politics of the Georgic in Vita Sackville-West's *The Garden* (1946)'. Unpublished paper presented at the conference 'Reworking Georgic' at the School of English, University of Leeds, 10 September 2019.

Martindale, Charles. 'Green Politics'. In *The Cambridge Companion to Virgil*, 2nd edn, edited by C. Martindale and F. Mac Góráin, 173–92. Cambridge: Cambridge University Press, 2019.

Martindale, Charles. 'Introduction: The Classic of All Europe'. In *The Cambridge Companion to Virgil*, 2nd edn, edited by C. Martindale and F. Mac Góráin, 1–19. Cambridge: Cambridge University Press, 2019.

Martindale, Charles. 'Paradise Metamorphosed: Ovid in Milton'. *Comparative Literature* 37 (1985): 301–33.

Martindale, Charles. 'Ruins of Rome: T. S. Eliot and the Presence of the Past'. *Arion* 3/2–3 (1995–6): 102–40.

Martindale, Charles. 'Thinking through Reception'. In *Classics and the Uses of Reception*, edited by C. Martindale and R. F. Thomas, 1–13. Malden, MA: Wiley-Blackwell.

Martindale, Charles. *Redeeming the Text: Latin Poetics and the Hermeneutics of Reception*. Cambridge: Cambridge University Press, 1993.

May, Robert. 'The Best Possible Time to Be Alive: The Logistic Map'. In *It Must Be Beautiful: Great Equations of Modern Science*, edited by Graham Farmelo, 212–29. London: Granta, 2002.

McDonald, Peter. '"Weird Brightness" and the Riverbank: Seamus Heaney, Virgil, and the Need for Translation'. In *Seamus Heaney and the Classics: Bann Valley Muses*, edited by S. Harrison, F. Macintosh and H. Eastman, 160–79. Oxford: Oxford University Press, 2019.

McMaster, Graham, ed. *William Wordsworth: A Critical Anthology*. Harmondsworth: Penguin, 1972.

Meisel, Martin. *How Plays Work: Reading and Performance*. Oxford University Press, 2007.

Miller, John F. *Apollo, Augustus, and the Poets*. Cambridge: Cambridge University Press, 2009.

Miłosz, Czesław. *New and Collected Poems 1931–2001*, trans. C. Miłosz, Robert Hass, et al. New York: Ecco Press, 2003.

Morisco, Gabriella. 'Two Poets and a Kite: Seamus Heaney and Giovanni Pascoli'. *Linguae* 12/1 (2013): 35–45. doi: 10.7358/ling-2013-001-mori, http://www.ledonline.it\linguae, accessed 26 November 2019.

Morley, John. *The Life of William Ewart Gladstone*. 3 vols. Toronto: Morang, 1903.

Muecke, Frances. 'Virgil and the Nature of Pastoral'. *AUMLA* 44 (1975): 169–80.

Muldoon, Paul. 'Getting Round: Notes towards an *Ars Poetica*'. Bateson Lecture 1998. *Essays in Criticism* 48 (1998): 107–38.

Muldoon, Paul. *Meeting the British*. London: Faber, 1987.

Muldoon, Paul. *The Annals of Chile*. New York: Farrar, Straus and Giroux, 1994.

Muldoon, Paul. *Why Brownlee Left*. London: Faber, 1980.

Murphy, Kevin. 'Heaney Translating Heaney: Coupling and Uncoupling the Human Chain'. *Texas Studies in Literature and Language* 58 (2016): 352–68.

Nagel, Rebecca. 'Farming Poetry: Vita Sackville-West and Virgil's *Georgics*'. *Classical and Modern Literature* 24 (2004): 1–22.

Nagel, Rebecca. 'Naming Plants in *The Garden* by Vita Sackville-West'. *Interdisciplinary Studies in Literature and Environment* (2015): 241–63.

Nelis, Damien. *Vergil's Aeneid and the Argonautica of Apollonius Rhodius*. London: Francis Cairns, 2001.

Nelson, Stephanie. *God and the Land: The Metaphysics of Farming in Hesiod and Vergil*. Oxford: Oxford University Press, 1998.

Nicolson, Harold. *Diaries and Letters*, ed. Nigel Nicolson. 3 vols. London: Collins, 1966–8.

Norton Anthology of English Literature, ed. Stephen Greenblatt et al. 9th edn. 6 vols. New York: Norton, 2012.

O'Donoghue, Bernard. 'Dante's Versatility and Seamus Heaney's Modernism'. In *Dante's Modern Afterlife: Reception and Response from Blake to Heaney,* edited by Nick Havely, 242–57. London: Macmillan, 1998.

O'Donoghue, Bernard. 'Heaney, Yeats, and the Language of Pastoral'. In *Seamus Heaney and the Classics: Bann Valley Muses*, edited by S. Harrison, F. Macintosh and H. Eastman, 147–59. Oxford: Oxford University Press, 2019.

O'Donoghue, Bernard. 'Heaney's *ars poetica*: *The Government of the Tongue*'. In *The Art of Seamus Heaney*, 4th edn, edited by Tony Curtis, 181–90. Brigend: Seren, 2001.

O'Donoghue, Bernard. 'Heaney's Classics and the Bucolic'. In *The Cambridge Companion to Seamus Heaney*, edited by B. O'Donoghue, 106–21. Cambridge: Cambridge University Press, 2009.

O'Donoghue, Bernard. *Seamus Heaney and the Language of Poetry*. London: Routledge, 1994.

O'Donogue, Bernard. 'The Aisling'. In *A Companion to Poetic Genre*, edited by Erik Martiny, 420–34. Malden, MA: Wiley-Blackwell 2012.

O'Donoghue, Heather. 'Heaney, *Beowulf,* and the Medieval Literature of the North'. In *The Cambridge Companion to Seamus Heaney*, edited by B. O'Donoghue, 192–205. Cambridge: Cambridge University Press, 2009.

O'Driscoll, Dennis. *Stepping Stones: Interviews with Seamus Heaney*. London: Faber, 2008.

O'Rourke, Donncha. 'The Representation and Misrepresentation of Virgilian Poetry in Propertius 2.34'. *AJP* 132 (2011): 457–97.

Ovid. *Epistulae ex Ponto, Book I,* ed. Jan Felix Gaertner. Oxford: Oxford University Press, 2005.

Ovid. *Erotic Poems,* trans. Peter Green. Harmondsworth: Penguin, 1982.

Oxford Classical Dictionary, ed. Simon Hornblower and Antony Spawforth. 3rd edn. Oxford: Oxford University Press, 1996.

Oxford English Dictionary, database version.

Oxford Latin Dictionary. ed. P. G. W. Glare. 1996. Oxford: Clarendon Press, 2007 (reprint).

Panofsky, Erwin. 'Et in Arcadia Ego: On the Conception of Transience in Poussin and Watteau'. In *Philosophy & History: Essays presented to Ernst Cassirer,* edited by Raymond Klibansky and H. J. Paton, 223–54. Oxford: Clarendon Press, 1936.

Panofsky, Erwin. 'Et In Arcadia Ego: Poussin and the Elegiac Tradition'. In Panofsky, *Meaning in the Visual Arts: Papers In and On Art History,* 295–320. Garden City, NY: Doubleday, 1955.

Papaioannou, Sophia. 'Founder, Civilizer and Leader: Virgil's Evander and His Role in the Origins of Rome'. *Mnemosyne* 56 (2003): 680–703.

Parker, Michael R. 'Past Master: Czesław Miłosz and his impact on the poetry of Seamus Heaney'. *Textual Practice* 27 (2013): 825–50.

Parker, Michael. '"His Nibs": Self-Reflexivity and the Significance of Translation in Seamus Heaney's *Human Chain*'. *Irish University Review* 42/2 (2012): 327–50.

Parker, Michael. *Seamus Heaney: The Making of the Poet*. London: Macmillan, 1993.

Parry, Adam. 'The Two Voices of Virgil's *Aeneid*'. *Arion,* 1st series, 2 (1963): 66–80.

Pater, Walter. *Appreciations, with an Essay on Style*. London: Macmillan, 1907.

Peirano, Irene. 'Illo ego qui quondam: on authorial (an)onymity'. In *The Author's Voice in Classical and Late Antiquity,* ed. Anna Marmodoro and Jonathan Hill. Oxford: Oxford University Press, 2013.

Pellicer, J. C. 'Pastoral and Georgic'. In *The Oxford History of Classical Reception in English Literature,* vol. 3, 1660–1790, edited by Charles Martindale and David Hopkins, 287–321. Oxford: Oxford University Press, 2012.

Pellicer, J. C. 'Reception, Wit, and the Unity of Virgil's *Georgics*'. *Symbolae Oslenses* 82 (2007): 90–115.

Perkell, Christine G. *The Poet's Truth: A Study of the Poet in Virgil's Georgics*. Berkeley: University of California Press, 1989.

Perkell, Christine. 'The Golden Age and Its Contradictions in the Poetry of Vergil'. *Vergilius* 48 (2002): 3–39.

Philips, John. *Cider, A Poem in Two Books, by John Philips. With notes provincial, historical, and classical,* ed. Charles Dunster. London: Cadell, 1791.

Philips, John. *Cyder. A Poem in Two Books* (1708), ed. John Goodridge and J. C. Pellicer. Cheltenham: Cyder Press, 2001.

Pigman III, G. W. 'Versions of Imitation in the Renaissance'. *Renaissance Quarterly* 33 (1980): 1–32.

Pomeroy, Elizabeth W. 'Within Living Memory: Vita Sackville-West's Poems of Land and Garden'. *Twentieth-Century Literature* 28 (1982): 269–89.

Pope, Alexander. *The Dunciad in Four Books,* ed. Valerie Rumbold. Rev. edn. London: Pearson Longman, 2009.

Pöschl, Viktor. 'The Poetic Achievement of Virgil'. *Classical Journal* 56 (1961): 290–99.

Potts, Robert. 'The View from Olympia', *The Guardian,* 7 April 2001, https://www.theguardian.com/books/2001/apr/07/poetry.tseliotprizeforpoetry2001, accessed 5 November 2019.

Prigogine, Ilya, and Isabelle Stengers. *Order Out of Chaos: Man's New Dialogue with Nature.* New York: Bantam, 1984.

Putnam, Michael C. J. 'The *Aeneid* and *Paradise Lost*: Ends and Conclusions', *Literary Imagination* 8 (2006): 387–410; 406–7.

Putnam, Michael C. J. 'The Lyric Genius of the *Aeneid*'. *Arion* 3 (1996): 81–101.

Putnam, Michael C. J. 'Virgil and Heaney: "Route 110"'. *Arion* 19 (2012): 79–107.

Putnam, Michael C. J. *Virgil's Poem of the Earth: Studies in the Georgics.* Princeton: Princeton University Press, 1979.

Quint, David. 'The Virgilian Coordinates of *Paradise Lost*'. *Materiali e discussioni per l'analisi dei testi classici* 52 (Re-Presenting Virgil: Special Issue in Honor of Michael C. J. Putnam) (2004): 177–97.

Raitt, Suzanne. *Vita and Virginia: The Work and Friendship of V. Sackville-West and Virginia Woolf.* Oxford: Clarendon Press, 1993.

Reckford, K. J. 'Recognizing Venus I: Aeneas Meets His Mother'. *Arion* 3 (1995–6): 1–42.

Review of Sackville-West, *The Land. TLS*, 21 October 1926, 716.

Review of Sackville-West, *The Land. The Bookman*, November 1926, 112.

Ricks, Christopher. 'Growing Up: Review of *Death of a Naturalist*'. (*New Statesman*, 27 May 1966, p. 778). In *Seamus Heaney* (New Casebooks Series), edited by Michael Allen, 21–3. Basingstoke: Macmillan, 1997.

Riley, Kathleen. '"The Forewarned Journey Back": *Katabasis* as *Nostos* in the Poetry of Seamus Heaney'. In *Seamus Heaney and the Classics: Bann Valley Muses,* edited by S. Harrison, F. Macintosh and H. Eastman, 205–22. Oxford: Oxford University Press, 2019.

Rogers, Pat. 'Rhythm and Recoil in Pope's *Pastorals*'. *Eighteenth-Century Studies* 14 (1980): 1–17.

Rosenmeyer, Thomas G. *The Green Cabinet: Theocritus and the European Pastoral Lyric* (1969). Bristol: Bristol Classical Press, 2004.

Sackville-West, V. *The Land.* (1926) Rev. edn. London: Heinemann, 1941 (reset 1955, reprinted 1976).

Sackville-West, V. *Selected Writings,* ed. Mary Ann Caws. London: Palgrave, 2002.

Sackville-West, V. *The Garden* (1946). London: Frances Lincoln, 2004.

Sackville-West, V. Typescript/manuscript of *The Land*, 1926, Huntington Library HM 41088. Microfilm. *The Vita Sackville-West and Harold Nicolson Manuscripts, Letters, and Diaries*. Reels 2 and 3. Brighton: Harvester Microform, 1988.

Sambrook, James. *English Pastoral Poetry*. Boston, MA: Twayne, 1983.

Saunders, Tim. 'Making an Example out of Marsyas'. In *Classics and the Uses of Reception*, edited by C. Martindale and R. F. Thomas, 32–43. Malden, MA: Wiley-Blackwell, 2006.

Saunders, Timothy. *Bucolic Ecology: Virgil's Eclogues and the Environmental Literary Tradition*. London: Duckworth, 2008.

Schein, Seth L. 'Reading Homer in Dark Times: Rachel Bespaloff's *On the Iliad*'. *Arion* 26/1 (2018): 17–36.

Schmidt, Ernst A. 'Arcadia: Modern Occident and Classical Antiquity' (1975). In *Vergil's Eclogues* (Oxford Readings in Classical Studies), edited by Katharina Volk, 16–47. Oxford: Oxford University Press, 2008.

Scodel, R. S., and Richard Thomas. 'Virgil and the Euphrates'. *AJP* 105 (1984): 339.

Shapin, Steven, and Simon Schaffer, *Leviathan and the Air-Pump: Hobbes, Boyle, and the Experimental Life*. Princeton: Princeton University Press, 1985.

Sheeler, Jessie. *Little Sparta: The Garden of Ian Hamilton Finlay*. Photographs by Andrew Lawson. London: Frances Lincoln, 2003.

Skoie, Mathilde. 'Passing on the Panpipes: Genre and Reception'. In *Classics and the Uses of Reception*, edited by C. Martindale and R. F. Thomas, 92–103. Malden, MA: Wiley-Blackwell, 2006.

Snyder, Susan. *Pastoral Process: Spenser, Marvell, Milton*. Stanford: Stanford University Press, 1998.

Spurr M. S. 'Agriculture and *the Georgics*'. *Greece & Rome* 33 (1986): 164–87.

Squire J. C. 'Books of the Day: British Georgics'. *Observer* 10 October 1926, 6.

Squire J. C., 'Poetry'. *London Mercury* January 1927, 318–21.

Stallworthy, Jon 'The Poet as Archaeologist: W. B. Yeats and Seamus Heaney'. *RES* 33 (1982), 158–74.

Stewart, Ian. *Does God Play Dice? The New Mathematics of Chaos* (1989). 2nd edn. London: Penguin, 1997.

Stoppard, Tom. *Arcadia*. London: Faber, 1993 ('reprinted with corrections, 1993', reset 2000).

Stoppard, Tom. *Arcadia*. London: Faber, 2009 ('reprinted with revisions').

Stoppard, Tom. *Rosencrantz and Guildenstern Are Dead*. London: Faber, 1968 (reset 2000).

Stoppard, Tom. *Travesties* (1975). Rev. edn. London: Faber, 1993.

Stoppard, Tom. *Travesties* (1975). Rev. edn. London: Faber, 2017.

Summers, Claude J. '"Or One Could Weep Because Another Wept": The Counterplot of Auden's "The Shield of Achilles"'. *JEGP* 83 (1984): 214–32.

Taplin, Oliver. 'The Shield of Achilles within the *Iliad*'. *Greece & Rome* 27 (1980): 1–21, at 15.

Tarrant R. J. 'Poetry and Power: Virgil's Poetry in Contemporary Context'. In *The Cambridge Companion to Virgil*, 2nd edn, edited by C. Martindale and F. Mac Góráin, 243–62. Cambridge: Cambridge University Press, 2019.

Tatum, James. 'Mrs Vergil's Horrid Wars'. *Arion* 21 (2013): 3–46.

Theocritus. *A Selection: Idylls 1, 3, 4, 6, 10, 11 and 13,* ed. Richard Hunter. Cambridge: Cambridge University Press, 1999.

Theocritus. *Idylls,* trans. Anthony Verity. Oxford: Oxford University Press, 2003.

Theodorakopoulos, Elena. 'Closure and the Book of Virgil'. In *The Cambridge Companion to Virgil*, 2nd edn, edited by C. Martindale and F. Mac Góráin, 226–39. Cambridge: Cambridge University Press, 2019.

Thibodeau, Philip. *Playing the Farmer: Representations of Rural Life in Vergil's Georgics.* Berkeley: University of California Press, 2011.

Thomas, Richard F. 'Virgil's Ekphrastic Centerpieces'. *Harvard Studies in Classical Philology* 87 (1983): 175–84.

Thomas, Richard. 'The *Georgics* of Resistance: From Virgil to Heaney'. *Vergilius* 47 (2001): 117–47.

Thomas. Richard F. *Virgil and the Augustan Reception.* Cambridge: Cambridge University Press, 2001.

Thomas H. B. M., and D. Küchemann, 'Sidney Barrington Gates. 1893–1973'. *Biographical Memoirs of the Royal Society* 20 (1974): 181–212.

Thoreau, Henry David. *Walden,* ed. Stephen Fender. Oxford: Oxford University Press, 1997.

Trilling, Lionel. 'The Fate of Pleasure'. In *Beyond Culture: Essays on Literature and Learning,* 57–87. London: Secker & Warburg, 1966.

Vendler, Helen. *Our Secret Discipline: Yeats and Lyric Form.* Cambridge, MA: Harvard University Press, 2007.

Vendler, Helen. *Seamus Heaney.* London: HarperCollins, 1998.

Vickers, Brian. 'Leisure and idleness in the Renaissance: The ambivalence of *otium*', Part 1. *Renaissance Studies* 4 (1990): 1–37.

Vickers, Brian. 'Leisure and idleness in the Renaissance: The ambivalence of *otium*', Part 2. *Renaissance Studies* 4 (1990): 107–54.

Vida, M. G. *The De Arte Poetica of Marco Girolamo Vida,* trans. Ralph G. Williams. New York: University of Columbia Press, 1976.

Virgil. *Aeneidos Liber Primus,* ed. R. G. Austin. 1971. Oxford: Clarendon Press, 2004.

Virgil. *Aeneidos IV,* ed. R. G. Austin. 1955. Oxford: Clarendon Press, 2007 (reprint).

Virgil. *Aeneidos Liber Sextus,* ed. R. G. Austin. 1977. Oxford: Clarendon Press, 2009 (reprint).

Virgil. *Aeneid Book VI,* trans. Seamus Heaney. London: Faber, 2016.

Virgil. *Eclogues,* ed. Robert Coleman. Cambridge: Cambridge University Press, 1977.

Virgil. *The Eclogues,* trans. Guy Lee. Rev. edn. London: Penguin, 1984.

Virgil. *Georgics,* ed. R. A. B. Mynors. 1990. Oxford: Clarendon Press, 2000 (reprint).

Virgil. *Georgics,* ed. Richard Thomas. 2 vols. Cambridge: Cambridge University Press, 1988.

Virgil. *Georgics,* trans. Kristina Chew. Indianapolis: Hackett, 2002.

Virgil. *Virgil,* ed. and trans. H. R. Fairclough, rev. G. P. Goold. 2000. Loeb Classical Library 63–4. 2 vols. Cambridge, MA: Harvard University Press, 2002 (reprint).

Volk, Katharina. *The Poetics of Latin Didactic: Lucretius, Vergil, Ovid, Manilius.* Oxford: Oxford University Press, 2002.

Wall, Richard. 'A Dialect Glossary for Seamus Heaney's Works'. *Irish University Review* 28/1, ed. Anthony Roche (1998): 68–86.

Ware, Catherine. 'The Ashplant and the Golden Bough: Heaney in Vergil's Labyrinth'. *Classical Receptions Journal* 10 (2018): 229–48.

Warren, C. Henry. 'Gems and Coloured Glass'. *Spectator Literary Supplement*, 30 October 1926, 758.

Warren, Geoff. 'C. Henry Warren: A Contented Countryman?'. *Landscape* 12 (2011): 1–23.

Weil, Simone. 'The *Iliad*, of the Poem of Force' (1940, trans. 1945). In Simone Weil/ Rachel Bespaloff, *War and the Iliad,* trans. Mary McCarthy. Intro. Christopher Benfey, 3–37. New York: New York Review of Books, 2005.

West, D. A. '*Cernere erat*: The Shield of Aeneas'. In *Oxford Readings in Vergil's Aeneid,* edited by S. J. Harrison, 295–304. Oxford: Oxford University Press, 1990.

Westlake, J. H. J. 'W. H. Auden's "The Shield of Achilles": An Interpretation'. *Literatur in Wissenschaft und Unterricht* 1 (1968): 50–8.

Wheatley, David. 'Professing Poetry: Heaney as Critic'. In *The Cambridge Companion to Seamus Heaney*, edited by B. O'Donoghue, 127–8. Cambridge: Cambridge University Press, 2009.

Whitmarsh, Tim. 'True Histories: Lucian, Bakhtin, and the Pragmatics of Reception'. In *Classics and the Uses of Reception*, edited by C. Martindale and R. F. Thomas, 104–15. Malden, MA: Wiley-Blackwell, 2006.

Wilkinson L. P. *The Georgics of Virgil: A Critical Survey* (1969). Bristol: Bristol Classical Press, 1997.

Williams, Mary Frances. 'Seamus Heaney's *Exposure* and Vergil's *Aeneid*'. *Classical and Modern Literature* 19 (1999): 243–56.

Williams, Raymond. *The Country and the City* (1973). London, Hogarth Press, 1985.

Woolf, Virginia. *Orlando: A Biography,* ed. Michael H. Whitworth. Oxford: Oxford University Press, 2015.

Woolf, Virginia. *The Common Reader*, vol. 1, ed. Andrew McNeillie. London: Vintage, 2003.

Woolf, Virginia. *The Letters of Virginia Woolf,* ed. Nigel Nicolson and Joanne Trautmann. 6 vols. London: Hogarth Press, 1975–80.

Wordsworth, William, and S. T. Coleridge. *Lyrical Ballads,* ed. Michael Mason. 2nd edn. Harlow: Pearson Longman, 2007.

Wordsworth, William. *Early Poems and Fragments, 1785–1797,* ed. Carol Landon and
    Jared Curtis. Ithaca, NY: Cornell University Press, 1997.

Wordsworth, William. *The Excursion,* ed. Sally Bushell et al. Ithaca, NY: Cornell
    University Press, 2007.

Wordsworth, William. *Translations of Chaucer and Virgil,* ed. Bruce E. Graver. Ithaca:
    Cornell University Press, 1998.

Wu, Duncan (ed.). *Wordsworth's Poets.* Manchester: Carcanet, 2003.

Yeats, W. B. *The Major Works,* ed. Edward Larrissy. Rev. edn. Oxford: Oxford University
    Press, 2001.

Zeifman, Hersh. 'The comedy of eros: Stoppard in love'. (2001). In *The Cambridge
    Companion to Tom Stoppard*, edited by Katherine E. Kelly, 185–200. Cambridge:
    Cambridge University Press, 2002 (reprint).

Ziolkowski, Theodore. 'Robert Frost in Roman Mode'. *Arion* 24 (2016): 1–13.

Ziolkowski, Theodore. *Virgil and the Moderns.* Princeton: Princeton University Press,
    1993.

Index

Index Locorum

Poems and passages by Heaney, Homer, Ovid and Virgil
(for other authors, see general index)

www.ingramcontent.com/pod-product-compliance
Lightning Source LLC
Chambersburg PA
CBHW070837030726
47504CB00005B/1132